# NECROPOLIS

## *London and Its Dead*

D0170079

## CATHARINE ARNOLD

POCKET
BOOKS

LONDON • SYDNEY • NEW YORK • TORONTO

First published in Great Britain by Simon & Schuster UK Ltd, 2006
This edition first published by Pocket Books, 2007
An imprint of Simon & Schuster UK Ltd
A CBS COMPANY

7 9 10 8

Simon & Schuster UK Ltd
1st Floor
222 Gray's Inn Road
London WC1X 8HB


www.simonandschuster.co.uk

Simon & Schuster Australia
Sydney

A CIP catalogue record for this book
is available from the British Library.

ISBN-13: 978-1-4165-0248-7

Typeset in Granjon by M Rules
Printed and bound in Great Britain by
CPI Cox & Wyman, Reading, RG1 8EX

**Picture credits**
The Art Archive: p. 27
Corbis Images: p. 231
The Highgate Literary and Scientific Institution: p. 268
The Museum of London: p. 13, p. 58, p. 107, p. 184
The Illustrated London News: p. 130, p. 152, p. 208, p. 212
The Victoria and Albert Museum: p. 76

*For my parents*
*In Memoriam*

# Contents

# NECROPOLIS

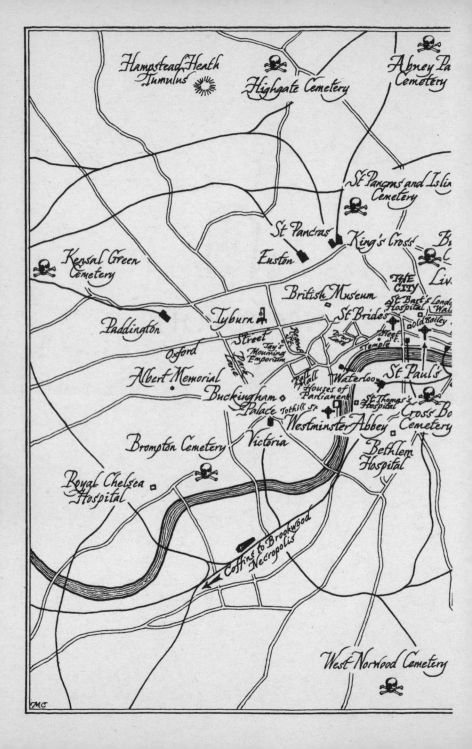

West Ham Cemetery

Victoria Park Cemetery

nhill Fields emetery

erpool St

Bank of England

Monument

Whitechapel

Tower Hamlets Cemetery

Ratcliff Highway

Tower of London

Guy's Hospital

nes

Nunhead Cemetery

*London in the 1880s*

# Acknowledgements

Many people have helped me in the creation of this book, taking time and trouble to give me their advice and sources for further reference. I would like to take this opportunity to thank the following: Jean Pateman and the Friends of Highgate Cemetery; Ron Woollacott and the Friends of Nunhead Cemetery; Robert Stephenson and the Friends of Brompton Cemetery; Roger Arber of The Cremation Society of Great Britain; Henry Vivian-Neal and the Friends of Kensal Green Cemetery; Stephen White; John M. Clarke; Brookwood Cemetery Society; the Reverend Dr Peter Jupp; Andrew Gordon and Edwina Barstow at Simon & Schuster; Joan Deitch; Dr Sarah Niblock; Simon Cadman; Sarah Crichton and Guy Martin of Brooklyn, New York, for assisting with my American research; the British Library; the University Library, Cambridge; the Hallward Library, University of Nottingham; the Museum of London; the Victoria and Albert Museum; Vanessa Dale; my agent, Charlie Viney; and last but not least, my family, particularly my husband, whose constant encouragement and support sustained me throughout writing *Necropolis*.

# Introduction

When Sir Christopher Wren was commissioned to rebuild St Paul's Cathedral after it had been destroyed by the Great Fire of London in 1666, he made an astonishing discovery. As Mrs Isabella Holmes reveals in her marvellous book of 1898, *The London Burial Grounds*:

> Upon digging the foundation of the present fabrick of St Paul's, he found under the graves of the latter ages, in a row below them, the Burial-places of the Saxon times – the Saxons, as it appeared, were accustomed to line their graves with chalk-stones, though some more eminent were entombed in coffins of whole stones. Below these were British graves, where were found ivory and wooden pins of a hard wood, seemingly box, in abundance, of about six inches long; it seems the bodies were only wrapped up, and pinned in wooden shrouds, which being consumed, the pins remained entire. In the same row, and deeper, were Roman urns intermixed. This was eighteen feet deep or more, and belonged to the colony, where Romans and Britons lived and died together.

Wren's discovery reminds us that London is one giant grave. So many generations have lived and died here within such a small span – pagan, Roman, mediaeval, Victorian – and left intriguing traces of their lives: like the skulls of Romans, murdered by

1

Boudicca, recovered from the Thames, and the clay pipes of plague victims, discovered during excavations for the Piccadilly Line. In fact, the tunnel curves between Knightsbridge and South Kensington stations because it was impossible to drill through the mass of skeletal remains buried in Hyde Park. London, from six feet under, is not just Cobbett's 'Great Wen', it is the city a horrified young Thomas Carlyle dubbed 'the Great Maw'!

Death provides a fascinating mirror through which to view London, as it has grown and changed. This book does not claim to be an exhaustive survey of every burial ground; for that, we must turn to Isabella Holmes, who chronicled every cemetery in London, and to Hugh Meller's excellent *Gazeteer*. The intention is to examine how London has coped with its dead from the pagan era to the present day, and the men and women who have played a part, from the mysterious Roman lady of Spitalfields to Graham Greene and his experience of the Blitz; from the cortège of Queen Elizabeth I to the funeral of Diana, Princess of Wales, 400 years later; and from the Dickensian horrors of the overcrowded inner-city churchyards to the Victorian Valhallas of Kensal Green, Highgate and Brompton.

My own interest in graveyards began in childhood, when I used to walk home from school through Nottingham's Rock Cemetery, with its magnificent marble angels and sandstone catacombs. When I moved to London, and longed for green tranquil spaces, I spent weekends exploring the great Victorian burial grounds. The word 'cemetery' derives from the Greek *koimeterion* or 'dormitory', and these 'great gardens of sleep' seemed tranquil indeed.

Each had its unique appeal: the grandeur of Brompton, designed as an outdoor cathedral; Kensal Green, with its elegant Neo-classical tombs; and, most fascinating of all, Highgate – last resting-place of Karl Marx and poor Lizzie Siddal, the Pre-Raphaelite muse who was exhumed so that her husband could recover the book of poetry buried with her.

Highgate was the inspiration for *Necropolis*. I was sitting in a café at the top of Highgate Hill one bright May morning, sipping coffee and watching the world go by, when a laden hearse drove straight past my window, reminding me that the great cemetery lay but a few steps away. From planning to write about Highgate, I began to explore the places which inspired it, including Paris's Père Lachaise, and those that followed, such as Green-Wood, in New York. But London seemed peculiarly suited to a narrative about the dead. As I roamed the cemeteries, and examined dusty tomes in silent libraries, I realized that London possesses a Dickensian aura of mystery, a pervasive melancholy . . .

Writing *Necropolis* has enhanced my vision of London as a city of ghosts: famous and infamous, they dart along like shadows. The shade of Virginia Woolf flickers through Bloomsbury; forgotten scribblers materialize on Fleet Street near the Wig and Pen; and at Westminster, I sense the phantoms of a thousand Scottish soldiers, interned by Cromwell after the Battle of Worcester in 1651, and buried in the plague pits near the Houses of Parliament.

Meanwhile, we have carved out a place for ourselves among the dead; the glittering pinnacles of commerce rise along the skyline, their foundations sunk in a charnel house; and the lost lie forgotten below us as, overhead, we persuade ourselves that we are immortal and carry on the business of life.

*Catharine Arnold*
*January, 2006*

# 1 : A PAGAN PLACE

*Celtic Golgotha and the Roman Cemeteries*

High above London stands one of the city's oldest burial grounds. The Bronze Age tumulus on Parliament Hill Fields predates Kensal Green and Highgate cemeteries by over 4,000 years. This tumulus, which dates from around 2,400 BC, is characteristic of the peaceful, remote spots where the earliest Londoners went to join their ancestors, although the city, as such, did not yet exist. The region was merely a series of rudimentary villages, inhabited by tribes who survived by farming and fishing in the marshy land around the tidal river.

The tumulus is a reminder that, since time immemorial, humans have demonstrated a universal propensity to bury their dead, to mourn their passing and to mark their passage into the next world with a series of mortuary rituals and religious ceremonies.

The earliest form of interment, during the Neolithic period (4,000–2,500 BC), consisted of long barrows. These were vast walk-in burial chambers covered by mounds of earth. Today, those barrows which remain are grassy mounds, but at the time they were decorated with stones or cobbles and had elaborate wooden entrances, sealed with massive rocks which could be rolled away when the occasion demanded. Used and adapted over the centuries, these communal barrows contained large numbers of 'crouched inhumations' (bodies buried in the foetal position).[1]

When they first opened Neolithic barrows in the nineteenth century, Victorian antiquaries found that many skeletons had been disarticulated, and had bones missing, indicating that they had been moved about before full decomposition had taken place. It appeared then, that Neolithic people did not simply dispose of their dead – they handled them repeatedly and shifted them about.[2] The Victorians interpreted this as evidence of lack of respect, ritual sacrifice and even cannibalism – a view supported by Classical authors.

A more recent interpretation, in 1999, suggests that the bodies had been moved for a different purpose; it was possible that members of the tribe who had died and been buried elsewhere were exhumed and reinterred alongside their kith and kin, just as the bodies of loved ones are flown home today, for burial in the family plot. Repellent as the practice of reburial may have seemed to the Victorians, there are also anthropological explanations for placing the dead in specific locations, in order to 'invest the monument with the spiritual power of the dead person'.[3]

There were no individual gravestones in the burial chambers, but the bodies were often framed by rudimentary rows of stones and buried with 'grave goods' – personal items to accompany the dead person into the afterlife. These included arrowheads, pots, and jewellery made from shells or jet. Many graves also contained the remains of cattle, sheep and even reindeer, and there is evidence that cherished domestic animals followed their owners to the grave; archaeologists have found the bones of dogs and cats in Neolithic barrows.

By the Bronze Age, the long barrows had fallen into disuse. Cremation had become the primary means of disposal, with bodies burned in pits and the cremated remains buried in collared urns beneath smaller, rounded burial mounds. These tended to be the preserve of chieftains, whilst more humble members of the community were consigned to a shallow grave or ditch. The hero's funeral in *Beowulf* conveys the spectacular nature of such an event:

> *The warriors kindled the bale* [bonfire] *on the barrow,*
> *Wakened the greatest of funeral fires,*
> *Dark o'er the blaze the wood-smoke mounted;*
> *The winds were still, and the sound of weeping*
> *Rose with the roar of the surging flame*
> *Till the heat of the fire had broken the body* . . .[4]

Beowulf's comrades spend ten days fashioning a mound high on a cliff, where the hero's ashes are buried along with his hoard of treasure. Twelve warriors then parade around the burial mound, singing dirges, praising his deeds and 'bemourning the fall of their mighty lord'. *Beowulf* was, of course, composed around AD 800, nearly 3,000 years after the Bronze Age, but it provides a superb poetic evocation of the event, allowing us to imagine a similar procession on Parliament Hill Fields, as the Beaker People bade farewell to a slain warlord or tribal elder beneath his newly constructed tumulus.

The death and burial of warriors would prove to be a recurring theme, for over the following centuries, many Ancient Britons and Roman soldiers were to be slain in battle.

Although Julius Caesar had attempted to conquer Britain in 55 and 54 BC, the Romans did not mount a successful invasion until AD 43, under Claudius. Arriving at the south coast, the Romans made their way up the Thames Estuary. Finding a spot where the tidal river proved deep enough for shipping but narrow enough for a crossing, they immediately grasped its strategic significance and created a makeshift settlement of forty acres along the waterfront. 'Londinium', capital of the Province of Britannia, was born. But Londinium soon became a target for the oppressed Britons.

In A.D. 60, the Britons, led by Queen Boudicca, rebelled. According to the Roman historian Tacitus, Boudicca hated the Romans as they had stolen her land when she was widowed, flogged her and raped her daughters. Intent on wiping out their oppressors, Boudicca's army descended on London and burned it to the ground. This first Great Fire of London was so intense that it melted bronze coins, scorching the earth so profoundly that archaeologists discovered a seared layer of soil centuries later. Boudicca took no prisoners. Tacitus recorded that over 70,000 Romans and their allies – men, women *and* children – perished in the massacre; they were lynched, burned and even crucified. Romans were beheaded and thrown into the river. The number of skulls recovered from the Walbrook near Finsbury Circus, and the Thames around Battersea and Mortlake prompted the Victorian archaeologist Henry Syer Cuming to name the river 'our Celtic Golgotha'.

The Romans soon retaliated, however, crushing the insurgents and, once they had regained control, set about creating London in the image of a Roman city. A defensive wall, nine feet wide, eighteen feet high and nearly two miles long was constructed – sections of which survive to this very day. Inside the wall was the Forum (on what is now Gracechurch Street in the City), a combination of law court, council chamber and shopping mall. With their passion for town planning, the Romans laid out streets, villas and temples. In a policy shift which the historian Guy de la Bédoyère has compared with modern Western Imperialism, the Romans converted militant Britons to their way of life with consumer enticements, introducing them to the urbane pleasures of hot spas and fine dining, encouraging them to wear togas and speak Latin.[5]

This cultural imperialism extended to the Roman way of death. Roman law forbade burial *in urbe*. To preserve the sanctity of the living, cemeteries were located on roads leading out of town, such as the Appian Way. These laws derived from a need to keep the dead at a distance. The Romans *feared* their dead. In fact, Roman funeral customs derived from a need to propitiate the sensibilities of the departed.[6] The very word *funus* may be translated as dead body, funeral ceremony, or murder. There was genuine concern that, if not treated appropriately, the spirits of the dead, or *manes*, would return to wreak revenge.

Technically, all that was necessary to make burial legal under Roman law was to scatter a handful of earth over the body. However, funerals were as significant to the Romans as they would later be to the Victorians. A lavish funeral, conducted by professional undertakers, was considered essential. Burial clubs enabled individuals to save for their last rites; even slaves could join.[7] Funerals normally took place three days after death. The corpse was washed and anointed with oils, as it was believed that the body was polluted by death and would not rest easy without ceremonial cleansing. It was then wrapped in a special toga and placed on a bier. This was carried from the house as a chorus of paid mourners wailed, in contrast to the studied calm of the household. The funeral procession observed strict hierarchy, with the heir at the forefront, dressed in a black toga, the folds of which he held before his face, his hair deliberately dishevelled to signify bereavement. The wearing of black was significant, as black garments were thought to confer invisibility upon the bereaved, protecting them from vengeful spirits.

Following directly behind the bier were the servants who would, in earlier times, have been slaughtered at the graveside, along with a warrior's horse. Musicians and torchbearers came next, with the rear taken up by the mimes – sinister, silent figures in wax masks modelled on dead members of the family. The cortège would stop at the Forum, where a funeral oration was given, before the procession made its way out of the city walls to the cemetery where, after burial, a funeral feast took place at the graveside, with libations poured to appease the spirit of the dear departed.

The Romans, like the British, practised cremation; in their case, the custom derived from the Greeks and the Etruscans. Cremation was well established in London by the first century AD. In *Urne Burial*, the seventeenth-century divine Sir Thomas Browne referred to the urns of '*Spittle* Fields by *London,* which contained the Coynes of *Claudius*, *Vespasian*, *Commodus*, *Antonius*, attended with Lacrymatories, Lamps, Bottles of Liquor, and other appurtenances of affectionate superstition'.[8] Browne also reminds us that, in Classical Antiquity, there was an element of noble sentiment to cremation. More than a hygienic method of disposing of the dead, cremation enabled lovers and comrades to be mingled together for eternity:

> The ashes of *Domitian* were mingled with those of *Julia*; of *Achilles* with those of *Patroclus*; All Urnes contained not single ashes; Without confused burnings they affectionately compounded their bones; passionately endeavouring to continue their living Unions. And when distance of death denied such conjunctions, unsatisfied affections conceived some satisfaction to be neighbours in the grave, to lye Urne by Urne, and touch but in their names.[9]

Members of the aspiring British middle class, persuaded to embrace all things Roman, had little difficulty in embracing the Roman way of death, as many of the practices, such as burying the cremains in a sanctified spot, corresponded with existing ritual. Under Roman conditions, the body was burned in a special pit at the cemetery. The bones were removed, washed, and placed in an amphora for the family to bury. A small number of urns were available, although sometimes cooking pots, which had cracked during the firing process and were not suitable for tableware, would be used. This practice was similar to the Beaker custom of burying the cremains in collared jars. The major cultural difference was that, instead of barrows, the Romans buried their dead in purpose-built cemeteries.

The remains of three major Roman cemeteries have been found on roads leading west, north and east out of London.[10] Recent excavations at Prescot Street, near Aldgate, have uncovered over 670 burials and 134 cremations. The original site, which lies on either side of the Colchester Road, covered fifty-one acres and contained over 100,000 dead from the 400 years during which it was used. Burial took place in a series of plots, divided by ditches. As well as the major road which dissected the cemetery and formed a route for funeral processions, a number of smaller roads were created and a quarry dug nearby for producing brick. Many of the plots had been used several times during the life of the cemetery, and the remains of lead coffins were found, along with traces of mausolea. Overlapping graves indicate that overcrowding was a problem, even in those days.

Grave goods included jars of food and wine (one motto beaker, now at the Museum of London, bears the inscription *utere*: use me), chickens, always buried to the left of the body, and coins for Charon, the ferryman, to row the deceased across the Styx. Hobnailed boots, for the long walk to the Underworld, were provided for both adults and children. Many grave goods offer clues to their owner's personality. The Harper Road Woman, who died around AD 70, was buried with her bronze torc necklace, a mirror and a jug of wine, suggesting a pleasure-loving character. At West Tenter Street, near Aldgate, another woman was sent on her way with two Medusa amulets to ward off the evil eye, a gaming set, to prevent boredom in the Netherworld, and a jet pendant. The Romans believed jet possessed magical properties to ward off evil spirits.

The Romans practised cremation up until AD 200, when it began to fall out of favour. Under the influence of Christianity, which emphasized the physical resurrection of the body, the first wooden coffins were introduced. Christian burial rites, derived from Judaic law, included washing the corpse before burial and anointing it with oils. Once the corpse had been washed, and the orifices plugged to prevent leakage, it was wrapped in a shroud. The belief persisted that a body must be entire for resurrection on Judgement Day, so, when possible, items such as missing teeth and even amputated limbs were carefully preserved and buried with the corpse.

Traditionally, bodies went on display for at least two days before burial, so that mourners could pay their last respects, and the important practice of 'watching', also derived from ancient Jewish ritual, might be observed. 'Watching' also seemed to develop from a natural reluctance to leave the dead person to whom so much care had been devoted during their final hours.

Roman coffins ranged from the simple wooden box to the elaborately decorated sarcophagus, placed in a marble mausoleum large enough to accommodate an entire family. The concept of the mausoleum was inspired by the monument to King Mausolus of Halicarnassus, one of the Seven Wonders of the World. Raised by the King's devoted wife, Artemisia, it consisted of a massive marble tomb, surmounted by an Ionic colonnade supporting a roof-like pyramid. At its foot stood a four-horse chariot containing statues of the King and Queen. Since then, the term 'mausoleum' has been applied to any massive tomb containing shelves upon which the dead could be laid in lead coffins.

The most remarkable discovery of recent years is that of the Spitalfields Woman.[11] In 1999, archaeologists were working on the excavation of a site earmarked for a new office block. They were expecting to find the remains of one of the largest hospitals in England (Spitalfields derives from 'St Mary's Hospital Fields'), but a greater discovery lay beneath. Under a layer of 8,000 mediaeval burials, they uncovered a cemetery, situated on Ermine Street, the major route north out of London. There were over 200 burials, the most spectacular of which consisted of a stone sarcophagus, dating from the fourth century AD. One of four high-profile burials, it had been placed on a raised area of the cemetery, designed to be seen from the main road. This feature had its drawbacks. Two of the tombs had been broken into, probably during the Late Roman period, and grave robbers had even created a ramp to make it easier to steal the sarcophagus. The latter had been enclosed in a timber mausoleum, long since rotten, although traces of the joists remained. Nearby were the remains of a child.

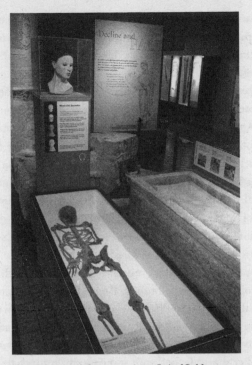

*The skeleton of the mysterious Spitalfields woman
and the reconstruction of her face.*

Unlike the other three, this sarcophagus had never been tampered with. Distracted, perhaps, by another find, or interrupted in their work, the grave robbers had left it intact. Perhaps they intended to return at a later date.

By the thirteenth century, the graves had been built over, which had preserved the sarcophagus for posterity. After scanning with a metal detector indicated that there was something precious inside, the lid was raised to show an elaborately decorated lead coffin, surrounded by mud. Inside was an intricate hair ornament made of jet, and a beautiful glass perfume bottle, suggesting that the inhabitant was a woman.

When the coffin was opened, it revealed the skeleton of a young woman, perfectly preserved, lying on a pillow of bay leaves and wrapped in an elaborate robe of Chinese silk, decorated with gold thread from Syria.

The Spitalfields Woman had been prosperous. She came from a wealthy family, the wife or daughter of a senior Government official. DNA testing revealed that she was probably of Spanish origin. Her sarcophagus was limestone, quarried in the East Midlands, possibly selected from a number of sarcophagi kept on hand for important burials by the precursors of the London undertaking trade. Tall for her day at five feet four inches, she showed little evidence of injury or disease; the cause of death was thought to have been an infection. And she had never given birth. DNA testing indicated that the child buried nearby was not related.

The Spitalfields Woman now resides in her coffin, at the Museum of London, for all to see. Reconstruction techniques, pioneered in the discipline of forensic science, have allowed experts to recreate her face. For all the Roman horror of the dead, there is nothing to fear here. We can look into her eyes, and consider the details of her short life, and gain some insight into what it was like to live and die in London, almost 2,000 years ago.

An earlier version of the bustling commercial melting pot that it has become today, London flourished under the Romans. However, as the Roman Empire declined, so did London. In AD 410 the Emperor Honorius withdrew his army from Britannia, abandoning London to a wave of barbarians from Denmark, Germany and the Lower Rhine. These new arrivals, who displaced the Celts and Romans, became known as the Anglo-Saxons. Like the nomadic tribes which had roamed London before the Roman invasion, the Anglo-Saxons were pagans, their religious beliefs shaped by Nordic mythology. Although many Roman buildings fell into disrepair – like their predecessors, the Anglo-Saxons preferred to live in simple village settlements – the newcomers made good use of the existing cemeteries.

The most spectacular and elaborate of all Saxon burials was not in London at all, but at Sutton Hoo in Suffolk, where, in the seventh century AD, an entire ship was dragged up from the river and equipped with priceless treasures for a king's last voyage to Valhalla. This is echoed in the epic poem *Beowulf*, believed to have been composed in the eighth century AD Beowulf's father, Scyld, was carried down to the shore and placed in 'a ring-prowed ship, straining at anchor and sheeted with ice', filled with battle armour, swords and gems. In keeping with tradition, Scyld's ship was launched into the 'unknown deep and trackless seas'[12]; but the ship at Sutton Hoo, the ultimate in grave goods, was buried, a fittingly glorious end to what must have been a glorious life.

The advent of Christianity brought such magnificent examples of paganism to a close. The Church imposed its own pattern on burial, but there was still plenty of opportunity for extravagant funerals and elaborate monuments. There would also be a new challenge to Londoners on how they coped with their dead *en masse*, in the form of the Black Death.

# 2: *DANSE MACABRE*

## *London and the Black Death*

Mediaeval London was dominated by the Church. More than thirty monasteries, convents, priories and hospitals lined its narrow streets. At this stage in its development, England's capital consisted of the City of London, roughly one square mile, surrounded by the mighty wall which had endured since the days of the Romans. The Tower of London, built by William the Conqueror in the eleventh century, occupied the eastern boundary. To the north lay Cripple Gate and Bishop's Gate; to the west stood New Gate and Blackfriars; while, along the south bank, the Thames formed a natural defence. Beyond the wall, Westminster, the seat of Government, lay to the west, 'Hole Bourn' and 'Clerks Well' to the north and, across the river, St Thomas's Spital (ancestor of the great London teaching hospital) and St Mary Overey's Priory.

Space was at a premium, and enterprising Londoners constructed houses, shops and even a church on London Bridge. Trade flourished here, in the largest and wealthiest city in England. Entire streets were devoted to one trade and their names survive today: Apothecary Street; Shoe Lane; Stonecutter Street; Pudding Lane.

London was one vast factory, drawing workers from all over the country.

In administrative terms, London was divided into parishes, like a series of overlapping villages, which took responsibility for all who dwelled in them, the living and the dead. Named after the churches which governed them, parishes were controlled by churchwardens and overseen by 'vestries', the precursors of modern district councils or boroughs.

The religious Orders played a vital role in the community, carrying out the majority of charity work, tending the sick, burying the dead and praying for the dead and the living. The monks' behaviour, however, was sometimes less than perfect. Despite the Christian injunction to fasting and abstinence, monks ate better than the laity. Recent excavations at Bermondsey Abbey yielded skeletons with the symptoms of arthritis and obesity. Living on a diet heavy in saturated fats and wine, London's monks were condemned by Peter the Venerable, Abbot of Cluny, for 'wearing furs and eating fat'.[1]

The cloisters of St Bartholomew's Priory, West Smithfield, were notorious for lowlife: 'lords and ladies, aldermen and their wives, squires and fiddlers, citizens and rope-dancers, jack-puddings [clowns] and lawyers, mistresses and maids, masters and 'prentices' meeting up for 'plays, lotteries, farces and all the temptations to destruction'.[2] Occasionally, scholars from St Paul's and other grammar schools would meet in St Bartholomew's churchyard for learned debates, but these events inevitably degenerated into street fights and had to be discontinued.[3]

Influential convents and monasteries included the Greyfriars or Franciscans, later Christ's Hospital, which took in underprivileged children; the Blackfriars or Dominicans; and the Crossed or Crouched Friars by Fenchurch Street. Outside the City walls were the Whitefriars or Carmelites, south of Fleet Street; the Abbey and Convent at Westminster; St Mary Spital, outside Bishopsgate; and Bermondsey Abbey. Some Orders were mendicants (beggars), who had no burial place of their own, but most establishments had a large cemetery or 'cloister garth' for monks and nuns. At the Church of the Crutched Friars, by Fenchurch Street, rules for burial stated that:

> When any Brother of Suster of the same Bretherhede is dede, he or she shall have 4 Torchys of Wex of the Bretherhede, to bring the Body in Erthe: And every Brother or Suster shall come to his Masse of Requiem, and offer I$^d$ and abide still to the Tyme the Body be buryed, uppon Pain of a l.Wex, yf he or she be within the Cite.[4]

Despite the reference to torches and tapers, burials did not always take place in the evenings. They were conducted after Mass, before dinner, and with as little delay as possible. These were solemn proceedings, particularly if the deceased had been a Prior, or a Canon, with an impressive procession of monks bearing lighted tapers, chanting Psalms, sprinkling holy water, and the celebration of Requiem Mass. At Christ's Hospital, this practice persisted into the eighteenth century, with the Christ's Hospital scholar or 'blue' carried in a torchlight procession and buried within the school grounds as his fellow students sang the thirty-ninth Psalm. The boys also participated in London's ceremonial funerals. Whenever a worthy died, one boy for each year of the man's life marched in his cortège.

Builders demolishing the remains of the Blackfriars monastery after the Great Fire of London discovered four heads, in pewter pots, in a wall. The heads, which were embalmed, had tonsured hair. The historian Strype speculated that these were the heads of 'some zealous priests or friars executed for treason, or for denying the King's Supremacy; and here privately deposited by these Black Friars'.[5]

The monastic Orders were responsible for a number of hospitals, which had their own burial grounds. These included St Bartholomew's in the City and St Thomas's in Southwark, devoted to the care of the 'wounded, maimed, sick and diseased'. Greyfriars or Bridewell, a house 'for the correction of vagabonds', near the Embankment, also had its own burial ground, which continued to be used into the nineteenth century.

As the distinguished historian Dr Vanessa Harding has observed, the dead were everywhere in mediaeval London, 'neither out of sight, nor out of mind'.[6] The Romans had feared their dead, and banished them to distant cemeteries; by the Middle Ages, Christians buried their dead close to home. Londoners were born, baptized, married and buried in the Church. Literally, in many instances, as burial within the walls and vaults was considered the most distinguished form of interment.

Although St John Chrysostom had directed Christians to continue the Roman practice in the fourth century AD, warning them that burial in the church was analogous to placing a rotting cadaver near the limbs of Christ, his caution was ignored.[7] The custom of burying within the church derived from the concept of martyrdom. Christians revered those who had died for their faith, turning their tombs into shrines. The faithful clamoured to be buried alongside the martyrs, as close as possible to the venerable remains, a custom which, in anthropological terms, recalls Neolithic beliefs that certain human remains possessed supernatural properties. It was believed that canonized saints did not rot, like lesser mortals, but that their corpses were miraculously preserved and emanated an odour of sanctity, a sweet floral smell, for years after death. In forensic terms, such preservation is likely to be a result of natural mummification in hot, dry conditions.

The tradition of martyrdom informed a different attitude towards human remains. Corpses *per se* were not regarded as objects of fear. Nowhere was this more evident than in the charnel house of St Paul's. Built over a shrine to St Erkenwald, an Anglo-Saxon bishop of London, following a great fire, beneath its soil lay the graves of Britons, Saxons and Romans. St Paul's was London's principal church after Westminster Abbey. Weddings were celebrated here, sermons preached, plays enacted and burials conducted.

The institution of the charnel house was a particularly gruesome aspect of mediaeval burial. Christians then had little concept of one man, one grave, and many, of course, could not afford an elaborate burial. Fees consisted of payments to the gravedigger for breaking the ground, to the priest and to the parish church, and to the sexton, who tolled the passing bell. Those who could not pay were buried 'on the parish', in pits, wrapped in shrouds. When one pit was full, it was covered in earth, and a previous one reopened. The bones were dug up, and taken to the charnel house for safekeeping. The term derives from the French *charnier:* flesh. In France and Italy, skeletal remains were used to create artistic displays, including chandeliers, which were exhibited in the ossuary – a gallery above a charnel house.

Eventually, even the bodies of the wealthy, buried under the stone flags of the church, submitted to this fate. But it was not regarded as violation. The French historian Philippe Ariès has observed that the significant thing was to be buried in or near the church. What actually happened to your body after that was immaterial. Tombs and headstones were reserved for the nobility. Although the faithful visited the shrines of saints, the concept of returning to the grave of a loved one, and communing with their memory, was unknown.

The dead were also at the heart of the city. Saturated with Christian theology, the attitude of the average Londoner was, in the words of Ariès, *'et moriemur* – and we shall all die'. With land at a premium, churchyards were communal spaces at the core of parish life, more like streetmarkets than parks. Laundry fluttered above the graves; chickens and pigs jostled for scraps. Bands of travelling players enacted dramas, and desecration was inevitable, with 'boisterous churls' playing football, dancing, drinking and fighting on the hallowed ground. Just how rough these activities got is indicated by entries in parish registers of deaths resulting from participation in such pastimes. Church services were frequently disturbed, and the erection of booths for the sale of food and drink caused serious damage to the graves. Before condemning such irreverence, we should remember that the bond between the living and the dead was very different from today. It was an extension of the mediaeval belief that the dead were, in some sense, still close by, and probably grateful to hear the merrymaking.

Under normal conditions, London possessed enough burial space to satisfy demand, but the arrival of the Black Death in 1348 placed existing resources under enormous strain, leading to the creation of London's first cemeteries since Roman times.

The epidemic of 1348 was the most severe, but it was not the first. For centuries, the plague had been, according to Victorian historian Mrs Isabella Holmes, a 'constant and dreaded visitor to Britain'. London was first ravaged by the plague in 664, and it returned again and again, constantly driving kings, courtiers and wealthier citizens to flee to the country for safety. However, the strain which struck England in 1348 was so virulent that previous outbreaks paled into insignificance. Although historians such as John Stow wrote that 'scarce the tenth person of all sorts was left alive', it is now believed that the Black Death wiped out a third to half the population of London, and up to 50 per cent of the population of Europe.

Originating in the deserts of Mongolia in the 1320s, it spread to China and, by 1351, had killed two-thirds of the population there. Mongolian nomads then carried it west, along trade routes. The Black Death wiped out millions as it rampaged through these trade routes. Thousands perished in Constantinople in 1347. The following year, two-fifths of the population died in Cairo. Corpses were piled so high in the Egyptian village of Bilbais that bandits hid behind them during ambushes. One third of the Islamic world died as the plague spread on to Damascus, Jerusalem and Mecca. The Black Death derived its name from the internal bleeding that caused black bruises to appear on the skin. There were three, inter-related forms of plague: bubonic, which caused buboes or tumours on the neck, armpit and groin, and from which victims occasionally recovered; pneumatic plague, which attacked the respiratory system; and septicaemic plague, which attacked the blood system and was always fatal.[8]

In 1346, Genovese merchants travelled to Caffa (now Feodosia) in the Crimea, where they came under siege from Tartar warlords. When plague broke out among the Tartars, their leader, Janibeg, ordered the survivors to catapult the corpses over the walls into the city. The Genovese fled, bringing the plague back to Italy late in 1347. Thousands died, and were thrown into mass graves. In Siena, one Agnolo di Tura buried his five children with his own hands. 'So many died,' he wrote, 'they believed it was the end of the world.' In *The Decameron*, Giovanni Boccaccio noted: 'Such was the cruelty of heaven and, to a great degree, of man, that, between March 1348 and the following July, it is esti-mated that more than one hundred thousand human beings lost their lives within the walls of Florence, what with the ravages attendant on the plague and the barbarity of the survivors towards the sick.'[9]

Many Italian citizens felt that the only solution to the plague was to leave their families, their homes and their city. Neighbours avoided one another. Brother deserted brother. Worst of all, parents abandoned their children.

As the corpses piled up, the churches ran out of consecrated ground and the authorities were forced to dig mass graves, where bodies were buried by the hundred. 'They stowed them away like bales in the hold of a ship,' wrote Boccaccio, 'and covered them with a little earth, until the whole trench was full.' Another commentator observed that the mass graves looked like lasagne.

The Black Death soon reached France, killing over half the pop-ulation of Marseilles. At Montpelier, only seven out of one hundred and forty Dominican friars survived. Attempts to treat the symptoms with Theriac, a remedy which included crushed snakes, failed dismally. Cattle were slaughtered in the belief that they spread disease. Huge fires were lit to fumigate the streets. One theory was that the air had become stiff and needed to be dispersed: bells were rung and birds were released to fly around rooms. Eventually, the authorities realized that quarantine was the only way of containing the outbreak, and entire households were walled up. Many believed the plague was a punishment sent from God. An Order of Flagellants sprang up, who lashed themselves in an attempt to stop God attacking the world. As mass hysteria broke out, the populace sought a scapegoat for the epidemic. First lepers, then the Jews, were held responsible. In towns and villages across Europe, thousands of Jews were accused of poisoning the water sources and burned alive. In Frankfurt, the Flagellants organized the wholesale massacre of the entire Jewish population.

The plague struck England in June 1348, arriving by ship at Melcombe Regis (Weymouth) on bales of cloth from Burgundy infested with rat fleas. Spreading like wildfire from Bristol to Gloucester to Oxford, it attacked London in November 1348 and flourished in the city's filthy conditions. London was a heaving anthill of overhanging timber-frame houses, where jutting rooftops met across narrow alleyways, trapping fetid air beneath. Pigs and cattle roamed between the houses; industrial waste, from the tanneries which boiled up wool and leather using animal excrement in the process, littered the banks of the river. Butchers turned out their offal into the open drains, which were no more than sewers. Edward III complained that, 'When passing along the water of the Thames, we have beheld dung and lay stools and other filth accumulated in diverse places within the city, and have also perceived the fumes and other abominable stenches arising therefrom.'

Crammed together in rat-infested rookeries, the populace were vulnerable to infection, with the poor the inevitable victims; ideal conditions for a deadly virus to take hold. London was a death trap.

By January 1349, the 'deadly pestilence' had become such a threat that Parliament was prorogued (suspended but not dissolved), because 'grave fears were entertained for the safety of those coming here at the time', according to Robert of Avesbury, an eyewitness. Avesbury recalled that:

Those marked for death were scarce permitted to live longer than three or four days. It showed favour to no-one, except a very few of the wealthy. On the same day, twenty or forty or sixty bodies, and on many occasions many more, might be committed for burial together in the same pit. The pestilence arrived in London at about the feast of All Saints [1 November] and daily deprived many of life. It grew so powerful that between Candlemass [2 February] and Easter [12 April] more than two hundred corpses were buried almost every day in the new burial ground made next to Smithfield, and this was in addition to the bodies buried in other graveyards in the city.[10]

According to William Maitland, who compiled a massive *History of London* in 1756, the new burial ground came into being because the plague:

. . . continued to rage in a most deplorable and dreadful Manner, till the common Cemeteries were not capacious enough to receive the vast Number of Bodies so that several well-disposed Persons were induced to purchase Ground to supply that Defect: Amongst whom we find Ralph *Stratford*, Bishop of *London*, who in 1348, bought a Piece of Ground called *No-Man's Land*, which he enclosed with a Brick Wall, and dedicated to the Burial of the Dead.[11]

The Bishop of London consecrated this new cemetery, but it became so full that an extension had to be opened:

... a Place called *Spittle-Croft*, the Property of *St Bartholomew's Hospital*, containing thirteen acres and a Rod of Ground, which was also purchased and appropriated to the same Use of burying the Dead by *Sir Walter Manny*; in which were buried 50,000 Persons, who died of the Plague, as recorded by antient Historians and was long remembered by the following Inscription fixed on a Stone Cross upon the Premises: *A great Plague raging in the Year of our Lord 1349, this Burial-Ground was consecrated, wherein, and within the Bounds of the Present Monastery, were buried more than fifty thousand Bodies of the Dead, besides many others thenceforward to the present Time: Whose Souls the Lord have Mercy upon.*[12]

Another cemetery was subsequently opened at East Smithfield by 'one *John Corey*, a Clergyman, for the same Use' later that same year; dedicated to the Holy Trinity, 'in which were also buried innumerable Bodies, during the Time of this Pestilence'. Maitland believed that, 'With the Addition of those buried in other Grounds, Church-yards, and Churches, may convince us of the Assertion, that not one in ten survived this divine Visitation, and that there could not die less than 100,000 Persons in the whole.'[13]

Archaeologist Duncan Hawkins of the Museum of London has taken issue with Maitland's figures. The population of London between 1300 and 1348 has been estimated at around forty to one hundred thousand. Of these, between a third to half perished during the Black Death. Whatever the figures involved, Hawkins argues, it is obvious that the victims of the Black Death overwhelmed the existing provision for the dead in churchyards and religious institutions. Recent excavations suggest that between ten and twelve thousand bodies were buried at the new cemeteries.[14]

Hawkins discovered that Londoners who succumbed to the Black Death were treated with considerably more reverence than in Italy. Between 1986 and 1988, Hawkins led excavations at the East Smithfield cemeteries, which lie beneath the Royal Mint; these revealed that, far from being hurled into mass graves, the majority of the dead were stacked neatly, five deep, with their heads at the west and feet to the east, in keeping with the Christian practice that bodies should be facing the right direction when they were resurrected on Judgement Day. Even at the height of the plague, many victims were decently interred, in shrouds and coffins.

The cemeteries did not remain as such once the first wave of the plague had abated in London in 1350. Real estate was already at a premium in England's capital. Spittle Croft, where more than five thousand bodies were buried over a twenty-year period, became the site of the Charterhouse or Carthusian Priory, built in 1371. At the cemetery of the Holy Trinity, 'just without the wall', the Abbey of St Mary of Grace was founded, for Cistercian monks. The development covered the victualizing office and adjoining houses.

Only No-Man's Land retained its identity as a cemetery. Subsequently referred to as the Pardon Churchyard, it was used for the burial of the outcast and excluded, like heretics, executed people and suicides.

This was not the last Londoners saw of the plague. In 1361, another outbreak caused Edward III to order all cattle to be slaughtered, from Stratford in the east of London to Knightsbridge in the west. To no avail, as twelve hundred people died in forty-eight hours.

London recovered, eventually, but the aftermath of the Black Death was devastating. The epidemic destroyed the economy, causing mass starvation and anarchy. The shortage of men and women available to join and run the monasteries, and the decline in numbers of men who could enter the priesthood, undermined the authority of the Church.[15] On a theoretical level, the Black Death led the devout to question the very nature of existence. Death, once the inevitable conclusion of a good Christian life, now became a terrifying apparition, striking without warning and wiping out an entire generation. This new manifestation of death was epitomized by the *danse macabre*.

*Dancing with Dr Machabre (from a mediaeval woodcut).*

The *danse macabre* was a traditional form of iconography, popu-lar throughout Europe, depicting Death engaged in a dialogue with every member of society, from the Pope to the common labourer. Death is portrayed as a 'transi' or half-decomposed corpse, enticing the living to join him, and serving to remind us all that *memento mori*: remember you must die, while the dance itself is not so much a dance as a procession, with the subjects advancing gravely and reluctantly, as though participating in a funeral procession. 'Dances of death' actually took place at European cathedrals following Mass, with the participants paid in wine.[16]

The message of the *danse macabre* consisted of three elements: first came the notion that we are all equal in the presence of death. Second was the idea of confronting the living with the dead, a familiar mediaeval theme reinforcing the vanity of human grandeur, and the third was the dance itself, which appears to have been an offshoot of the morbid ecclesiastical imagination, designed to frighten sinners into repentance.

Accounts from Europe indicate that the *danse macabre* took

another form, inspired by the Black Death, rather like our children's rhyme 'Ring o' Ring o' Roses', which refers to the Great Plague. In 1374, a fanatical sect of dancers appeared in the Rhine, convinced that they could put an end to the epidemic by dancing for days and allowing other people to trample on their bodies. It is not recorded whether they recovered but, incredibly, they began to raise money from bystanders. By the time they reached Cologne they were 500 strong, dancing like demons, half-naked with flowers in their hair. Regarded as a menace by the authorities, these dancers macabre were threatened with excommunication.[17]

In London, the *danse macabre* became the central feature of a chapel in the Pardon Churchyard, which formed part of the old St Paul's. Founded by Gilbert Becket, and rebuilt in Henry V's time by Dean Moore, the chapel was surrounded by a cloister decorated with a mural depicting the *danse macabre*, described thus by the writer John Stow in 1601:

> About this Cloyster was artificially and richly painted the dance of Machabray, or dance of death, commonly called the dance of Pauls: the like whereof, was painted about S. Innocents cloister, at Paris in France: the metres or poesie of this daunce, were translated out of French into England by John Lidgate, the Monke of Bery, & with y$^e$ picture of Death, leading all estates painted about the Cloyster: at the speciall request and dispence of Jankin Carpenter, in the Raigne of Henry the 6. In the Cloyster were buried many persons, some of worship and others of honour; the monuments of whom, in number and curious workemanship, passed all other that were in that church.[18]

Jankin Carpenter, who really deserves the credit for persuading England's leading poet John Lydgate to translate the verses, was the executor of the famous Lord Mayor of London, Richard Whittington. The people of all estates who appear in the poem and were depicted on the wall represented every level of society, facing the inexorable power of Death. Pope, Emperor, Cardinal, Empress, Patriarch, King, Archbishop, Prince, Bishop, Earl or Baron, Abbot or Prior, Abbess, Justice, Knight or Squire, Mayor, Canon, 'Woman Sworn Chaste' [a nun], Gentlewoman, Astronomer, Physician, Merchant, Labourer, Minstrel, Child and finally, Hermit. *All erthely creatures to obey my noblynes*, states Death: there is no getting away from 'Dr Machabre'. *Ryche & pore must daunce in pe same way.*[19]

The mural of the *danse macabre* made a profound impression on Sir Thomas More. Speaking of the remembrance of Death, he says:

> But if we not only here this word Death, but also let sink into our heartes, the very fantasye and depe imaginacion thereof, we shall parceive therby that we wer never so gretly moved by the behold-ing of the Daunce of Death pictured in Poules [Paul's], as we shal fele ourself stered and altered by the feling of that imaginacion in our hertes. And no marvell. For these pictures expresse only y$^e$ lothely figure of our dead bony bodies, bitten away y$^e$ flesh.[20]

More himself was executed on the orders of Henry VIII in 1535, after opposing the Reformation. In 1549, the *danse macabre* also fell victim, when the chapel was destroyed on the orders of the Duke of Somerset, the Lord Protector, who was salvaging materials to build his mansion on the Strand. According to Stow:

> In the year 1549, on the tenth of Aprill, the said Chappell by commaundement of the Duke of Summerset, was begun to bee pulled downe, with the whole Cloystrie, the daunce of Death, the Tombes, and monuments: so that nothing thereof was left, but the bare plot ground, which is since converted into a garden, for the Pety Canons.[21]

The *danse macabre* might have been destroyed, but Lydgate's senti-ments had impressed themselves on generations of Londoners: *Deth spareth not/pore ne blode royal.*[22] Death was universal; but the manner in which that death was observed was another matter. Doctor Machabre would knock on a palace door, just as he did on the door of a humble minstrel. But the funeral of a royal conjured up a unique blend of religious and dramatic elements: it would become the Theatre of Death.

# 3: *MEMENTO MORI*

## The Theatre of Death

*When beggars die, there are no comets seen;*
*The heavens themselves blaze forth the death of princes.*[1]

Life for the Elizabethans was nasty, brutish and short. Londoners lived with the constant prospect of violent death. There were, for instance, the lethal knife-fights, such as the one that killed dramatist Kit Marlowe in the Deptford Tavern; public executions; and, of course, the plague, which continued to menace the city from the outskirts of town, 'pitching his tent in the polluted suburbs, like a Spanish leaguer, or stalking Tamberlaine', according to the excitable polemicist, Thomas Dekker.

Long before the epidemic of 1665, London endured a series of outbreaks of the plague, the worst of which occurred in the year of the Queen's death, 1603. In his ironically entitled *The Wonderful Year*,[2] Dekker portrayed London as one vast burial ground, gaping with a hundred hungry graves. So many coffins harassed the churches that there was no room left for weddings, and every individual faced a grisly end, and 'must one day be thrown, like stinking carrion, into a rank and common grave'.

Death and burial were a public spectacle. Shakespeare may have seen for himself the gravediggers at St Ann's, Soho, playing skittles with skulls and bones.[3] There is an echo of this in *Hamlet*, as the tragic hero commands Yorick's skull: 'Now get you to my lady's chamber, and tell her, let her paint an inch thick, to this favour she must come; make her laugh at that.'[4]

*Hamlet*'s gravediggers are hearty artisans, who regard themselves akin to Adam, the first man and the original gardener, and see no shame in their occupation. They are not unsympathetic creations. Public opinion, however, had already revealed a degree of antipathy to those who made a living from death. Dekker referred to 'merry sextons, hungry coffin-sellers, and nasty grave-makers, employed, like moles, in casting up of earth and digging of trenches'. Bosola, about to murder the Duchess of Malfi in Webster's tragedy of the same name, describes himself as a tomb-maker, and in Act 4, Scene 2, asks: 'Do we grow fantastical in our death bed? Do we affect fashion in the grave?' Bosola, who enters another scene with a human leg over one shoulder, is a grotesque creation, a necrophiliac monster, but a monster familiar to the audiences of his time.

The sixteenth century was still a period when the living shared their space with the dead; churchyards continued to be employed for a variety of activities. St Paul's Churchyard, which extended further to the north than it does today, was a worldly place, put to a number of uses that would today be condemned as inappropriate. The historian William Maitland noted that in 1569, 'A Lottery was set on Foot in St Paul's Churchyard, where it was begun to be drawn at the West Door of the Church on the 11th of January, and continued incessantly drawing, Day and Night, till the 6th of May following.'[5]

The Cathedral became a judgment-hall for foreign heretics who were condemned to be burned at Smithfield. One tract describes the south aisle in the late sixteenth century as being a centre of 'usury and popery and the north side for simony' (buying or selling of ecclesiastical preferment). In addition to all kinds of rendezvous and brawls, intrigues and conspiracies, there was a horse-fair, and the middle aisle, Paul's Walk, was a fashionable promenading ground for the rich and eccentric every morning and afternoon.

St Paul's was also the venue for another vital Elizabethan activity: religious and political controversy. St Paul's Cross, at the north-east corner of the Cathedral, was constructed of timber and mounted upon steps of stone covered with lead. Dating from 1299, its original purpose was to inspire passers-by to pray for the repose of the dead, in keeping with Catholic doctrine. However, the cross soon became a popular soapbox, the Speaker's Corner of its day, from which announcements and harangues on all such matters as the authorities judged to be of public concern were poured into the ear and heart of the populace. The cross featured all shades of opinion, from clerics to charlatans and cranks. Bishops Latimer and Ridley frequently preached at St Paul's Cross, proclaiming to crowds of eager listeners the opinions that later cost them their lives. They needed bodyguards to protect them from the crowd, and eventually, on the orders of Mary Tudor, they were burned at the stake in 1555.

There was a strong link between drama and death. In addition to famous clerics thundering out their message from the pulpit (and suffering public execution), mystery plays had been performed in churches from the tenth century onwards. At the church of St Catherine Cree, Leadenhall Street, plays included *The Massacre of the Innocents*, the shepherds feeding their flocks on Christmas Eve, and scenes from the life of St Catherine. Originally, plays took place inside the church, but these were banned during the Reformation by the Bishop of London. After this, troupes of strolling players performed a more advanced form of drama in the churchyards. An old parish record includes the following entry: 'Receyved of Hugh Grymes, for lycens geven to certen players to playe their enterludes in the churche-yarde from the feast of Easter, An D'ni. 1560, untyll the feaste of Seynt Mychaell Tharchangell next comynge, every holydaye, to the use of the parysshe, the some of 27s and 8d.'[6]

Two funerals represent the extremes of sixteenth-century death: that of Anne Boleyn, discarded wife and victim of a public execution in 1536; and that of her daughter, Elizabeth I, the supreme monarch, whose funeral in 1603 was one of the most spectacular London has ever seen, in its combination of tradition, religion, political gesture and theatrical event.

Death by public execution was a common fate in sixteenth-century London. England under the Tudors was a police state, and there was no telling where the axe might fall. A trusted statesman, Sir Thomas More, Speaker of the House of Commons, was executed in 1535; as was a beautiful young Queen. Something more than the ubiquitous threat of plague inspired the English pamphleteer and playwright Thomas Nashe when he reflected in 1600 that:

> *Brightness falls from the air*
> *Queens have died young and fair*[7]

Brightness could also be the blade of a sword, flashing down on a pretty neck. Dishonoured and discarded, condemned on trumped-up charges, Anne Bolyen was sent to the Tower of London on 2 May 1536. King Henry VIII had tired of his twenty-nine-year-old Queen after a marriage of less than three years, and her failure to bear him a male heir. After she miscarried a boy, he accused her of witchcraft, adultery and incest.

A barge carried Anne from Greenwich, along the same route that she had taken to prepare for her Coronation, and, handed over to a Constable at Traitor's Gate, she became hysterical, laughing and crying by turns. Anne was escorted to her last home – a cell in the Lieutenant's lodgings, fourteen foot square by eight foot high, with a casement window looking out over Tower Green. The sheer drop beneath left no prospect of escape. Few people emerged alive from the Tower. From being a mighty fortress, designed to impress Londoners and foreigners alike, it had become England's state prison.

During the Tudor period, the Tower had four known burial grounds, consisting of the churchyard of St Peter Ad Vincula, its vaults, and the outer graveyard, as well as a little strip by the eastern wall, that was used for the burial of prisoners and members of the household. Burial also took place within the Tower. In 1674, the remains of two young children were discovered buried at the foot of the staircase of the White Tower. 'Meetly deep in the ground, under a great heap of stones,' describes Holmes. Assuming these to be the bodies of the two little Princes murdered on the orders of Richard III, Charles II had them reinterred in Westminster Abbey.[8]

It was from the Tower that Anne wrote her last letter to Henry. Pleading for mercy towards 'the infant princess, your daughter', Anne begged for a fair trial: 'Let not my sworn enemies sit as my accusers and my judges; yea, let me receive an open trial, for my truth shall fear no open shame.' Imploring pardon for 'those poor gentlemen who are in prisonment for my sake', Anne was unable to resist a snide reference to Jane Seymour, 'that party for whose sake I am now as I am'.[9]

It made no difference, of course. Henry had long resolved to be rid of her. After a show trial on 15 May, before 200 people, Anne was acquitted of incest, for which the traditional punishment was being burned at the stake. She was, however, found guilty of treason. Anne went to the scaffold on Tower Green on 19 May, in a dark grey gown with a crimson petticoat. Her executioner, from Calais, was said to be an expert in his field. Joking that she was in a safe pair of hands and pointing out that 'I have a little neck!' Anne forgave those who had brought her to this pass, prayed for her husband, and was blindfolded. According to Stow, the executioner smote off her head at one stroke with a sword. Next day, dressed in white, Henry married Jane Seymour.

There was to be no heraldic funeral for Anne. Instead, her body, with the head, was placed in a narrow chest, in the choir of the Chapel Royal of St Peter Ad Vincula, adjacent to the Tower. This church was the last resting-place of executed nobility and those who had died awaiting capital punishment in London's Death Row. The Earl of Arundel, the Dukes of Somerset, Monmouth, Norfolk and Northumberland were buried there, and Anne was later joined by another of Henry's wives, Catherine Howard, and Lady Jane Grey, the Nine Days' Queen. An item claimed to be the head of Lady Jane's father, the Duke of Suffolk, was put on show at the nearby Holy Trinity Church, Minories, late into the nineteenth century. Displayed in a glass case, it was preserved like leather, with strands of hair still clinging to the scalp, and a wound visible where the axeman had struck a first, unsuccessful blow.

Anne's body was identified during renovations to the chapel in 1876, and she was reinterred, her final resting-place marked on the marble floor. Macaulay later wrote of St Peter's that:

> . . . there is no sadder spot on earth . . . Death is there associated, not, as in Westminster and St Paul's, with genius and virtue, with public veneration and with imperishable renown; not, as in our humblest churches and churchyards, with everything that is most endearing in social and domestic charities: but with whatever is darkest in human nature and in human destiny; with the savage triumph of implacable enemies, with the inconstancy, the ingratitude, the cowardice of friends, with all the miseries of fallen greatness and of blighted fame. Thither have been carried through successive ages, by the rude hands of gaolers, without one mourner following, the bleeding relics of men, who had been the captains of armies, the leaders of parties, the oracles of senates, and the ornaments of Courts.[10]

The Tower, eight centuries of tragedy and suffering within its walls, has inevitably attracted more than its fair share of ghost stories. Sir Walter Raleigh's phantom is said to flit about the cells; the white figure of a woman has appeared on Tower Green and, just as suddenly, vanished. In 1864, a sentry posted beneath the window of Anne Boleyn's chamber was found unconscious. Court-martialled for being asleep at his post, the soldier claimed he had been approached by a figure. He challenged it, but the figure bore down on him relentlessly. When he charged it with his bayonet and met no resistance, he collapsed in a faint. At his court martial, two witnesses said they had looked out of the window of the Bloody Tower before going to bed. In the clear, cold moonlight they too had seen a figure approach the sentry, and seen everything happen just as he had described. The sentry was acquitted.

Anne met an ignominious fate, laid to rest in the furtive manner of a political prisoner. Almost seventy years later, her daughter, 'Gloriana', was buried in one of the most elaborate examples of the heraldic funeral London had ever seen.

The heraldic funeral derived its name from the College of Heralds, part of the Royal Household. The original role of heralds had been to organize tournaments. The knights who fought in tournaments were recognized by the arms on their shields and the crests on their helmets, which were hereditary. As a result, the College of Heralds became experts in family coats of arms, and genealogy. Part of their remit soon came to include organizing funerals, derived from the elaborate funerals of the French court in the thirteenth century. The Earl Marshall (always the Duke of Norfolk) ran the College of Heralds, and it was his role to order the Court into mourning, and specify the funeral arrangements.

Elizabeth I died in Richmond on 24 March 1603, 'mildly like a lamb, easily like a ripe apple from the tree', according to her physician, Dr John Manningham. The Queen's body, surrounded by her ladies-in-waiting, was taken from Richmond to Whitehall on a barge draped with black. The coffin then lay in state at Westminster in a room 'hung with mourning', decked from ceiling to floor with great swags of heavy black fabric, which had remained the traditional colour of mourning since Roman times. Only Mary Queen of Scots challenged the prevailing orthodoxy when she wore white to mourn the death of Lord Darnley in 1567, earning the title of 'The White Queen'.

On previous occasions, displays of mourning had been reckoned so extravagant as to threaten the monarch's authority. Over 900 black gowns were distributed at the funeral of the Earl of Oxford, who had been heavily fined by Henry VII for excessive display of power and wealth. However, not everyone who was entitled to an elaborate funeral received one. When Jane Seymour died in 1537, a fortnight after the birth of Edward VI, Henry VIII made strenuous attempts to restrict extravagant mourning. A big state funeral was deemed inadvisable for political reasons. The Lords decided: 'that the wearing of doole [from the Latin, *doleo,* to grieve] and such outward demonstration of mourning . . . did not profit the dead . . . Private men should reserve their private sorrows to their own houses, and not diminish the presence of their Prince with doleful tokens.'[11]

Although Elizabeth had a horror of being embalmed and directed her remains to be wrapped up in cerecloth (waxed linen), sources suggest she probably *was* embalmed, as this was standard practice for royalty at the time. As heraldic funerals inevitably took time to organize, a rudimentary form of embalming had to be carried out, so that the body could be paraded through the streets at the head of the procession.

According to the historian Dr Julian Litten, the procedure consisted of eviscerating the corpse, with internal organs buried elsewhere or placed in a pot. The inner cavities were then sluiced out and disinfected with aromatic oils, and then sewn up. The exterior was preserved by rubbing it with spices. Finally it was wrapped in cerecloth, and the seams sealed with beeswax to keep it airtight. Then it was placed in a lead coffin. Commoners' bones may have been dug up again and slung into a charnel house: for royalty, burial was for ever.

Another embalming technique, especially if the person had died abroad, was the *mos teutonicus* method. This involved chopping up the body, boiling it in wine or vinegar until it became skeletalized (the flesh falling from the bones), then shipping the remains home for burial. When Henry V died in France in 1422, his remains were subjected to *mos teutonicus*, so that he could be brought back to England, but the operation was not a success, and the body was in no condition for display. As an alternative, an effigy of the King was constructed from leather and dressed in his clothes; a wax death mask served as a face. The effigy headed the procession and was later displayed in Westminster Abbey.

Heraldic funerals impressed through sheer weight of numbers. The more elevated the status of the deceased, the bigger the funeral. Part of the impact of the heraldic funeral was the amount of time it took the serried ranks of mourners, clad in their 'blackes', to parade through the streets of London. Unlike the swift removal of Anne Boleyn's remains, the funeral procession of her illustrious daughter took many hours. On the morning of 28 April 1603, no less than 1,600 people followed the funeral procession of The Right High and Mightie Princesse Elizabeth Queene of England, France and Ireland from the Palace of Whitehall to Westminster Abbey. This spectacular funeral brought together three key elements of life and death in Tudor London: the pageantry of the heraldic funeral; the civic pride of the big London funeral; and the dramatic spectacle of the royal funeral.

According to Dekker: 'Never did the English nation behold so much black worn as there was at her funeral. Her hearse seemed to be an island swimming in water, for round about it there rained showers of tears.'[12] In *Englandes Mourning Garment*, Henry Chettle invokes Shakespeare's *Rape of Lucretia*, comparing Elizabeth's death with a form of *danse macabre*:

> *Death now hath ceaz'd her in his ycie armes,*
> *That sometime was the Sun of our delight:*
> *And pittilesse of any after-harmes,*
> *Hath veyld her glory in the cloude of night . . .*
> *Shepheard remember our Elizabeth,*
> *And sing her Rape, done by that Tarquin, Death.*[13]

In an eyewitness account, Chettle describes how Elizabeth's funeral followed the traditional heraldic format. Every member of the Royal Household attended, from the most exalted to the most obscure, with those of highest status closest to the coffin. The procession was led by 'the Knight Marshals man, to make way'. Then came 240 poor women, followed by servants of gentlemen, esquires and knights. After two porters, there were four trumpeters. Music was a vital part of funeral processions and trumpets were associated with royalty. Behind the Standard of the Dragon, symbolizing Elizabeth's Welsh roots, came the Children of the Woodyard; the Children of the Skullery; and groups simply described by Chettle as 'The Skalding House', 'The Larder', 'Maker of Spice-bags', 'Kitchin'.

From further up the social scale came the noblemen, and the French and Venetian Ambassadors, followed by four more trumpeters and the Standard of the Lion. Behind these could be glimpsed the banners of Cornwall, and Ireland, the Lord Mayor of

*The Chariott drawne by foure Horses vpon which Charret stood the Coffin couered with purple Veluett and vpon that the representation. The Canopy borne by six Knights.*

*The funeral procession of Elizabeth I.*

London, Sir Robert Cecil (Secretary of State and Elizabeth's spin doctor), and the members of the aristocracy – the Barons, Bishops, Earls and Viscounts, and the Archbishop of Canterbury. At the centre of the procession, hemmed in like a queen bee, beneath a canopy held up by four noblemen, was Elizabeth herself:

> Covered with velvet, borne in a chariot, drawn by foure horses trapt in black velvet. About it sixe Banner Rolls [wide banners, bearing symbols associated with Elizabeth's ancestors] on each side: Gentlemen pensioners with their Axes downeward.

Behind the chariot marched the women of the Royal Household. The Lady Marchioness of Northampton was the chief mourner, her train supported by a vice-Chamberlaine attended by Viscountesses, and the daughters of Earls and Barons. Under Elizabeth's modernizing influence, they were permitted to wear farthingales, the wide hooped skirts

made fashionable by the Spanish Court, instead of the traditional mediaeval mourning robes. Finally, the Captain of the Guard, 'with all the Guard following', brought up the rear, 'their halberds downeward'.

The most extraordinary aspect of this procession was the life-size effigy of the Queen lying on top of the coffin. Carved from wood, with a wax death mask for a face, the effigy had flaming red hair and staring blue eyes, and was dressed in a crimson gown trimmed with ermine, beneath the Parliamentary robes. On its head was the crown, and, in each hand, the orb and sceptre.

This creation was so lifelike that it caused consternation. According to John Stow:

> They beheld her statue and picture lying upon the coffin set forth in Royall Robes ... there was such a generall signing and groning, and weeping, and the like hath not beene seene or knowne in the memorie of man. At the sight thereof, divers of the beholders fell a weeping.

Although Thomas Dekker wrote at about the same time that: 'The report of her death, like a thunderclap was able to kill thousands, it took away hearts from millions,' we should resist the temptation to take these outpourings of national grief at face value. By 1603, Elizabeth I had become unpopular. Many of her citizens were eager for James I to succeed to the throne, considering it an indignity to be ruled by a woman; after all, there had been two Queens in a row. At Court, Elizabeth was frequently lampooned as a bad-tempered old woman, much given to stamping her foot and swearing at people, and forgetting to change her clothes. Crop failures over three successive years had resulted in famine, with food prices soaring and people starving to death. But if, as Dekker concluded, the whole kingdom seemed a wilderness, and the people in it transformed into wild men, Elizabeth's funeral constituted a final show of strength: the heraldic funeral as social control. A big state funeral served to calm and reassure the public and reinforce the power of the monarchy. Elizabeth's funeral was a political gesture and a dramatic spectacle, conducted during a period of intense theatricality. Jennifer Woodward, in her excellent book of the same name, refers to this phenomenon as 'The Theatre of Death'. Elizabeth Tudor was dead, but the monarchy, symbolized by her effigy, remained.

James I, who was to be crowned in July 1603, was not permitted to attend the funeral. He was not even admitted to the capital until it was over. Elizabeth's dead body was a mere cadaver; her effigy represented the body politic. 'Display of Elizabeth's effigy in the funeral procession, by perpetuating the public ruler image of the dead Queen, filled the ceremonial gap, demonstrating a continuity of rulership until the arrival of the new King.'[14]

In its pomp and pageantry, Elizabeth's funeral was the dramatic embodiment of the *danse macabre*. Its function was to confirm that, 'the Queen is dead – long live the Queen!'

Although London was to see many lavish funerals over the following centuries, Elizabeth's was, to a certain extent, the last of the great heraldic funerals. The sheer expense, which involved payment to the College of Heralds and a nominal fee for participants such as the children of Christ's Hospital, militated against these events. They took weeks to plan, and the processions clogged the streets of an already bustling metropolis.

The Puritan ethic, during the Commonwealth, condemned elaborate funerals and ostentatious displays of mourning. Although Oliver Cromwell's funeral in 1658 was lavish, as befitted a Head of State, costing a total of £60,000 with a £4,000 hearse, the Lord Protector did not rest in peace. 'Tried' for regicide after his death and the Restoration of Charles II, in 1661 Cromwell's remains were disinterred from Westminster Abbey and left to swing from a gibbet. Cromwell's skull was placed on a pole outside Westminster Hall, where it remained for twenty years before being dislodged. The skull subsequently passed through many pairs of hands, displayed in local pubs for the benefit of the curious. One rumour circulated that Cromwell's ghost haunted the Wig and Pen Club in

Fleet Street, where the skull was exhibited. Eventually, after forensic tests proved it to be genuine, Cromwell's skull was offered to his old Cambridge college, and is buried at an unmarked spot in Sidney Sussex.

However lavish the state funerals of the great and good, the majority of Londoners were interred without ceremony in overcrowded churchyards. St Paul's continued to be used for burials after the Reformation but, however robust Elizabethan attitudes, its condition was giving cause for concern. During an outbreak of the plague in 1552, Bishop Latimer had preached:

> The citizens of Naim had their burying places without the city, which, no doubt, is a laudable thing; and I do marvel that London, being so great a city, hath not a burial-place without: for no doubt it is an unwholesome thing to bury within the city, especially at such a time, when there be great sicknesses, and many die together. I think verily that many a man taketh his death in St Paul's Churchyard, and this I speak of experience; for I myself, when I have been there on some morning to hear the sermons, have felt such an ill-savoured, unwholesome savour, that I was the worse for it a great while after, and I think no less – but it is the occasion of great sickness and disease.[15]

Following another outbreak in 1563, the Mayor and Aldermen of the City of London realized that they faced a lack of sufficient burial space, particularly if there were to be further epidemics. This factor, and the poor state of St Paul's burial ground, led to the creation of a new site at Moorfields, on land owned by Bethlem Hospital. Walled in at the expense of the Lord Mayor, Sir Thomas Rowe, the burial ground was known as the New Churchyard, and was used by parishes which had run out of space.

Another burial ground was already in the making: following the demolition of the Pardon Chapel at St Paul's in 1549, 1,000 cartloads of bones from the vault and the charnel house were reinterred in

Finsbury Fields, 'with great respect and care, decently piled together'. A century later, this site would become Bunhill Fields, one of London's most celebrated cemeteries.

The condition of its churchyard was but one symptom of a malaise which afflicted St Paul's. Long before it was destroyed by fire, the building had begun to fall into decay. Struck by lightning during the reign of Elizabeth I, repair work had been abandoned and the scaffolding dismantled. By 1645, the Cathedral was being used as 'horse quarters' for soldiers. For Cromwell's followers, St Paul's had become a symbol of oppression. Staunch Parliamentarian Robert Greville, Lord Brooke, passing by upon the Thames on 13 March 1640, told his fellow passengers that he hoped they would live to see 'no one stone left upon another of that building'.

Sir William Dugdale, an antiquary, concerned about the effects the Civil War would have on church architecture, 'foreseeing that God would be turned out of churches into Barnes; & from thence again into the fields and mountains, and under hedges',[16] recorded St Paul's in great detail in the 1650s, drawing the monuments, copying the epitaphs and noting the arms on the walls, 'that by Inke & paper, the shadows of them, with their inscriptions, might be Preserved for posterity'. Dugdale's record of the old St Paul's was invaluable. But even he could not have predicted that while St Paul's might survive the ravages of the Commonwealth, it would be destroyed by the Great Fire; still less could he have foreseen the devastating epidemic which was to afflict London in 1665.

# 4: PESTILENCE

*Diary of a Plague Year*

In December 1664, a mysterious comet appeared in the skies above London. Pale and languid, slow and lethargic, it seemed a sinister portent. People heard voices, warning them to flee. Others saw visions in the sky: coffins, hearses, heaps of dead bodies. A ghost appeared several times near Bishopsgate, bowing out whenever the clocks struck eleven. Radical dissenter Solomon Eagle ran naked through the streets with a pan of burning charcoal on his head, warning Londoners to repent their wicked ways. Daniel, a patient at Bethlem Hospital, gazed at the cloud formations and saw an angel in white unsheathing the sword of pestilence over a guilty city.[1] And, at Long Acre, Covent Garden, in the parish of St Giles's, doctors in their sinister beaked masks and waxed black gowns stormed a Frenchman's house. Rumours circulated, whipping up hysteria. It was claimed that, alerted by neighbours, the doctors had removed the bodies of two plague victims.

But Londoners had no inkling of the horrors that awaited them, nor that their capital was about to become a necropolis.

London beneath the sickly comet was a city ripe for pestilence. Following the Restoration of the Monarchy in 1660, people had flocked to the capital, increasing the population to 200,000. Royalist families who had survived Cromwell's Commonwealth were back in town. Ex-servicemen set up in trade. Fashionistas responded to the Court's incessant demand for novelty. Tailors, wigmakers, clothiers and weavers streamed into the garment district of the East End, packing out the parishes of Whitechapel, Shoreditch and Spitalfields. William Dunbar, one of the first of many literary Scots to seek fame in London, might have praised the capital as 'the flour of Cities all'[2] but London was a dirty old town. An Act of Parliament in 1662 described London's highways as foul, dangerous and inconvenient to the inhabitants.

Narrow streets were open drains of raw sewage, ditches and rivers dumping grounds for the carcases of dead animals and occasionally humans. Cromwell's former chaplain, Hugh Peter, complained bitterly that it was impossible to walk anywhere without getting covered in dog shit and worse.

With the Great Plague of 1665, London faced its supreme challenge in burying the dead since the Black Death in 1348. A challenge that it would not meet again for over 200 years, when cholera struck.

As rumours spread in the stagnant air, two very different men chronicled the epidemic's progress: Samuel Pepys, diarist, Civil Service mandarin and *bon viveur*, and Henry Foe, a saddler living in the East End, who followed events voraciously, as far as any man could, in an era where Cromwell had banned newspapers, and gossip was the only mass medium. Henry's experiences were chronicled by nephew Daniel Defoe in *A Journal of the Plague Year* (1722), a triumph of investigative journalism. Reading Defoe, we live through the plague with Henry, witnessing the horrors he describes.

It was early in September 1664, before the comet had cast its melancholy influence across London, when Henry Foe first heard rumours that the plague had returned to Holland, where it had been virulent in the past.

The very word 'plague' was designed to strike horror into the seventeenth-century mindset. Bubonic plague had haunted England for centuries, most notoriously in the outbreak of 1348–9. Once again, the pestilence stalked westwards, obliterating entire communities, leaving the dead to litter the streets and no one left to bury them. A series of epidemics culminated in the outbreak of 1625, when 40,000 Londoners died. The memory of that last epidemic was still fresh. And, even by seventeenth-century standards, the plague was a horrible way to die. The symptoms were unmistakable. Inflamed glands or 'bubos', about the size of a nutmeg, appeared in the victim's groin, surrounded by areas of blackened skin. Plague spots or 'tokens' erupted – little silver pennies of gangrenous flesh – accompanied by violent headaches and vomiting. Death was inevitable.

'Several Counsels were held about Ways to prevent its coming over, but all was kept very private,' noted Henry.[3] The rumours faded away, and people forgot about it until December 1664, when the grim discovery of the two dead Frenchmen was made in Long Acre. Despite the family's attempts at a cover-up, these two unfortunates were the first recorded victims of the epidemic, appearing on the weekly Bill of Mortality – a list of deaths published by each parish.

Henry and his fellow Londoners gave a collective shudder, there were a few outbreaks of panic, and then the event was forgotten – until early January 1665, when a third Frenchman from the same house in Long Acre died of the plague, followed by a fourth man six weeks later.

People started to avoid St Giles's. They didn't go there unless they had to. And if business did take them to Drury Lane, they walked right down the middle of the street, avoiding any contagion that might lurk in the doorways.

Henry learned that burials in London had increased. The usual number hovered at around 240 to 300 per week. But by early January 1665 (from 27 December to 3 January), these figures were rising to 349, and between 17 January to 24 January, to 474. To a general feeling of relief, cold weather had set in by February 1665, and appeared to see off the infection, although burials at St Giles's continued to be disturbingly high. By March, rumours multiplied.

Henry heard that two more victims had been recorded, and twelve cases of 'the spotted fever', a variation of the plague virus. Pepys's first reference appeared on 30 April: 'Great fears of the sickness here in the city, it being said that two or three houses are already shut up. God preserve us all.'[4]

Londoners panicked. Warm April weather, summer on the way, and the plague was spreading to other parishes: St Andrew's, Holborn; St Clement Dane's, the Strand; and the parish of St Mary Woolchurch, in Bearbinder Lane near the Stock Market. The casualty in Bearbinder Lane was a recent arrival in the City of London. Last Christmas the victim had been living in Long Acre, at the same address as the Frenchmen who were the first recorded victims of the epidemic. Desperate to escape infection, he had spread it to another part of town.

By May, the weather was clement, with no threat of a heatwave to incubate the pestilence. Londoners prayed that the plague would pass them by. The population of the City appeared healthy, only fifty-four recorded plague victims had been buried out of the entire ninety-seven parishes, and it looked as though the plague would be contained within the parishes it had already afflicted. The mortality rate was low. St Giles's had buried thirty-two in one week, true, but only one was a plague victim. Listening to the word on the street, Henry Foe remained positive and concentrated on running his business.

But not for long. The *Bills of Mortality* were exposed as a pack of lies. Forty people were buried in the parish of St Giles's in the second week of May, but they were not officially recorded as plague victims, for fear of the consequences. 'Knavery and collusion' by parish authorities to avoid panic and quarantine was rife. The death toll was higher than anyone could have imagined.[5] By the end of May, the figure in St Giles's had risen to fifty-three, but still only nine deaths were ascribed to the plague. By June, the authorities were facing an epidemic. The Court, with Charles II, moved to Oxford. Entire households were dying in St Giles's. And it was at this point, when the spectre of the plague threatened the city, that the Lord Mayor and aldermen turned London into a police state.

Endowed with Draconian powers, the Privy Council appointed Searchers to seize dying victims, hidden by their families, and quarantine their households. On 7 June Pepys noted: 'This day I did in Drury Lane see two or three houses marked with a red cross upon the doors, and "Lord Have Mercy Upon Us" writ there which was a sad sight to me, being the first of that kind that to my remembrance I ever saw.'[6]

The red cross, the fatal handwriting of death, became a horribly familiar sight over the following months as house after house was quarantined. With a plague victim in the family, a home became a prison without bars. As soon as an infected person had been identified, a period of twenty-eight days must pass before they (if they survived) or their family were allowed out. If one person had just emerged from quarantine, and then another member fell sick, the entire wretched procedure had to be repeated all over again. Families were plunged into despair: 'The consternation of those who were thus separated from all society, unless with the infected, was inexpressible; and the dismal apprehensions it laid them under, made them but an easier prey to the devouring enemy.'[7]

Watchers were appointed to ensure that members of infected households could not escape. Nurses, who could do little to alleviate the suffering, were sent in, but soon became the stuff of urban myth, accused of suffocating and robbing their unfortunate patients, or succumbing to the plague themselves, dressed in their mistresses' stolen finery. And then, after the merciful release, the bearers would arrive to take away the dead.

Appointed by the parish, these officials inevitably became victims themselves. A shortage of carts, horses and even coffins made matters worse, with coffins used over and over again to transport the dead to their burial place. The small sums due to nurses, bearers and watchmen continued to be paid regularly, putting a strain on meagre parish funds. As the death toll rose, the sum increased, but there were still not enough people to bury the dead, although, as Henry Foe noted, the poor displayed a kind of brutal courage by taking on the work, because they needed the money.

By June, London shimmered in the heat of the most baleful summer it had ever known. With the Court gone to Oxford, and entire neighbourhoods in quarantine, the streets were deserted yet somehow menacing. Sparkling Restoration nightlife was a thing of the past. A curfew shut pubs by nine. Public dancing rooms, gaming tables, music houses, puppet shows, had all been closed down. London was a ghost-town, eerily quiet, without so much as a dog's bark to disturb the silence. Recognizing that they spread infection via fleas, the authorities had ordered a massive cull. All domestic animals were destroyed. The dog-catcher for St Margaret's, Westminster, was paid for burying 353 dog corpses. The City Corporation prohibited the keeping of pigs, dogs, cats, weasels, pigeons and rabbits. The Corporation dog-catcher claimed payment for 4,380 dogs slaughtered. Figures for cats were considerably higher, as most households contained about half a dozen.

Inevitably, Londoners rebelled against these ruthless measures. Healthy people, driven to distraction by being incarcerated for a month at a time with their own families, made vigorous attempts to escape, through back doors, over walls, out of windows, down alleyways. Watchmen were distracted, in two cases attacked. One was even blown up with gunpowder.

Pepys's neighbour, a Mr Marr, related the tale of an absconding servant girl:

How a maid-servant of Mr John Wright's falling sick of the plague, she was removed to an out-house, and a nurse appointed to look to her, who being at once absent, the maid got out of the house at the window and run away. The nurse coming and knocking, and having no answer, believed she was dead, and went and told Mr Wright so; who, and his lady, were in great strait what to do to get her buried. At last resolved to go to Burntwood hard by, being in that parish, and there get people to do it but they would not; so he went home full of trouble, and in the way met the wench walking over the Common, which frighted him worse than before. And was forced to send people to take her; which he did, and they got one of the pest coaches [a secure sedan chair] and put her into it to carry her to a pest-house. And passing in a narrow lane, Sir Anthony Browne, with his brother and some friends in the coach, met this coach with the curtains drawn close. The brother being a young man, and believing there might be some lady in it that would not be seen, and the way being narrow, he thrust his head out of his own into her coach to look, and there saw somebody look very ill, and in a sick dress and stunk mightily; which the coachman also cried out upon. And presently they came up to some people that stood looking after it; and told our gallants that it was a maid of Mr Wright's carried away sick of the plague which put the young gentleman into a fright and almost cost him his life, but is now well again.[8]

Pepys did not tell us what became of the maid.

The pest house, to which the wretched girl was removed, was no novelty in Restoration London. Pest houses, similar in spirit to the isolation hospitals of the nineteenth century, were holding places for the diseased and dying. Henry referred to two pest houses, 'one in the fields beyond Old Street, and one in Westminster'.[9] Demand was overwhelming, with the sick desperate to gain a place. And they were efficient, too, despite the deadly virus:

For very many were sent out again whole, and very good
Physicians were appointed to those Places, so that many People
did very well there . . . and they were so well look'd after there in
all the time of the visitation, there was but 156 buried in all at the
*London* Pest-house, and 159 at that of *Westminster*.[10]

The first pest house in London had been set up in 1630 by Sir
Theodore de Mayerne, Charles I's physician, inspired by the
L'Hôpital St Louis in Paris. It served as a hospital for nine out-
parishes. On the approach of the long but less harmful Plague of
1640–7, it was acquired by St Giles's for its own patients, and the
building then converted into a workhouse.

As the outbreak of 1665 gathered terrifying force, the authorities
ordered the construction of a new pest house to cope with the victims from St Giles's. A meadow near the village of Marylebone,
known as Mutton Field, appeared to be the perfect location, and the
owner was willing to sell. But, in a predictable burst of nimbyism,
there was uproar among the villagers. The Privy Council rushed
the sale through despite all protests, offering local residents use of
the pest house if they became infected. The building was rapidly
constructed. Like others, it was timber-framed upon a foundation
course of brick. The site was walled in, and a surgeon named Fisher
appointed.[11]

Magistrates also ordered a pest house to be built in St Martin-in-
the-Fields. It was erected on five acres of ground called Clayfield in
Soho Fields. Dr Tristran Inard, a physician, became master of the
pest house. Paid £170, he also had a practice in Long Acre, where he
sold his Grand Preservative or Antidote Epidemical, one of the
many spurious patent medicines circulating during the epidemic.
For, with antibiotics long in the future, there was little to be done to
'cure' the plague. Herbal remedies, fumigation, leeches and poul-
tices were the only means of alleviating the symptoms.

Accommodating over ninety patients, the Soho pest house was
the largest in London. At the height of the plague it served not only

St Martin's, but St Clement Dane's, St Paul's, Covent Garden and St Mary Savoy as well. Pest houses even provided a rudimentary form of medical research. Dr Nathaniel Hodges and other leading lights of the medical profession took on the plague as it continued its merciless advance across London. The pioneering Dr George Thompson carried out a post mortem on a plague victim in a desperate attempt to find a cure and almost died in the attempt.

At Westminster, a pest house was improvised at Tothill Fields, opposite the Abbey, in the area now known as The Sanctuary, behind Victoria Street. Surrounded by a ditch with access gained by a bridge, it was also equipped with its own burial ground, since pestilence and death were near neighbours. Known as 'The Five Houses' or 'The Seven Chimneys', these establishments were still standing at the beginning of the nineteenth century.[12]

Tothill Fields had been the site of a plague pit during earlier epidemics. According to the Victorian historian Mrs Isabella Holmes, Tothill Fields had also served as a burial ground for over 1,000 Scottish prisoners and their wives, captured during the Civil War and interred in the churchyard of St Margaret's, Westminster.[13]

By the second week of June 1665, temperatures were soaring, along with the mortality rate. One hundred and twenty people had been buried in St Giles's. Officially, sixty-eight of these died of the plague, although one hundred was a more accurate figure. Up until this point, with the exception of the unfortunate Frenchmen in Bearbinder Lane, the City had remained plague free. But in this second week, four deaths were reported – one in Wood Street, another in Fenchurch Street, and two in Crooked Lane.

Henry Foe lived in Aldgate, near Whitechapel, and the pestilence had not reached his side of the city. This neighbourhood remained buoyant. Up West, panic had set in. On 10 June, Samuel Pepys heard that the plague was coming into the City. By 15 June, 'the town grows very sickly'.[14] On 17 June, he had a terrifying experience during a trip from the Treasury to Holborn. Pepys's driver abruptly stopped the coach and 'came down hardly able to stand

and told me he was suddenly struck very sick and almost blind, he could not see'.[15] By 23 June, Pepys was observing that travelling by Hackney coach is 'very dangerous nowadays, the sickness increasing mightily'.[16]

By 18 July, he was offering his friends the Mitchells a pint of wine, since they, like so many others, were getting out of town. And a week later, he had another scare when his clerk, Will, complained of a severe headache and went for a lie-down on Pepys's bed, 'which put me in extraordinary fear!'[17]

'A Plague is a formidable Enemy,' observed Henry Foe. And the only way to escape the plague was to run away from it. Anybody who could do so, left town. In a seventeenth-century *War of the Worlds* moment, the narrow streets were jammed with terrified citizens heading out of London. The aristocracy and wealthy merchants escaped to their second homes in the country, clutching the certificates of health issued by the Mayor of London that enabled them to travel. The frenzy to escape was exacerbated by rumours of Government plans to install turnpikes, roadblocks and armed guards to turn back Londoners and prevent them spreading the plague. London Bridge was gridlocked with carriages, carts, horses and people, fleeing for their lives. It filled Henry with 'very serious Thoughts of the Misery that was coming upon the City, and the unhappy Condition of those that would be left in it'.[18]

Although Whitechapel appeared safe, Henry's brother pleaded with him to come to Northamptonshire. But Henry had his business to consider, with a client base in America built up over many years. And, although a bachelor, he had a family of servants, a shop and a warehouse. He was also religious, with a fatalistic turn of mind. Much to his brother's disgust, he felt it was his destiny to stay in London.

As rumours reached him of life outside the capital, Henry had less cause to regret his choice. Many escaped only to meet a grim and lonely end. Fleeing to the country, they were turned back by mobs of vigilantes, armed with pitchforks and flaming torches.

Others became messengers of death, carrying the contagion to the remotest parts of the kingdom. Wherever the plague spread, in all the great cities of England, exiled Londoners were held responsible.

Taking pity, some country people left food, at a safe distance. And when the victims died, they dug pits and dragged the bodies into them, using poles and hooks, careful to operate wind-ward of the corpses, for fear of contagion. Long experience of the depredations of the murrain (a cattle disease) had taught country people to bury deep and stay away. Once filled in, the pits remained undisturbed, although their function and location remained a source of anecdote for generations. Stoke Newington, Camberwell, Gypsy Hill – these and many other fields outside London become unofficial burial grounds, their contents unknown and unmourned.

These interments possessed a simple dignity that was lacking back in London, where the very nature of burial was changing as the plague taxed the resources, the patience, and the energy of the authorities in a manner that was unprecedented. Under the emergency legislation, burial of plague victims followed a strict procedure, with interment taking place at night, between sunset and sunrise, with only the church-wardens or Constables in attendance. Family and friends were banned from attending, on pain of quarantine or imprisonment. The consequences for those who flouted the rules could be fatal. Many attended the funeral of a friend one evening, only to go to their own long home the next.

By August, when Pepys's parish bell was hoarse with tolling for the dead six times a day, the authorities were forced to reconsider their position: 'The people die so, that now it seems they are fain to carry the dead to be buried by daylight, the nights not sufficing to do it in. And my Lord Mayor commands people to be within at nine at night, that the sick may have liberty to go abroad for air.'[19]

By the end of August, death stared London in the face. Pepys's own physician, Dr Burnett, died after performing a post mortem on a plague victim. 'It is feared the true number of the dead this week is near ten thousand, partly from the poor that cannot be taken notice through the greatness of the number, and partly from the Quakers and others that will not have any bell ring for them,' noted Pepys on 31 August.[20]

And even life's little luxuries were tainted, a source of anxiety. On 3 September Pepys put on a new silk suit, and unpacked his new periwig: 'but darst not wear it because the plague was in Westminster when I bought it. And it is a wonder what will be the fashion after the plague is done as to periwigs, for nobody will dare to buy any hair for fear of the infection that it had been cut off the heads of people dead of the plague.'[21]

Far worse was to come. A shortage of coffins was one thing, but then London began running out of graves. Despite the burgeoning population during the Restoration, no serious attempt had been made to increase the number of available burial grounds. One or two pest houses had their consecrated graveyards, but otherwise burial was limited to existing churchyards and hospitals such as Bethlem and St Bartholomew's. Conditions at Bethlem were grim, with complaints to the Court of Aldermen about noisome stenches arising from the great numbers of dead bodies buried there.

These existing facilities were totally insufficient for the crisis that loomed in August: the disposal of thousands of rotting corpses. Today, we would regard this as a public health issue, but in the London of 1665, the cost of burial was the major concern. With so many families dead and dying, few could afford to pay for funeral services, the burden of which fell on the parish. The authorities had no option but to dig mass graves.

For the faithful, there was another dimension to this horror. The Bishop of London refused to consecrate land that could not be held in perpetuity, meaning that plague pits were unconsecrated. All plague-pit burials took place without benefit of religious ceremony. The devout poor, unable to afford the extortionate fees necessary to procure an oversubscribed space in the churchyard, viewed this development with alarm. Pepys was much troubled this day to hear at Westminster how the officers do bury the dead in the open Tuttle-fields [Tothill Fields, Westminster], pretending want of room elsewhere; whereas the New-Chapel church-yard was walled in at the public charge in the last plague time merely for want of room, and now none but such as are able to pay dear for it can be buried there.[22]

Meanwhile, Henry Foe observed that: 'They Died in Heaps, and were buried in Heaps,' as he witnessed the excavation of several plague pits in his native East End. Safe for so long, his own neighbourhood was now threatened. The plague had been a long time coming, but when it did, 'there was no Parish in or about *London* where it raged with such Violence as in the two parishes of *Aldgate* and *WhiteChapel*.'[23]

Once the dead-carts start to circulate, at the beginning of August, the first plague pits receive fifty or sixty bodies each. Then larger holes were dug:

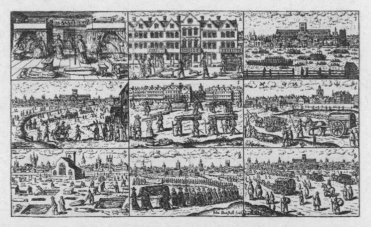

*'They died in heaps and were buried in heaps.' (Daniel Defoe in* A Journal of the Plague Year, *1722)*

wherein they buried all that the Cart brought in a Week, which by
the middle, to the End of *August*, came to, from 200 to 400 a Week;
and they could not well dig them larger, because of the Order of
the Magistrates, confining them to leave no Bodies within six Foot
of the Surface; and the Water coming on, at about 17 or 18 Foot.[24]

As the pestilence stalked across London, frantic efforts were
made to bury the dead. The precise number of casualties will never
be known, for thousands of deaths went unrecorded. The dead carts
were filled and emptied and filled again from sunset to dawn, and
no account was kept of the numbers thrown into the plague pits.

In Stepney, 1,000 people died in a week. The churchyard was
full, so a pit was dug at the corner of Mile End Road, followed by
another at the site of the old Roman cemetery in Spitalfields. In
Southwark, vast numbers were interred in Deadman's Place (now
Park Street, behind Tate Modern). Pepys witnessed two or three
burials in broad daylight on Bankside, with at least forty or fifty
mourners publicly flouting the law against funeral processions.[25]

When space ran out in Westminster, bodies were brought
to the burial ground of the pest house in Tothill Fields, where
a rough cemetery had been staked out, enclosed with a stout
fence. Cartloads arrived daily, each with its grim harvest of
thirty, forty, fifty bodies. Meanwhile, in west London, the army
dug trenches in Hyde Park, and great pits were sunk in the
remote village of Knightsbridge. Further west still, the orchards
at Lillie Road, Fulham, were choked with human remains.

Visiting the plague pits was forbidden. Initially, this was to prevent infection, and subsequently, because the bereaved and the
dying gravitated to the pits in a spirit of despair. Nearing their end,
victims hurled themselves into the mass graves, while officials had
the unenviable task of dragging them out again. At the pit in
Finsbury bodies were discovered still warm, buried alive. An entire
cart and horses plunged into a pit when the driver lost control; he
was later identified by his whip.

The bearers, who collected the corpses, were foul-mouthed, frightening onlookers with their swearing and cursing as they brought out the dead. One particularly unpleasant specimen was an individual named Buckingham, infamous for his habit of picking up the body of a young child by one leg, holding it upside down, and bawling: 'Faggots, faggots, five for sixpence!'[26] At the lip of the gaping pit, he took ghoulish pleasure in exposing the naked bodies of young women to public view. Subsequently arrested, he was publicly flogged and sentenced to one year in gaol.

The plague pits exerted a form of morbid fascination over Londoners, despite their toxic state. On 30 August, Pepys walked to the plague pit at Moorfields to see it for himself ('God forgive my presumption.') He was relieved to be spared the sight 'of any corpse going to the grave', although 'everybody's looks and discourse in the street is of death and nothing else'.[27]

Henry Foe, haunting the desolate streets of London in his inky cloak and broad-brimmed hat, provided the most powerful description of a plague pit – the great pit of Aldgate. Forty foot long, and about fifteen or sixteen foot broad, the pit was designed to serve Aldgate for a month or more. It was excavated to a depth of twenty feet in places, until the labourers could dig no deeper because of the water rising through the ground. The sheer scale of the pit made Henry suspect that the churchwardens were preparing to bury the entire parish. The pit was finished on 4 September; burials began on 6 September and, less than a fortnight later, it had consumed 1,114 bodies.[28]

Henry arrived at the pit late on the night of 10 September, and attempted to bluff his way in. The sexton warned him off. It was his job to risk his life, not Henry's. But Henry's curiosity got the better of him. He felt he could learn something from the sight, he told the sexton. It would be instructive. The sexton replied that the prospect before him was the best sermon he had ever heard in his life. And with that he threw open the door, and said: 'Go, if you will.'

Shocked by his tone, Henry hesitated on the threshold. At that instant, two links, or flaming funeral torches, emerged from the gloom, accompanied by the ominous clang of the plague bell, and a dead cart, laden with corpses, rumbled towards him through the empty streets. Following the cart, Henry could see nobody at first except the bearers, and the fellow who led the horse and cart. But as they approached the pit, he witnessed a man in an extreme state of distress, pacing up and down. Assuming him to be ill, or deranged, the bearers prepared to lead him away. Then they realized that he was in utter despair, having accompanied the bodies of his wife and children to the plague pit. He was distressed, but lucid, claiming he would only stay to see his family buried.

The man's family were not the only bodies on the cart. Another sixteen or seventeen corpses were shot into the pit, some swathed in sheets or blankets, others naked. Beyond hurt, it mattered not to them whether they were buried with dignity or formality, huddled together in the common grave of mankind, where no distinction existed between rich and poor. But the bereft husband and father was horrified to see his family's remains dumped in a ditch, without benefit of ceremony. He yelled out and collapsed, and the bearers ran to pick him up. As they ushered him past the mass grave, he stared into it again. Glowing lanterns had been placed all round the sides, but there was nothing to be seen. The mortal remains of his own family had already disappeared under a layer of soil. With a gentleness belying their normally brutal reputation, the bearers helped the widower to his local, the Pye Tavern in Houndsditch, and Henry, shocked and sickened by the scene, returned home.

Later, unable to sleep despite the fact it was one o'clock in the morning by then, he headed down to the Pye Tavern. The bereft father, a regular, was still there. The landlord had overlooked the curfew and done his best to comfort the man, despite the risk of infection. As Henry listened to his story, the man was targeted by a group of youths who had witnessed the entire incident from the pub window. Jeering, they wanted to know why he didn't just go ahead and jump in the plague pit. A bookish type, not usually the sort to start a fight in a pub, Henry reproved the youths sharply. So they turned on him, demanding to know what *he* was doing out of his grave!

Despite this outburst, Henry took to drinking at the Pye, trying to keep up the spirits of the bereaved family man, who survived the epidemic. About a week later, one of the youths who had taunted them was himself struck down. Within days, he and his mates had all been carried off to the great pit themselves.

Henry Foe, Samuel Pepys, and others who had bravely remained or were too poor to leave, occupied a sinister, desolate London, a city drained by death.

> *Ladyes who wore black patches out of pride*
> *Now weare them their plague sores to hide*
> *Into the vallies are the bodyes throwne*
> *Valley no more but now dead mountains grown*
> *Thick grass and moss begins to growe*
> *Out of the Putrified corps and now*
> *The Cattell did the men devoure*
> *As greedily as men did them before.*[29]

There were no boats upon the river, and grass grew down Whitehall. Front doors stood open, casement windows swung in the breeze, with no one to close them. Death was a midwife, with infants passing straight from the womb to the grave. Marriage beds were sepulchres, unhappy couples meeting with death during their first embrace. One woman 'deliberately drew her husband into her embraces, which ended his life with hers'; and the dead carts circulated endlessly, operating throughout the city, not confined to particular parishes any more, but carrying all to the pit, in a desperate attempt to contain the epidemic. '*Quis tali fundo temperet a lachymie*,' mused Dr Nathaniel Hodges. 'Who could look upon this place and not weep?'[30]

Soon smog was added to the other hazards. On 6 September, the

Lord Mayor ordered fires to be lit in the street throughout the city in an attempt at fumigation. This measure simply exacerbated matters. People choked to death on the suffocating fumes. The watchmen, eyes watering from the smoke, looked as if they were weeping for their fatal mistake. The 'wet constitution' of the air created by fumigation caused the most fatal night of the entire epidemic, when more than 4,000 people expired.

On 14 September, Pepys met a 'dead corpse of the plague, carried to be buried close to me at noonday through the city'. One of his own watermen was dead and another had buried a child and was dead himself. 'In great apprehension of melancholy, and with good reason' Pepys returned home to a stiff drink, 'which I am fain to allow myself during this plague time, by advice of all, my physician being dead and surgeon out of the way, whose advice I am obliged to take.'

Just as the plague reached crisis point, and it seemed as if nobody would emerge unscathed, the epidemic began to recede. Henry's friend, Dr Heath, observed that the Bills of Mortality for the past week indicated 8,000 dead, and not the 20,000 that he had predicted. Even more encouraging, the duration of the disease had grown from two days to five, and one in five people actually recovered.

In October, the mortality rate continued to fall. But, lulled by a false sense of security, citizens became careless. Returning from the country, they were desperate to socialize. 'The People were so tir'd with being so long from *London*, and so eager to come back, that they flock'd to Town without Fear or Forecast, and began to shew themselves in the Streets, as if all the Danger was over.'[31]

This rash conduct cost many their lives. There was a brief resurgence of the pestilence, with the bills increasing again by 400 in the first week of November. But the plague was on its way out: 'The Distemper was spent, the Contagion was exhausted, and also the Winter Weather came on apace, and the Air was clear and cold, with some sharp Frosts; . . . most of those that had fallen sick recover'd, and the Health of the City began to return.'[32]

As London began to recover from the pestilence, one of the first tasks was to seal the plague pits and churchyards to prevent reinfection. Fearing that disturbance of the plague-laden earth would scatter infection, the Privy Council prohibited further burials in City churches and churchyards. Most of these had already ceased, because the ground was choked with plague victims. All churchyards were to be covered with twelve inches of lime, a caustic alkaline substance which dissolves flesh. However, lime was not obtainable in such vast quantities, so it had to be mixed with fresh earth. And despite the best efforts of the authorities, not all plague pits were undisturbed. Some were converted for other uses, or even built on. A piece of ground beyond Goswell Street, along the old lines of the City fortifications, where hundreds of victims from Clerkenwell and Aldersgate were buried, subsequently became a physic garden, one of the first examples of a London burial ground being turned into a park. Another piece of land at the end of Holloway Lane, in Shoreditch, became a yard for keeping hogs.

Originally a green field, there was a massive plague pit for the dead of Bishopsgate at the upper end of Hand Alley. Two or three years after the plague was ended, it came into the possession of Sir Robert Clayton, who built a large, handsome house on the land. However, laying the foundations meant digging up the bodies. When the ground was opened, some of the corpses were so well-preserved that it was possible to distinguish the women from the men by the length of their hair, and the flesh that remained. After a public outcry, and the fear that disinterring the corpses might reactivate the plague, the remains were carted off to another part of the site and thrown into a deep pit, which was not built on, but became a passage known as Rose Alley. Cordoned off, this site held the remains of over 2,000 plague victims. Plague pits were never memorialized. There were no gravestones. They were dug in fields, and filled in as soon as full. At the height of the epidemic, one pit might only be used for a couple of days before being filled in and a new one dug alongside. Not all owners were paid for the land, requisitioned by the authorities, so it reverted to them once the plague was past, and to former use.

As time passed, London has constructed houses, churches, streets, entire railway stations, over these mass graves, and it is only by chance that they come to light due to building excavations. During the nineteenth century, skeletal remains were reinterred elsewhere, destroying vital archaeological evidence and leaving nothing but anecdote. The pest fields of Tothill, Westminster, disappeared beneath St Vincent's Square, according to Mrs Holmes, and became the playground of St Paul's School. In Gower's Walk, Whitechapel, human remains were discovered during building excavations in 1893. The pit consisted of one layer of black earth, intermingled with bones, without coffins, sandwiched between two layers of gravel, strongly suggesting a mass grave.

Liverpool Street Station now stands on the site of a forgotten plague pit. In an excavation of nearby Broad Street in 1863, the dig yielded between three and four hundred skeletons, the soil being full of them below surface level to a depth of eight or ten feet. The bones lay in disorder. Only a few of the first committals were in coffins, these being found in one corner. The corpses had been thrown indiscriminately into pits. So many leather shoes were dug up as to suggest that they died with their boots on.

Cartloads of human remains were discovered at Beak Street, Golden Square and Poland Street, Soho, during the nineteenth century. Quantities of bones were found when the old Marylebone courthouse was built in 1727 and the new one in 1822, suggesting this was close to the Marylebone pest house which had caused such uproar among the locals. When a bookshop in Oxford Street was rebuilt in the early 1920s, numbers of human bones were found eight feet down, not in rows, but buried indiscriminately, as if the bodies had been flung in.

At the spot where Brompton Road and Knightsbridge now meet, excavations for the Piccadilly Line between Knightsbridge and South Kensington Underground stations unearthed a pit so dense with human remains that it could not be tunnelled through. This is said to account for the curving nature of the track between the two stations.

Plague pits figure in the mythology of haunted London. During the nineteenth century, 50 Berkeley Square, the home of the eccentric and reclusive Mr Myers, attracted considerable press coverage. A widower, Myers kept to himself, and the room he favoured was described as having a terrifying, chilling atmosphere. A maid went insane with fear. A man who stayed the night for a wager was found dead in bed. Other researchers referred to a 'shapeless, slithering, horrible mass', and suggested that this manifestation resembles the sheeted corpses of pestilence victims. Like so many houses in London, it is entirely possible that 50 Berkeley Square *is* built on a plague pit. The ghouls are a matter for speculation.[33]

Unlike the victims of the Great Fire, who are commemorated by Wren's Monument on Cannon Street, there is no official memorial to those who perished in the London plague. Dr Nathaniel Hodges' tablet in St Stephen's, Walbrook, said merely that he had survived it. In Surrey, a stone in a churchyard refers simply to two children, 'dying young in the great sickness, AD 1665'.[34]

Early in January 1666, Pepys visited the Church of St Olave's, Hart Street, for the first time in a year. He and his family survived the plague; despite everything, he had enjoyed one of the most successful years of his life. Nevertheless, he felt lucky to be alive. Evensong, and twilight had already set in:

> This is the first time I have been in this church since the plague, and it frightened me indeed to go through the church more than I thought it could have done, to see so many graves lie so high upon the churchyard where people have been buried of the plague.[35]

With a shiver, Pepys glanced at the raised ground and went on his way. Meanwhile, Henry Foe stepped out into the cold night air. His business revived, his household secure, he headed for the Pye Tavern, and the widower who had become a cherished friend. The shape of the Aldgate Pit reared in the darkness, like one great grave covered in brown earth. Then snowflakes began to fall, whirling faster and faster in the gloom, spinning a pall of white.

By the following spring, grass, weeds and wildflowers will have covered this burial mound, as Nature reclaims the scarred earth. And, within a year, London will be engulfed by another tragedy, which will erase almost all traces of the plague: the Great Fire of 1666.

# 5: *ET IN ARCADIA EGO*

## *A Vision of Elysian Fields*

A year after the Great Plague, London was destroyed by fire. Seventy per cent of its houses vanished into the flames. St Paul's Cathedral, the Royal Exchange, Christ's Hospital and the north end of London Bridge were engulfed. Thirteen thousand buildings, including eighty-nine churches, disappeared for ever. Fifty-one churches were rebuilt by Sir Christopher Wren and his followers, including Nicholas Hawksmoor, but thirty-three were never replaced.

In addition to the churches, Wren was commissioned to design and build a new St Paul's. Faced with this opportunity to forge another London from the wreck of the old, Wren did not neglect the dead in his plans and proposed suburban cemeteries on the outskirts of town. As an architect, Wren deplored the concept of intra-mural interment, since he understood that the practice contributed to rot, damp and subsidence. He may also have been motivated by the appalling scenes that ensued during demolition work of the old St Paul's, when mummified corpses, their tombs smashed by falling debris, were salvaged and propped up in the Convocation House yard for the amusement of sightseers. The remains of John Colet, founder of St Paul's School, became the focus of a grisly scientific experiment:

> After the Conflagration, his monument being broken, his coffin, which was lead, was full of a liquor which conserved the body. Mr Wyld and Ralph Greatorex tasted it and 'twas of a kind of insipid taste, something of an ironish taste. The body felt, to the probe of a stick which they thrust into a chink, like brawne. The coffin was of lead and layd in the wall about 2 foot ½ above the surface of the floor.[1]

Wren was not alone in his distaste for intra-mural burial. His contemporary, the diarist John Evelyn, also deplored the state of London's churchyards: 'I observed that most of the churchyards (though some were large enough) were filled up with earth, or rather the congestion of dead bodies one above the other, to the very top of the walls, and some above the walls, so that the churches seemed to be built in pits.'[2]

The Great Fire should have provided the perfect opportunity to obliterate the plague pits, and do away with London's overcrowded churchyards. According to the writer and historian, Mrs Isabella Holmes, Wren:

> wished to see suburban cemeteries established, and burials in churches and churchyards discontinued, partly because he considered the constant raising of the level of a churchyard rendered the church damp and more liable to premature decay. But Wren's plans for rebuilding the city were not carried out; they were approved by the King and Parliament, but disapproved of by the Corporation [the municipal governing body of the City of London].[3]

The churches were rebuilt on the old sites, the churchyards were used again, and the sites of those churches which were not rebuilt became additional parish burial-grounds. Despite Wren's reservations, the great and good continued to be interred at the new St Paul's, including the great architect himself, in 1723.

Although burial of the dead was the responsibility of the Church of England, another trend was emerging. Following the Reformation, many Londoners had turned away from the established Church to join sects such as the Baptists, Methodists and Quakers, and they wished to be buried somewhere other than the city's churchyards. While many historians conclude that the first purpose-built cemetery in Britain was the Rosary Cemetery, opened in Norwich in 1819, Bunhill Fields, established 1665, may lay claim to this title. This land, north of the City and adjacent to Finsbury Fields, the Artillery Ground and Windmill Hill, was known as Bone-hill or Bon-hill.

In the year 1549, when the Charnel Chapel in St Paul's Churchyard was pulled down:

> the bones of the dead, couched up in a charnel under the chapel, were conveyed from thence into Finsbury Field, by report of him who paid for the carriage, amounting to more than one thousand cartloads, and there laid on a moorish ground, which, in a short time after, being raised by the soilage of the City, was able to bear three windmills.[4]

The number of windmills was later on increased to five, and these appear on many old maps of London.

Regarded as a profitless wasteland, the bowmen and archers of the City of London used the area nearby for target practice, and it eventually became the training ground for the Honorary Artillery Company. This area had been something of an informal graveyard since Saxon times: heretics were buried at Moorfields. According to the historian Maitland, writing in 1756, the Mayor and Citizens of London set apart and consecrated Bonhill in 1665, 'as a common Cemetery, for the interment of such corps as could not have room in their parochial burial-grounds in that dreadful year of pestilence.'[5] However, it appears the land was not actually used for plague victims on that occasion, and instead was leased by one John Tyndall or Tindal, who 'converted it into a Burial-ground for the use of Dissenters'. A large plot to the north was added, and eventually the whole cemetery measured about five acres. From 1665 to 1852, when the ground was closed, 123,000 people were buried there, including vast numbers of Methodist, Baptist, Presbyterian and Independent ministers.

St Bride's Church, Fleet Street, rebuilt by Wren in 1675, represents a microcosm of London burial practices in the seventeenth and eighteenth century. A series of excavations has found evidence of burial here since Roman times. No less than seven churches have been built on the site of St Bride's over the past 2,000 years: earlier still, the land was occupied by a Roman temple. Samuel Pepys, baptised in St Bride's in 1633, visited the church in March, 1664, to:

> chose a place for my brother to lie in, just under my mother's pew. But to see how a man's tomb are at the mercy of such a fellow, that for 6d he would – in his own words – 'jostle them together but I will make room for him' – speaking of the fullness of the middle aisle, where he was to lie, and that he would for my father's sake do my brother that he is dead, all the civility he can; which was to disturb others' corps that are not quite rotten, to make room for him.[6]

Pepys's experience typifies the overcrowded intra-mural burials which Wren so deplored. But Pepys possessed the seventeenth-century's robust attitude to death. In February 1669, he took a group to Westminster Abbey:

> and there did show them all the tombs . . . there being other company this day to see the tombs, it being Shrove Tuesday; and here we did see, by particular favour, the body of Queen

Katherine of Valois; and I had the upper part of her body in my hands and I did kiss her mouth, reflecting upon it that I did kiss a Queen and that it was my birthday, thirty-six years old, that I first kissed a Queen.[7]

The body of Katherine de Valois, buried 1483, had been a grisly exhibit since she was dug up in 1502, when the chapel was demolished on the orders of Henry VII. Katherine's body was placed in a wooden box near her husband's tomb and Henry fully intended to have her reburied. But as he died the next day, this was never carried out and Katherine became one of the sights of Westminster Abbey. In 1631, John Weever wrote that: 'Katherine, Queen of England, lieth here, in a chest or coffin with a loose cover, to be seen and handled of any who will much desire it.' By the eighteenth century, the body was still on show, 'the bones being firmly united, and thinly clothed with flesh, like scrapings of tanned leather', according to Richard Gough, the eighteenth-century historian and genealogist.

Of late years the Westminster scholars amused themselves with tearing it to pieces; and one in particular, who bore a principal character in the police in India, lies under the imputation of having contributed in a special manner to that havoc. I can just remember seeing some shapeless mass of mummy of a whitish colour. It is now under lock and key near her husband's tomb, waiting for the next opening of the royal vault for her last repose.

This awful spectacle of frail immortality was at length removed from the public gaze into St Nicholas's Chapel and buried under the monument to George Villiers, when a vault was made for the remains of Elizabeth Percy, Duchess of Northumberland. Then the unfortunate creature was disinterred by the Dean of St Paul's in 1877, before eventually being reinterred near her husband in the Chantry Chapel in 1878.[8] St Bride's was re-opened in 1675, although the steeple, Wren's highest at 226 feet, was not completed until 1701.

Despite Wren's opinions on the subject, burial continued both outside and inside St Bride's. The majority of burials took place at the Upper Ground and Lower Ground cemeteries nearby. In the 1950s, a joint excavation by the Museum of London, the Natural History Museum and the University of Cambridge found a large quantity of human remains, including a mediaeval charnel house and 300 burials from the eighteenth and nineteenth centuries.

Burial records indicate that the crypt was reserved for local worthies, interred in lead coffins. These included Samuel Holden (1740), a Governor of the Bank of England; John Pridden (1807), a bookseller and churchwarden at St Bride's; John Jolliffe (1771), MP for Petersfield; and Henry Dolamore (1838), licensee of the Cheshire Cheese, the most famous pub in Fleet Street. Best known of all was Samuel Richardson (1761), novelist and printer. William Rich the pastrycook, who modelled his famous many-tiered wedding cakes on the steeple of St Bride's, was laid in the crypt in 1811. The occupations given for these burials – jeweller, Venetian blind maker, Lord Mayor (Robert Waithman, 1823) – place them fairly and squarely in London's emerging bourgeoisie. These were the new class of burials, and their funerals were to be every bit as elaborate as the lives they had departed.

In previous centuries, rich and poor lived together and died together. The greatest social distinction consisted of whether one was buried within the church or the churchyard. During the seventeenth century, the majority of Londoners continued to be buried close to home, in parish churchyards, with a series of religious and secular rituals that had changed little over the centuries. The historian Julian Litten refers to this rite of passage as 'the Common Funeral', the opposite of the heraldic or state funeral, a composite ritual performed by the community.

Many superstitions, centuries old, operated alongside the orthodox teaching of the Church. Death was often preceded by omens: a

raven or other dark-hued bird settling on a roof; white wax forming a shroud down one side of a candle; a broken mirror. Once
death had occurred, a window must be opened so that the spirit
could depart. The custom of placing money upon the eyes, derived
from the Classical conceit of paying Charon the ferryman, was still
current, centuries after the Romans had gone. Quantities of silver
and copper coins have been unearthed in churchyards over the
years, giving archaeologists valuable evidence as to the time of interment. Coins were a form of grave goods: cash, so vital in this world,
cannot entirely be dispensed with in the next.

Another practice which also persisted for centuries was that of
'telling the bees' when a death had occurred in the family. If this was
neglected, it was feared they would abandon their hives, never to
return. Death established, it was traditional to ring a passing bell;
this signified that a soul had passed on, and frightened off any evil
spirits making a concerted effort to obtain that soul at the time of
death. In a parish, the tolling of the bell indicated the loss of a resident. This communal attitude to death was reflected in Donne's
famous observation: 'No man is an *Island*, entire of it self. Any man's
*death* diminishes *me,* because I am involved in *Mankind*; And therefore never send to know for whom the *bell* tolls; It tolls for *thee*.'[9]

Caring for the dead was a dual role, for clergy and laity, with the
majority of the work done by the laity. They it was who performed
the secular rituals, preparing the corpse for burial, watching, providing refreshment for the mourners and transporting the body to
the grave. The corpse was washed and anointed in accordance with
traditional Christian teaching. The custom had a similar symbolic
function to that of washing a newborn, and was carried out by the
same people. The midwives who ushered new life into the world
also prepared dead bodies for the next one. Once the corpse had
been washed, and the orifices plugged to prevent leakage, it was
wrapped in a shroud.

In 1666, an Act designed to promote the wool industry came into
force, insisting that everyone should be buried in a woollen shroud.

Other fibres, such as silk or linen, were banned. A certificate had to be signed by a relative of the deceased, declaring that a woollen shroud had been used at the burial, and this was sworn as an affidavit before the local Justice of the Peace. The only exception was plague victims.

Many people resisted the idea of burial in wool, as linen was associated with the interment of Christ in the sepulchre following His crucifixion, but failure to comply incurred a fine of five pounds. This law, not repealed until 1814, protected the paper trade. As a result, no less than 200,000 pounds of rag were saved from the grave, and contributed to the rise of the printing industry. (Newspapers were originally made from recycled cloth, hence the word 'rag' as a term of derision.)

Grave clothes were part of a young woman's trousseau. These grim garments were sewn in the knowledge that they might be needed. For the same reason, a potential bride habitually prepared at least one set of burial clothes for any child she might bear. Babies dying within a month of baptism were buried in their baptismal robes and swaddling bands. Children were often elaborately dressed. In 1672, John Dwight produced a stoneware portrait of his six-year-old daughter, Lydia, on her deathbed, clutching a bunch of flowers, and wearing grave clothes, complete with a hood and broderie-anglaise pillow. A year later, he carved the stunning image of Lydia resurrected, on Judgement Day, a skull at her feet.

John Donne, who appears in a magnificent shroud in his effigy at St Paul's Cathedral, was quick to seize on the dramatic possibilities of the shroud, posing for his own effigy some years before his death.

Once the corpse had been dressed, complete with a nightcap which kept the jaw closed and created the impression that the dead person was but sleeping, it was placed in an open coffin. This was lined with a sawdust mattress, to absorb the by-products of early decomposition, and scattered with pungent herbs such as rosemary to disguise the smell. Traditionally, bodies went on display for at least two days before burial, so that mourners could pay their last

*Lydia Dwight on her deathbed, made by her father in 1672.*

respects, and the important practice of 'watching' might be observed. Prior to the Reformation, 'watching' had been allied to the Roman Catholic custom of praying for the departed and consoling the bereaved, and formed the origins of the Irish Wake.

Wakes, in their more exuberant form, did not form part of the conventional English funeral, but food and drink played an important role. A tradition of sharing a cup of wine, placed on the coffin for the purpose, persisted into Stuart times; in other instances, it was common to hold a glass to the lips of the corpse, as if drinking with them for the last time.

Just as the rituals of the heraldic funeral included welcoming in the heir – 'the King is dead – long live the King!' – the food offered during the common funeral had the same purpose. It celebrated the life of the deceased, and welcomed in his successor. The fare reflected the status of the family. The poor provided little more than a bread roll apiece, with a collection circulating to pay for the ale. Further up the social scale, the deceased often left elaborate instructions for baked meats, game, cakes and cheese, washed down with wine and ale. Specialities included prunes, appropriately black, served with a white 'posset' or fool. One funeral feast from 1673 clearly did not come up to scratch when mourners were offered: 'nothing but a bit of cheese, a draught of wine, a piece of rosemary and a pair of gloves'.[10]

After a period of two days or so, the corpse was taken for burial at the parish churchyard. If the body were in a coffin, this was placed on a stretcher or funeral bier. Burial in one's own parish was preferred, though in some cases bodies had to be transported longer distances, by funeral coach. These journeys were fraught with difficulty. The roads within London were narrow and uneven. When Charles II set out for Parliament in his State coach, bundles of sticks had to be thrown under the wheels to prevent them falling into potholes. The open roads consisted of a single high ridge with mud-filled ditches at either side. Lurid tales circulated of coaches overturned and coffins bursting open to display their sad cargo to the world.

Such trips were also expensive. John Evelyn had occasion to arrange the funeral of a friend: 'I caused her corpse to be embalmed, wrapped in lead and a brass plate soldered on, with an inscription and other circumstances due to her worth.' The body was taken to Cornwall, in a hearse with six horses, attended by two coaches of as many, with about thirty relations and servants. Every night, the corpse was removed from the hearse and placed in the house, surrounded by tapers and with servants in attendance. It is scarcely surprising to learn that this funeral cost over one thousand pounds.[11]

In many cases, where the family could not afford a coffin, the body was 'chested', or carried in a box to the graveside, and buried in nothing more than a shroud. The Order for the Burial of the Dead, from the *Book of Common Prayer*, introduced in 1554, does not even mention coffins: 'We therefore commit his body to the ground; earth to earth, ashes to ashes, dust to dust.'

It was traditional for the party to pause at the lych-gate, the roofed gateway of the churchyard. The term derives from the German 'leiche' or corpse, for it was here that the corpse rested while the first part of the burial service was read, in the days when it was thought inappropriate for the burial service to be conducted in the church.

Finally, the coffin was placed in its grave, with the head to the west and the feet to the east so that it would be standing in the right direction on Judgement Day.

Traditionally, although burials took place south, east and west of the church, the north was reserved for outsiders and outcasts. A suspected murderer might be buried on the north side; his victim in a place of honour – east, west or south.

Even in London, where space was at a premium, churchyards were traditionally filled with trees, evidence of a lasting pagan influence. However much the early Christian missionaries had struggled to make the English give up their tree-worshipping ways, paganism triumphed, retained in such traditions as holly and mistletoe at Christmas. The rowan or mountain ash with its vivid red berries protected against witchcraft. Yew trees, from which bows were made, had a symbolic value, guarding the churchyard from invasion, albeit that most churchyards would have been hard pushed to manufacture more than one bow out of their available stock. The cypress had been associated with death since Roman times, when it was customary to leave branches on the porches of villas to indicate that the family was in mourning.

But now, London was changing. Within fifty years of the Great Fire, London had become the largest city in Europe, and its inhabitants were polarized. Grasping the opportunities for property development, speculative builders bought up vast tracts of west London, which soon became the fashionable end of town. The poor drifted east, where the expanding docks offered employment. Burial customs were inevitably affected as a result. Among the poor, the rudimentary common burial continued, with families interring their dead as best they could, and the nobility maintaining their own traditions of the heraldic funeral. But a new social category was emerging: the merchant class, born from the commercial expansion that was transforming London. These were the people who had made a fortune trading in colonial goods such as tea, coffee and tobacco, or on the Stock Exchange, compensating for their perceived lack of gentility with lavish displays of conspicuous consumption. And for the nouveau riche, this extravagant approach extended to death itself. It was no longer enough to be chested to your graveside by devoted friends. Burial became an industry – and so the undertaking business was born.

Litten tells us that undertaking as a specific trade became established in London during the eighteenth century. Even then, undertakers were not popular. Regarded as hard-hearted men who made a living by exploiting the death of their fellows, they were mocked in dramas such as Richard Steele's *The Funeral, or, Grief A-la-Mode*. Anyone could set up as an undertaker. There were no exclusive guilds or chapels, and no written code of conduct, although, as Dr Litten has observed, there seems to have been an unofficial rule by which most contractors stuck to their own part of London.

The trade had three branches: coffin-making, undertaking and funeral furnishing. Coffin-making was a lucrative sideline for joiners and cabinetmakers, whilst the undertaker made coffins and also performed funerals. Like any other business, there was a hierarchy. France & Banting, undertakers to the Crown, ran a top-drawer operation and even had their own crest, featuring black chevrons and a silver unicorn. At the other end of the scale, coffins were built by local joiners, who frequently conducted the service themselves.

The majority of coffins and trappings were produced in Whitechapel and Southwark. Spitalfields was the centre of the 'black stuff' industry, producing the silks and velvets used in the trade. Matt black crape, the distinctive mourning fabric, was introduced by Huguenot refugees. Other manufacturers supplied coffin plates, sheets, carriages and feathers.

Like all salesmen, undertakers advertised vigorously. The trade card of William Boyce, whose premises were at *ye WHIGHT HART & COFFIN, in ye Grate Ould Bayley, near Newgeat* offers *all Sorts & Sizes of Coffins & Shrouds Ready Made*, while William Grinly, *At ye lower Corner of Fleet Lane at ye Signe of ye Naked Body & Coffin* promised *Coffins, Shrouds, Palls, Cloaks, Hearses and Gloves*, all on reasonable terms, in 1710.

Funerals became ostentatious social events, for which invitations were issued. William Hogarth designed one for Humphrey Drew, the Westminster undertaker, in 1720, depicting the street procession of a middle-class funeral. With Hogarth, a little satire creeps into the scene: a couple of mourners seem distracted by an event just out of sight; a slight altercation on the steps of the church between the priest and a flunkey suggests the group has arrived too early. Hogarth also depicted an undertaker's premises in *Gin Lane*, where the dismal trade is represented by a shop sign consisting of a coffin.

The change in funerals, and the development of the undertaking trade, was a reflection of shifting attitudes towards death on the part of the emerging middle class. Not for them the stiff upper lip of the aristocrat, or the stoical acceptance of the peasant. With the new class came the concept of the family as an affectionate unit. The notion of childhood was born, with offspring becoming lovable in their own right, rather than treated as miniature adults, spawned to continue the family line. With affection, inevitably, came bereavement, and the need for consolation in the form of some lasting memorial, something more than a simple stone. And burial need no longer take place in a mere churchyard.

The new middle class demanded a permanent memorial for their dead. One of the most influential books of the time was Gough's *Sepulchral Monuments* (1786), a massive two-volume survey of England's celebrated graves. This work, which combines a gazetteer with sombre reflection, was introduced by its author as: 'a mixture of private mixed with public life; a subject in which my countrymen have been anticipated by their neighbours'.[12] At its most extreme, this fashion took the form of a craze for mausolea, such as Vanbrugh's for Castle Howard in Yorkshire, which made such a terrific impression on the gothic novelist Horace Walpole that he observed it 'would tempt one to be buried alive!'[13]

Sir John Vanbrugh (1664–1726) had, like Wren, deplored burial in churches, and demanded that cemeteries be provided on the outskirts of towns. Vanbrugh had been inspired by a trip to the Colonies. In Calcutta, he visited the South Park Street Cemetery, where the English employees of the East India Company were buried. Both the design of the cemetery, with its Mogul tombs, and the layout of the new city that was to become the capital of British power in India, had impressed him. The craze soon caught on, with elaborate mausolea becoming a standard feature of the great English country houses. Rather than be buried in the family vault, the aristocracy found it infinitely more stylish to be interred in these temple-like constructions, among the rolling acres landscaped by such luminaries as Capability Brown to represent the Classical paradise of the Elysian fields.

By the mid-eighteenth century, another new attitude was emerging, one which encouraged reflection on death as a spiritual exercise and a valid form of artistic expression. The experts on Victorian death, James Stevens Curl and Chris Brooks, have described this tendency as, respectively, 'the cult of sepulchral melancholy' and 'graveyard gothic'. Melancholia had always been a consistent strain in the English character, as evidenced by the enduring popularity of *The Anatomy of Melancholy* (1621), a treatise on depression written by Robert Burton, a saturnine Oxford don rumoured to have hanged himself on completion of the work. But 'graveyard gothic' or 'the cult of sepulchral melancholy' focused specifically on death and bereavement.[14]

In its most benign manifestation, this fascination with death took the form of Gray's *Elegy* (1751), a meditation inspired by a traditional country churchyard. By modern standards the sentiments might appear self-indulgent, but such gentle melancholy was a legitimate poetic form. It was also, essentially, Romantic. Here was the author, describing his own feelings and inviting the reader to emote with him, at the prospect of his own death, and that of the reader's. Gone was the pragmatic acceptance of the peasant. To quote Ariès, the attitude had changed from *Et moriemur* – and we shall all die to *la mort de soi* – one's own death – and *la mort de toi* – the death of the other, whose loss and memory inspired a new cult of tombstones, cemeteries and a romantic attitude towards death.[15]

The poet Edward Young's *Night Thoughts* (1742) took as its theme the death of Narcissa, a pseudonym for his stepdaughter, Elizabeth Lee. Elizabeth was already terminally ill when she married Henry Temple in 1735. By the following autumn, Young and his wife accompanied the couple to the French Riviera, where it was thought the climate would be better for their daughter's advanced tuberculosis. When Elizabeth died on 8 October 1736, her corpse represented a familiar problem for English subjects dying abroad.

Where was she to be buried? As a Protestant, Elizabeth was 'denied a grave' within the local Roman Catholic cemetery. Although records indicate that Elizabeth was eventually buried, without incident, at a Protestant graveyard in Lyons, the fictional Narcissa suffers a more Gothic fate. The narrator breaks into an existing grave and places her there, 'more like her Murderer, than Friend'.[16]

Young was not alone in his relish of the macabre. In *The Grave* (1743), Robert Blair dwelt on 'the mansions of the dead', where, 'In grim array the grisly spectres rise, grin horrible, and obstinately sullen, pass and repass, hushed as the foot of night.'[17]

Wren's proposals for suburban cemeteries may have been rejected by the Corporation of London but, towards the end of the eighteenth century, planners in other capitals came to appreciate the hygienic and aesthetic possibilities of interring the dead on the outskirts of the city. Père Lachaise cemetery in Paris, founded by Napoleon in 1804, offered a magnificent example. Napoleon was the first leader to address the problems of the Paris cemeteries. Previously, burial had taken place in parish churchyards but, as the population soared, these had become full to overflowing and constituted a health hazard. The chief cemetery, Les Saint-Innocents, near Les Halles, was destroyed, and the bones transported to the catacombs, a series of deserted quarries underneath Paris.

The land, purchased by the urban planner Nicholas Frochot on Napoleon's orders in 1803, was originally a hill of the Champ l'Evêque, where a rich merchant built a house in 1430. Subsequently, Louis XIV named it after his confessor and the land was given to the Jesuits, who converted it into a hospice. The Jesuits sold the land in 1763 to pay off debts. Frochot's coup was to persuade the authorities to rebury the remains of Molière, La Fontaine, Abélard and Héloïse in the new cemetery – which soon led to Père Lachaise being the ultimate burial place for the rich and famous. As the social commentator Laman Blanchard observed in 1842, the Parisian man of wealth possessed a town house, a country house, a box at the Opera and a tomb in Père Lachaise.

Architect Théodore Brongniart, who also designed the Paris Stock Exchange, sought to emulate English garden designers such as Capability Brown, whose naturalistic landscapes were actually highly contrived: small hills were constructed, lakes sunk, trees planted at strategic locations. Although the style borrows from the English tradition, the result is quintessentially French. Père Lachaise is laid out like Central Paris itself, all avenues and boulevards rotating like spokes off a wheel from a series of significant architectural features, such as the massive rotunda to Casimir Perier (a disgraced politician) and the Bartholomé war memorial. The influences are formal and Classical, and the French culture of presentation is manifest. Along the Avenue de la Chapelle the majestic horse-chestnut trees are systematically pollarded to geometric exactitude. With its great and good, its eccentrics and mavericks, its war memorials and its important bourgeoisie, Père Lachaise is more like a small town than a garden. The little mausolea, with their narrow windows trimmed by ornamental grilles and their forbidding panelled doors, resemble apartment houses, inspiring one small child, when visiting, to ask his parents: 'Who lives here?' There are no weeds, or trailing growths of wild flowers and the planting is rigorous and schematic, more *haute couture* than the natural look.

In Edinburgh, Scottish architects also attempted to solve the problem of what to do with the dead. Carlton Hill Cemetery, which dates back to 1792, is situated on a hill 100 metres high, with panoramic views of Edinburgh, Holyrood, Arthur's Seat and the Firth of Forth. William Henry Playfair was commissioned to design a National Monument to honour the Scots killed in the Napoleonic Wars and, in keeping with the fashion for Classical architecture that characterized the Enlightenment, he came up with an impressive recreation of the Athens Parthenon, entirely fitting for 'the Athens of the North'. Building work commenced in 1822, then the money ran out. Just twelve columns stand today, towering over the city.

Over in Glasgow, John Strang developed the Glasgow

Necropolis. Opened in 1832, on a hillside like its predecessors, the Necropolis was designed to be non-denominational. It soon became like Westminster Abbey, supplying the final resting-place of Glasgow worthies from the 1830s to the 1870s.

The trend towards rural cemeteries spread to America. In Boston, New England, the authorities faced similar problems of overcrowded burial grounds. One difference was that in America, developers were free to build straight over graveyards, driven to do so by an ever-burgeoning population. Epidemics brought many burial grounds to the same pestiferous condition as their British counterparts, which led to the trend to bury out of town. There was another dimension: rapid urban growth, population mobility, booming business and commercial ventures, aggregations of surplus wealth, concentrations of educated and public-spirited people, revisions of religious doctrines and Romantic affectation – all combined to create a context in which the rural cemetery was a logical alternative to the burial places of an earlier era. Rural cemetery promoters wanted to change the image of the disgusting burial grounds of the past, and create peaceful retreats.

Established in 1831, in Cambridge, Massachusetts, Mount Auburn Cemetery was the first rural cemetery in America, and it set an example to the rest of America and to Europe, too. Landscape gardeners planned its layout around the natural contours of the site, with lazily meandering roads winding round already established tall shady trees. Mount Auburn became a sanctuary where mourners could commune with nature and their dead were buried with dignity within its spacious acres. It became such a popular destination that it led directly to the development of public parks. The City Fathers, somewhat perturbed to find citizens walking dogs and riding horses among the graves, agitated for more green spaces where the populace could promenade on sunny afternoons.[18]

Meanwhile, back in London, Victorian planners dreamed up bizarre and fantastic schemes to deal with the city's dead.

The influence of Père Lachaise was deeply felt. Architect Francis

Goodwin, responding to 'the prevention of the danger and inconvenience of burying the dead within the metropolis' designed a massive, 150-acre Neo-classical cemetery to be situated in north London, in Primrose Hill, or in south London, near Shooter's Hill. The plans included a 42-acre special section, a sort of British pantheon for 'the very wealthy and great and distinguished persons whose wisdom, bravery, genius and talent have conspicuously contributed to the glory of the county'. Enclosed by a double cloister through which visitors could promenade in wet weather, it featured facsimiles of the Temple of the Vestal Virgins at the Roman Forum and the Athenian Acropolis. Four figures, representing the Tower of the Winds in Athens were to stand at each corner of the cloister. There was to be a replica of Trajan's Column, the 30-metre-high monument to the Roman Emperor, dating from the first century AD, and catacombs. Outside this inner sanctum a secondary area, laid out like Père Lachaise, would cater for the middle classes, with the 'humbler class' of folk situated at a remove. Investors willing to buy into this grandiose proposal were offered 16,000 shares at £25 each.

Thomas Willson proposed a huge pyramid for Primrose Hill. At an estimated cost of £2,500, this massive mausoleum, higher than St Paul's, would contain five million Londoners. It was designed as an investment, with investors invited to apply for the 'Five Per Cent Pyramid Stock' in the Pyramid General Cemetery Company. The catacombs would be rented to parishes or individual families at £50 per vault. More than 40,000 bodies would be buried each year. A final profit was anticipated of £10,764,800.

Constructed from brick, with granite facing, the plans comprised a chapel, office, quarters for the Keeper, Clerk, Sexton and Superintendent, four entrances and a central ventilation shaft. A series of sloping paths would allow bodies to be moved. Each catacomb took up to twenty-four coffins and could be sealed up after all interments had been completed. Resembling a beehive, it would be a thing of awe and wonder to all who saw it:

> To trace the length of its shadow at sunrise and at eve and to toil
> up its singular passages to the summit will beguile the hours of
> the curious and impress feelings of solemn awe and admiration
> upon every beholder . . . a coup d'oeil of sepulchral magnificence
> unequalled in the world . . . the graceful proportions are partic-
> ularly adapted to sepulchral solemnity.[19]

The pyramid never left the drawing board but, undeterred, Thomas Willson went on to join the Board of the General Cemetery Company, responsible for Kensal Green, the first of London's magnificent nineteenth-century cemeteries.

The greatest British influence on the development of Kensal Green, and its successors, has been largely forgotten. It is to John Claudius Loudon[20] that we owe the London cemeteries and the impressive arboretums and botanical gardens which characterize our cities. Loudon (1783–1843) was a horticultural writer and designer who campaigned vigorously for burial reform; he suggested that the cemeteries of the past would become the parks of the future and predicted the development of cremation, forty years before it became legal in Britain.

Born in South Lanarkshire, Loudon was a polymath with a taste for horticulture. From his earliest years, he enjoyed laying out plots in the little garden his father had put aside for him, and when a relative brought tamarinds home from a missionary expedition, Loudon was happy to donate the fruit to his peers, as long as he got to keep the seeds. Although Loudon was destined for the Church, his father sympathized with his passion for plants and arranged for him to study with a landscape gardener from the age of fourteen. By the time Loudon arrived in London in 1803, armed with letters of introduction to some of the richest landowners in England, his reputation preceded him.

Determined, energetic and enthusiastic, Loudon opened a practice as a landscape architect at 4 Chapel Street, Bedford Row and made his mark upon the city at once, and for ever. Writing in *The*

*Literary Journal* about the gloomy nature of London's garden squares, he suggested planting plane trees, sycamores and almonds, which would stand up to the city's sooty atmosphere but counteract the existing funereal pines and firs. At a stroke of the pen, Loudon changed the city's appearance for ever – London without its spring blossom and distinctive plane trees is unimaginable.

The young man also worked on commissions in his native Scotland, including Brunswick House for the Duchess of Brunswick and Scone Palace in Perthshire for Lord Mansfield. Loudon's father moved south to join his son and took on Wood Hall Farm in Berkshire, where he successfully transplanted Scottish agricultural techniques; this led to Loudon Junior establishing one of the first agricultural colleges, at Great Tew. Both Loudons excelled in their careers, although they became victims of an extraordinary form of early nineteenth-century racism. 'North Britons', as these Scots were called, were bitterly resented in England for their professionalism, ambition and gritty determination.

Although literally crippled with arthritis – Loudon developed a limp in his twenties – he set out on 'The Grand Tour', the sightseeing trip to Europe and the Near East which marked a rite of passage for the young gentlemen of the era. Loudon was determined to visit the ruins of Classical Antiquity that had inspired Inigo Jones, Capability Brown and other landscape architects.

Europe in 1813 was still reeling from the effects of the Napoleonic wars. Arriving in Konigsberg, the former capital of East Prussia, Loudon found traces of war everywhere. The fields were littered with dead horses, their bones whitening in the sun; roads were broken up, houses in ruins. Refugee columns, possessions piled into carts, passed Loudon less than two miles from the marauding French army. Near Marienburg and Danzig, he encountered 2,000 Russian troops, who looked more like convicts than soldiers. By the time Loudon reached Berlin, he saw the long avenues of linden trees crowded with carriages and wagons, as people streamed into the city for protection, an extraordinary vision in the moonlight.

Travelling in Russia, Loudon was arrested as a spy when he paused to make architectural drawings in Riga, and had the bizarre experience of hearing his notebook read out in court, although the local magistrates could make head nor tale of his jottings and much was lost in translation. On the trip to Moscow, he fared little better. The roads were almost impassable, and on one occasion, when his carriage ran into a snowdrift, the coachmen unharnessed the horses and trotted away, leaving Loudon and his companions to the wolves, an experience which he endured with customary sang-froid. By the time Loudon got to Moscow, eager to sketch the grand designs, he found the houses black from a great fire, and the streets filled with the ruins of churches and aristocratic mansions. Instead of seeing the great palaces and gardens at first hand, he found only destruction and decay.

Loudon was a prolific author, in the magazine format which characterized Victorian publishing. Month after month he edited four periodicals and wrote encyclopaedias on gardening and agriculture. A workaholic with an iron constitution, he survived on four hours' sleep a night and copious cups of black coffee.

Not content with landscape gardening and journalism, Loudon developed an iron-glazing bar that made curved glazing possible in 1816 and built a prototype hothouse that influenced the great Paxton in his creations at Chatsworth and Crystal Palace. In 1826, wracked by rheumatism and arthritis, Loudon endured the amputation of his right shoulder after a botched operation to correct a broken arm and became addicted to the laudanum he was taking for the pain. But even this could not hold him back. Loudon learned to write and draw with his left hand, and hired a draughtsman to lay out his plans. Meanwhile, his opium habit was getting out of control; he was downing a wine-glass full of the drug every eight hours. Anxious to change this, he devised a characteristically ingenious solution, adding a wine-glass of water to his two-pint bottle of laudanum every time he took a wine-glass out. Diluted in this fashion, the mixture became gradually weaker every day, until Loudon had weaned himself off the drug.

In the same year, looking for a diversion from ill-health and overwork, Loudon reviewed a three-volume romance entitled *The Mummy's Tale – A Novel*, for *The Gardener's* magazine. Set in 2126, in an England that had reverted to absolute monarchy, this featured prototypes for espresso machines, air-conditioning and, most prophetically, 'a communication system that permitted instant world dissemination of news'. Intrigued, Loudon invited the anonymous author to lunch. To his astonishment, this early proponent of science fiction was a young woman of twenty-three, one Jane Webb. Left penniless at seventeen by her father's death, she had turned to writing as a means of support. Jane rapidly became Loudon's editor, wife, and mother of their only child, Agnes. With the arrival of Agnes, the Loudons' finances, always troubled, became desperate. Abandoning science fiction for the more remunerative genre of journalism, Jane developed into a successful author in her own right with a series of books designed to interest 'ladies' in gardening.

Loudon defined the main aim of a burial ground as disposing of the dead in such a way that their decomposition would not affect the living; he advocated cheap, temporary burial grounds for the poor, which could be recycled after seven years, or using part of the workhouse grounds as a cemetery, suggestions which led contemporary writers to accuse him of 'turning paupers into manure'.

Like Sir Christopher Wren before him, Loudon despised the concept of catacombs unless the cells were hermetically sealed:

What is this disgusting boxing up of dead bodies, as if to bid defiance of the law of nature? Surely it is pleasanter in idea, when looking on the statue of Dr Johnson in St Paul's, to think of his remains being covered by the green turf in the open grounds of a cemetery or churchyard than to think of them lying in black earth, saturated with putrescent moisture, under the damp paved floor of a crypt or cathedral.[21]

Loudon's solution to this unpleasant method of sepulchre was to tax it out of existence, rendering catacombs so expensive that the practice would be discontinued, any revenue to be spent elsewhere in the cemetery, in general upkeep and contributing to the burial of the poor. Family graves, which had to be reopened for serial interments, he disapproved of on health grounds.

A product of the Enlightenment, Loudon's cemeteries were characteristically functional. He advocated good drainage, spacious layout with sufficient space between graves so that diggers did not cut into existing graves while excavating new ones, and calculated that 1,361 graves per acre was ideal. If one estimated deaths of the town population at 3.1 per cent per annum, this acre would suffice for a population of 1,000 for forty-five years. Graves should be at least six feet deep to allow the gases of putrefaction to escape, filtered by the soil. There should be a gated entrance and holly hedges for security. He approved of the Lamb's Box, a device for gathering the earth from a freshly dug grave, so that the area around the mouth of the grave was not muddy, and the handcart for the funerals of the poor, considerably cheaper than a horse-drawn hearse. However, he condemned the presence of sheep in graveyards (a common solution to trimming the turf; the problem was that the sheep ate indiscriminately and nibbled young trees).

Loudon also demonstrated the ethical stance typical of the Victorian reformer. His cemeteries were not merely a place to bury the dead. They served to take on the role previously associated with churchyards and provide moral edification. Sermons in stones and spiritual uplift for the deserving poor:

> . . . the churchyard is their book of history, their biography, their
> instructor in architecture and sculpture, their model of taste, and
> an important source of moral improvement . . . the greenhouse

myrtle flourishes in the parterre dedicated to affection and love; the chaste forget-me-not blooms over the ashes of a faithful friend; the green laurel shades the cenotaph of the hero; and the drooping willow, planted by the hand of the orphan, weeps over the grave of the parent.

'Everything there is tasteful, Classical, poetical and elegant. Adorn the sepulchre, and the frightful visions which visit the midnight pillow will disappear.'[22]

By 1843, despite being wracked by rheumatism and arthritis, Loudon continued to work a punishing schedule, both as a designer and a journalist, contributing to West Norwood, Paddington and Brompton Cemeteries, and designing Birmingham Botanical Gardens and Derby Arboretum.

Ahead of his time, Loudon had taken on a commission for the first municipal cemetery in Britain, at Southampton, but it was to be his final project. A lifetime of ill-health and overwork had taken its toll. Loudon was in the final stages of lung cancer. Visiting him in Southampton, his wife 'took one look and knew that he was dying', and begged him to come home. But Loudon was determined to complete work on the cemetery and correct the proofs for his latest encyclopaedia, a guaranteed money-spinner. Despite Jane's entreaties, he went on to Bath, where he inspected the site for another cemetery, although he had to be wheeled around in a Bath chair. A visit to another potential client in Oxfordshire had the landowner offering to send Loudon back to London on the train, assisted by one of his servants.

Once home, Loudon's doctor informed him bluntly that his condition was terminal. Despite this, Loudon strove to see through all his projects, battling against the disease to complete drawings and finish manuscripts. Heavily in debt and pursued by his creditors, Loudon was anxious to provide for his family. He paced restlessly about the house, defiant to the end. One morning, as she was preparing to leave the house, Jane suddenly caught sight of a change in his expression. Darting forward, she caught her husband before he fell over. Loudon had literally died on his feet.

It is fitting that Loudon, whose work was such an inspiration to Kensal Green, was buried there. Loudon's grave in the 'tasteful, Classical, poetical and elegant' environs of Kensal Green was marked by a stylish Grecian urn. According to Jane, when the coffin was lowered into the grave, an unfamiliar man stepped forward from the crowd and threw in a few strips of ivy. He was a maker of artificial flowers, grateful that Loudon had sent him free tickets to a garden show, early in his career, when he had been too poor to attend. Never able to thank Loudon in person, this was his way of paying tribute.

Despite his publishing business and his inventions, Loudon died penniless. Jane struggled to make a living as a journalist and provide for Agnes, later a successful children's writer. Thirteen years after Loudon went to his grave, Jane joined him.

*On the Laying Out, Planting and Management of Cemeteries and the Improvement of Churchyards,* published posthumously in 1844, was to be Loudon's true memorial.

By the time of Loudon's death, London's graveyards had reached such a repulsive state that there was urgent need for reform. Loudon's lasting legacy was the contribution he made to the closure of these 'pestiferous grounds' and the development of the great London cemeteries.

# 6: GATHERINGS FROM GRAVEYARDS

*The Dead are Killing the Living*

By 1842, London had become the commercial capital of the world. Following the Battle of Waterloo in 1815, the population expanded from a mere one million to over two and a half million. The historian Thomas Carlyle was horrified by this city of swirling fog and thunderous noise, where coaches, carts, sheep, oxen and far too many people rushed on and on, bellowing and shrieking, as if the world had gone mad. Cobbett had dubbed the city 'the great Wen' (an archaic term for a boil or carbuncle); Carlyle went one better. 'It is a monstrous wen!' he wrote to his brother. 'The thick smoke of it beclouds a space of thirty square miles; and a million vehicles grind along its streets forever.'[1]

As London grew, so did her trail of dead – but the capital's 200 graveyards did not magically get any bigger. Burial was one aspect of metropolitan life which the planners had not yet confronted, even as they built the new Jerusalem. In shocking reality, London was more necropolis than metropolis, her bustling thoroughfares and sophisticated highways paved with gold for the fortunate few, her side-streets reeking of decay. By 1842, the life expectancy of a professional man was thirty. For a labourer, it was just seventeen. The burgeoning population, drawn to the city for employment, was rocked by a series of epidemics. The high infant death-rate and constant epidemics of cholera, typhoid, measles and smallpox meant that death was always present. No wonder that, according to historian Vanessa Harding, Londoners spent three million pounds a year on gin!

However, 1842 was a significant year, as it finally saw the Government recognize the scale of the problem of what to do with the dead. A Select Committee was appointed to investigate the capital's noxious and overcrowded burial grounds, but this only came about after a series of scandals, a wave of cholera epidemics and a long campaign by public health reformers Sir Edwin Chadwick and George Alfred Walker. Chadwick, a barrister and radical journalist, and Walker, an eminent surgeon, were pioneers who battled long and hard to improve the parlous state of things.

Graves were being crowded out by developers. City churches, with their old-world churchyards, were wedged in between huge modern office blocks, public buildings and railway stations. In a city where building land was at a premium, London was faced with a lack of burial space. Sir Edwin Chadwick, whose *Sanitary Report* proved to be a bestseller for the Stationery Office in 1842, confirmed that, every year, 20,000 adults and 30,000 youths and children were 'imperfectly interred' in less than 218 acres of burial ground, 'closely surrounded by the abodes of the living'.[2]

Available burial grounds fell into three categories: existing churches with their churchyards, stand-alone churchyards, and new developments. The satirical magazine *Punch*, at that period closer in spirit to today's *Private Eye,* editorialized that: 'A London churchyard is very like a London omnibus. It can be made to carry any number.'[3] St Mary's Churchyard, Islington, for example, was notoriously overcrowded. In 1835, Thomas Cromwell wrote that conditions were so bad it was necessary to remove the oldest tombstones to make way for the new. An engraving by Daniel Warner dating from the 1840s depicts it as jam-packed with looming mausolea rammed in among gravestones leaning at precarious angles.[4]

Despite the reservations of Wren, Vanbrugh and their successors, burial in vaults beneath churches had continued. The processes of decomposition, shaky foundations and the British disease of rising damp caused particular difficulties. Chadwick noted that, however solid the coffin, 'Sooner or later every corpse buried in the vault of a church spreads the products of decomposition through the air which is breathed, as readily as if it had never been enclosed.'

One example was the Rector's Vault beneath St Clement Dane's Church on the Strand, the entrance into which was in the aisle of the church, near the Communion table. When opened, the smell of decomposing flesh was so intense that lighted candles, passed through the opening into the vault, were instantly extinguished. Workmen were understandably reluctant to descend into the vault until it had been aired for two or three days.

One of the duties of a sexton consisted of 'tapping' coffins, 'so as to facilitate the escape of gases which would otherwise detonate from their confinement'.[5] On occasion, the build-up of corpse gas was so intense that coffins actually exploded. In the 1800s, fires beneath St Clement Dane's and Wren's Church of St James's in Jermyn Street destroyed many bodies and burned for days.

As well as fire, water was another problem. There had been a well to the east of St Clement Dane's, sunk in 1807, but the water became so offensive, probably as result of the infiltration of the products of human putrefaction, that it was bricked up. The water table had risen, with springs so close to the surface that coffins sank into a watery grave as soon as they were let down.

Churchyards where the churches had been destroyed in the Great Fire of 1666 but had never been rebuilt were used as burial grounds for the amalgamated parishes. But here, conditions were no better. The churchyards, the majority of which were controlled by the Church of England, were not big enough to cope with the number of dead. St Georges-in-the-East had three acres for a population of 40,000; St Matthew's, Bethnal Green, two acres for more than 70,000; St Mary's, Whitechapel, had under an acre for nearly 35,000 people.

Existing burial grounds included Cross Bones, an unconsecrated graveyard near Borough High Street, traditionally used for prostitutes, who were forbidden Christian burial. By the nineteenth century, Cross Bones was in the middle of one of the worst slums in London, choked with cholera victims – and a favourite with body-snatchers.

In addition to existing burial grounds, new ones were founded as speculative ventures by entrepreneurs. These were either attached to existing churches and chapels, or created on plots purchased by developers. There were fourteen of these by 1835, including Spa Fields, Clerkenwell, which had started life as a tea-rooms but was then converted to the rather more profitable purpose of human burial; New Bunhill Fields, Islington; Victoria Park Cemetery, Bethnal Green at Cambridge Fields (five acres); and Sheen's New Ground in Whitechapel (two acres). With the exception of the strictly-controlled Quaker and Jewish cemeteries, all these burial grounds were horribly congested. Charges for burial were cheaper than in churchyards, although services were not always conducted by ministers of religion. At Butler's Burial Ground in south London, the gravedigger donned a surplice to read the burial service; at Globe Fields in Mile End, proceedings were conducted by an ex-cobbler.[6]

George Alfred Walker carried out a shocking survey of forty-seven overcrowded London burial grounds. In *Gatherings from Graveyards* (1839) 'Walker of the Graveyards' confessed himself astonished that 'London, with its thousands of busy minds and observant eyes, anxiously exploring the dimly shadowed outlines of the future, should bear upon its breast these plague spots, the burial grounds.'[7] Walker believed that dead bodies actually *caused* disease – attributing outbreaks of typhus and cholera directly to them.

One of the most obscene examples chronicled by Walker was the site at Portugal Street, situated on St Clement's Lane, off the Strand,

and otherwise known as the 'Green Ground', although there was not a tree to be seen. 'It was a mass of putrefaction.' A 'burying place beyond memory of man', Portugal Street constituted a burial ground for a nearby workhouse, which was demolished to make way for King's College Hospital in the 1830s. Several slaughter-houses in the vicinity contributed to the stench of decay. Upwards of 5,500 bodies were interred there between 1823 and 1848.

'The soil of this ground is saturated, absolutely saturated, with human putrescence,' Walker noted incisively. 'The living here breathe on all sides an atmosphere impregnated with the odour of the dead.'[8] The effluvia from Portugal Street were so offensive that people living in St Clement's Lane were compelled to keep their windows closed. The walls of the Green Ground that adjoined the yards of local houses dripped with reeking fluid. Cholera, typhus and smallpox were rife.

In the course of his investigations, Walker interviewed an unfor-tunate man living at 33 St Clement's Lane. Clinically depressed and terminally ill, he lay in the back room of a filthy house, his wife and family at his bedside. Glancing out of the window, Walker saw an open grave within a few feet of the house. 'That's just been made for a poor fellow who died in the room upstairs,' said the man. 'He died of typhus fever, from which his wife has just recovered. They have kept him twelve days, and now they are going to put him under my nose, by way of a warning.'

Children were the primary victims of these filthy conditions and there were numerous anecdotes of undertakers temporarily storing the bodies of newborn infants in their own premises until there were enough dead babies to make it worthwhile giving them a decent burial. St James's Burying Ground, Clerkenwell, was exces-sively overcrowded. 'The mortality among children in this neighbourhood has been very great,' Walker observed. 'This will not occasion surprise when the locality of the burying ground, and the filth and wretchedness of the major part of the inhabitants are duly considered . . . in the poor ground, little regard is paid to the

depth of the graves, or the removal of the dead. In this filthy neighbourhood, fever prevails, and poverty and wretchedness go
hand-in-hand.'

Over 150 years later, George Alfred Walker's evidence is still
shocking. We examine it with a sense of outrage: how could such a
state of affairs have been condoned, in the most progressive city in
the world? Gladstone once said: 'Show me the manner in which a
nation cares for its dead, and I will measure with mathematical
exactness, the tender mercies of its people, their loyalty to high
ideals, and their regard for the laws of the land.'[9] From which we
may conclude that the standard of living and dying in early
Victorian London was desolate, to say the least. A lack of reverence
for the dead collided with denial to ruinous effect. Burial grounds
were so disgusting that the women of the family never accompanied
the coffin to the graveside. And the poor lived in such squalid and
overcrowded conditions that their grim interments were but an
extension of their oppressed and miserable lives.

Investigating the conditions of migrant workers in the East End,
George Godwin found a family of fourteen sharing one room in
Rosemary Lane, near the Tower of London. In an apartment in
Church-lane, St Giles's, less than fifteen feet square, (about the size
of the average modern bedroom), *thirty-seven* men, women and
children were huddled together on the floor. In New Court,
Charles Row, Whitechapel, which contained eight houses, there
was only one water closet for 300 people. The houses were dirty,
dilapidated, and teeming with vermin. Beds were no more than a
bundle of rags. Swarms of children, complexions pinched by mal-
nutrition, were dragged rather than brought up. Families got
evicted on a daily basis. The rent was two shillings and sixpence a
week, but the residents, many of them fresh off the boat from
Ireland, seldom earned more than three pennies a day.

On the frequent occasions when a child died, the need to raise
funds for the burial, combined with the Irish custom of keeping the
corpse in the house until the funeral, meant that a child's body

might lie among the living for a week. Dr Brouardel, a French physician, described the scene after a patient, who lived with his family in one room, died of smallpox. The doctor arrived to find a wake in full progress. 'There were bottles everywhere,' he wrote. 'Even on the abdomen of the deceased.' In some instances, the corpses of debtors were seized by bailiffs who refused to release the body for burial until the debts were paid.

Walker set up a Society for the Abolition of Burial in Towns, campaigning for the closure of the revolting inner-London burial grounds and the promotion of new suburban cemeteries, preferably municipal, 'to remove as far as possible from the living THE PESTIFEROUS EXHALATIONS OF THE DEAD'.[10] Walker's campaign attracted support from Sir Edwin Chadwick. A driven man, who worked fifteen hours a day and exhausted his subordinates, Chadwick had a characteristic Victorian devotion to the public good and turned his formidable intellect to the disgusting consequences of the city's overcrowded graveyards with *The Health of Towns and the Sanitary Condition of the Labouring Classes* (1842).

Although the relationship between the dapper, sardonic Walker and the dour Chadwick was a barbed one, their campaign flourished and attracted considerable public support. A correspondent to *The Times* claimed:

Passing along Portugal Street on Saturday evening, about ten minutes before seven, I was much shocked at seeing two men employed in carrying baskets of human bones from the corner of the ground next the old watch-house (where there was a tarpaulin hung over the rails to prevent their being seen, and where they appeared to be heaped up in a mound), to the back of the ground through a small gate.

Where this leads to I do not know; but I should be glad, through the medium of your invaluable journal to ask, why is this desecration? I feel more particularly than many might do, as I have seen twelve of my nearest and dearest relatives consigned to the grave in that ground; and I felt that, perhaps, I might at the moment be viewing, in the basket of skulls which passed before me, those of my own family thus brutally exhumed. At all events, for the sake of the community at large, it should be inquired into.[11]

St Giles's churchyard, where the first victims of the Great Plague had been buried, was infamous once again in the *Weekly Despatch*:

What a horrid place is St Giles's churchyard! It is full of coffins up to the surface. Coffins are broken up before they are decayed, and bodies are removed to the 'bone house' before they are sufficiently decayed to make their removal decent. The effect upon the atmosphere, in that very densely populated spot, must be very injurious. I had occasion to attend the church with several gentlemen, on Tuesday; being required to wait, we went into this Golgotha; near the east side we saw a finished grave, into which had projected a nearly sound coffin; half of the coffin had been chopped away to complete the shape of the new grave. A man was standing by with a barrowful of sound wood, and several bright coffin plates. I asked him: 'Why is all this?' and his answer was, 'Oh, it is all Irish.' [St Giles's had originally been consecrated as a Roman Catholic burial ground and was favoured by Irish immigrants.] We then crossed to the opposite corner, and there is the 'bone house' which is a large round pit; into this had been shot, from a wheelbarrow, the but partly-decayed inmates of the smashed coffins. Here, in this place of 'Christian burial', you may see human heads, covered with hair; and here, in this 'consecrated ground', are human heads with flesh still adhering to them. On the north side, a man was digging a grave; he was quite drunk, so indeed were all the gravediggers we saw. We looked into this grave, but the strench was abominable. We remained, however, long enough to see that a child's coffin, which had stopped the man's progress, had been cut, longitudinally, right in half; and there lay the child, which had been buried in it, wrapped in its shroud, resting upon the part of the coffin that remained. The shroud was but little decayed.[12]

Then, as now, Hanover Square was a good address. Yet, despite being in a fashionable neighbourhood, close to Marble Arch and surrounded by mansions, the burial ground of St George's Church was in a repulsive state. According to the journalist Thomas Miller, in this 'dimly lighted, breathless churchyard', freshly-buried bodies were moved from the more expensive section to the paupers' end, making room for more graves for which higher fees were paid. Families could never be certain that they were actually mourning their relatives. Miller describes headstones raised over the graves of strangers, as relations weep for someone they have never known, and the sexton and gravedigger watch from behind the nearby tombstones, clinking the silver in their pockets and chuckling. Meanwhile, the official residents had been removed, their remains serving as foundations for a new road, or ground up and sold as bone-meal for the market gardens of Kent.[13]

Charles Dickens, who began his career as a Parliamentary correspondent, was quick to add his voice to the campaign. In *The Uncommercial Traveller*, he noted that:

Such strange churchyards hide in the City of London; churchyards sometimes so entirely detached from churches, always pressed upon by houses; so small, so rank, so silent, so forgotten, except by the few people who ever look down into them from their smoky windows: St Ghastly Grim, with a ferocious strong spiked iron gates, ornamented with skulls and cross-bones, wrought in stone. These skulls grin aloft horribly, thrust through and through with iron spears.[14]

St Ghastly Grim or, to give it its real name, St Olave's Hart Street, was the same church where Pepys had been frightened by the graves of plague victims in January 1666. Despite the plague connection, the skull and crossbones date from 1633, and figure as a standard motif in a Dutch pattern book.

Dickens returned to the subject in his capacity as a novelist when he described 'Tom All Alone's' in *Bleak House*. 'Tom All Alone's' was actually Russell Court, Drury Lane, one of the most overcrowded burial grounds in London. Reached by a reeking little tunnel behind Drury Lane Theatre, it was surrounded by tall narrow tenement houses looking in on every side, rag and bone shops and a pawnbroker's. Originally located below the line of the buildings, by 1839 the burial ground had risen to the same level as the first-floor windows of the adjoining houses. A plumber, called to put in a drain at the west end of the burial ground, was obliged to cut through the wall of one residence. When his crew took up the ground floor, a huge quantity of human bones were discovered, dragged there by the vast number of rats which overran the neighbourhood.

In *Bleak House*, Jo the crossing sweeper brings the tragic Lady Dedlock to the burial ground near 'Tom All Alone's', so that she can locate the tomb of her dead lover:

> By many devious ways, reeking with offence of many kinds, they came to the tunnel of a court and to the gas-lamp (now lighted) and to the iron gate.
>
> 'That there berryin' ground,' said poor Jo, 'they laid him out as was werry good to me. He was put there,' says Jo, holding the bar and looking in.
>
> 'Where? Oh, what a scene of horror!'
>
> 'There,' says Jo, pointing, 'over yinder – among them piles of bones, and close to that there kitchen winder they put them werry nigh the top. They were obliged to stamp upon it to get it in. I could unkiver it for you with my broom if the gate was open; that's why they locks it, I s'pose.' Giving it a shake. 'It's always locked! Look at the rat! Hi! Look! There he goes! Ho! Into the ground.'[15]

Believe it or not, the horrors of 'Tom All Alone's' pale into insignificance compared with events at Enon Chapel. If name is destiny, there was definitely a clue to the Enon Chapel's future when it was opened in April 1822. Ostensibly a reference to John the Baptist baptizing converts at Enon near Salim (John 3:23), Enon has a more sinister interpretation. According to Hitchcock's *Bible Names Dictionary,* Enon means 'cloud; eye;' or, more ominously, 'mass of darkness'. Enon Chapel was to be one of the most infamous exhibits in the case for reforming the burial laws.

Built over an open sewer which passed uncovered through the vault, Enon Chapel was located on the west side of Clement's Lane, only yards away from one of the busiest streets in the world – the Strand. Access was through a gateway leading into a narrow and extremely dingy court, which opened out into Carey Street. It was surrounded by grim, dilapidated houses, crammed with the destitute.

Mr W. Howse, a Baptist minister, founded the chapel as a speculative venture. He opened the upper part for the worship of God, and devoted the lower to the burial of the dead. Worship there was a dangerous business; for members of the congregation frequently passed out – yet, because nobody guessed at the minister's appalling secret, it never occurred to them that the cause of their sickness lay beneath a flimsy layer of floorboards, in the vault of the chapel.

In warm, damp weather, local residents were assaulted by a peculiarly disgusting smell. Occasionally, when a fire was lit in a nearby building, an intolerable stench arose, which did not originate from the drains. Vast numbers of rats infested the houses; and meat exposed to the atmosphere turned putrid after an hour or two.

Soon after burials in the chapel vaults, a peculiar long narrow black fly was seen crawling out of many coffins. This insect was followed a few months later by another, which looked like a common bug with wings. The unfortunate children attending Sunday School in the chapel above saw these insects crawling in vast numbers during the summer, and named them 'body bugs'. The stench was frequently intolerable. One eyewitness complained of a peculiar taste in his mouth during worship that had him retching into his handkerchief.

Although the precise sequence of events is uncertain, according to Walker the scandal of Enon Chapel was uncovered in 1839, when the Commissioners of Sewers decided that a new sewer had to be carried under the building. This involved covering up the open sewer in the vault. What they found was a charnel house. Mr Howse had succeeded in burying around twelve thousand bodies into a space measuring fifty-nine feet by twelve, at fifteen shillings a time. Called to the scene, Walker was appalled to find the vault crowded with corpses from floor to ceiling. Entered by a trap door, it was a ramshackle construction. The rafters supporting the floor of the chapel were not even covered with lath and plaster; only a thick wooden floor separated the living from the festering dead. Pits had been dug and vast numbers of bodies placed in them, covered only by a few inches of earth.

One explanation as to why families had permitted their dearly beloved to be consigned to such a hell-hole was the lingering fear of body snatchers. They genuinely believed their dead were buried safely, away from the threat of the Resurrection Men. Gullible people were willing to disregard their own health and safety rather than suffer the anxiety that their loved ones had been brutally exhumed.

The pretext was the security of the dead; the real object was money. There was also the fact that burial was relatively cheap at Enon. Up the road, at St Clement Dane's, burial fees in the church-yard were £1 17s 2d for adults and £1 10s 2d for children, while Enon only charged fifteen shillings. Nor did Howse discriminate on the grounds of denomination. When it came to burial in 'the dust hole', all were welcome. This would include the children of Baptists. Unlike other Christian denominations, Baptists are not baptized automatically within weeks of birth. They have to attain a certain age before agreeing to undergo the procedure. As a result, many Baptist parents were anxious to secure graves for their children in the Dissenter cemeteries. It was either this, or the common grave. Walker visited 'this Golgotha' several times:

I was struck with the total disregard of decency exhibited – numbers of coffins were piled in confusion – large quantities of bones were mixed with the earth, and lying upon the floor of this cellar (for vault it ought not to be called ), lids of coffins might be trodden upon at almost every step. My reflections upon leaving the masses of corruption here exposed were painful in the extreme; I want language to express the intense feelings of pity, contempt, and abhorrence I experienced. Of the bodies found in the vault, not one was placed in lead. It was scarcely a Christian burial.[16]

Walker later told the Select Committee of 1842 that sixty loads of dirt and human remains had been carted away from the vault at various times, and thrown into the Thames. Vast quantities were used as landfill at Waterloo Bridge. Once, part of a load fell off in the street, and the crowd picked up a human skull.

Howse had also resorted to quicklime (commonly used to break down animal carcasses for swift burial). But quicklime did not devour coffins. Howse and his wife burned these for firewood.

The authorities had the chapel closed down but left the bodies to rot, oblivious to the consequences. In 1844, a new tenant, a Mr Fitzpatrick, moved in. As the kitchen ceiling was too low, he hired a builder, John Mars, to moonlight on Sunday afternoons. It was on just such a Sunday that Mars decided to lift all the flagstones, from the front of the house to the back, to lower the level of the kitchen floor. At this point, he made a grim discovery: huge quantities of bones. Mars's solution was barbaric but practical: he dug down another two feet in the chapel, and stashed the bones in the hole.

The building, renamed Clare Market Chapel, was let to a sect of teetotallers, who used it for tea-dances. These bizarre occasions were referred to locally as 'dances on the dead', where the giddy hoofed it over the mouldering remains, the previous generation turning to dust beneath the dancers' feet.

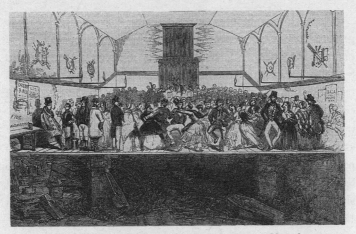

*Dancing on the dead – The scandal of Enon Chapel.*

Walker eventually took possession of the chapel in 1847. Exhumation commenced, and a pyramid of human bones was exposed to view, separated from piles of coffin wood in various stages of decay. About 6,000 people visited the site before four cartloads of bones were removed, and the human remains were decently interred in one pit at the recently opened Norwood Cemetery, at Walker's own expense. The coffin wood was piled up and burned.

Fear of body snatchers led many families to inter their dead in appalling places like Enon Chapel. The lamentable state of London's burial grounds, with their cheap, shoddy coffins and shallow graves, made corpses easy prey for the Resurrection Men. These ghoulish figures had been operating since the late eighteenth century. Far from resting in peace, Londoners feared that they would be disinterred, and their remains sold to anatomy schools. The prevailing Christian belief that bodies must remain intact for Resurrection made dissection particularly repulsive.

As a discipline, anatomy originated with Andreas Vesalius, who produced prints of dissected men in his *De Humanis Corporis Fabrica*, 1543. Henry VIII granted the College of Barbers and Surgeons (precursor of the Royal College of Surgeons) the right to take four hanged criminals a year for dissection. The bodies of criminals were the only legal source of cadavers, but by the eighteenth century, demand had outstripped supply. The science of anatomy was essential for doctors, particularly surgeons, who needed a thorough understanding of the human body in order to operate successfully. William Hunter (1718–83) ran the first anatomy course in London in 1747, joined by his brother John in 1748. A dissection room was established at St Thomas's in 1780, with Guy's and Bart's soon following suit. By the 1790s, there were about 200 anatomy students in London. By the 1820s, over 1,000 were working their way through 800 corpses a year.

Medical ethics did not stretch to questioning the source of cadavers, and dead bodies were accepted on a 'don't ask, don't tell' basis. In some cases, anatomy students were asked to provide their own cadavers. Bodies were snatched from Tyburn Gallows, still warm, triggering riots from a populace disgusted by the anatomists' activities.

The first prosecution for body snatching, but by no means the first case, came in 1777, when an attempt was made to steal a fresh corpse for dissection from the churchyard of St George the Martyr, Southwark. Although many body snatchers were ignorant louts, a professional class emerged who justified their activities on scientific grounds. Body snatching required skill, as well as guts. Far from opening the grave, they would dig an aperture through which the body could be removed, leaving the coffin and shroud intact. Taking these was construed as stealing, but a corpse had no intrinsic monetary value, unlike a dead pig or a sheep, the theft of which could mean transportation. The corpse was rolled up in a sack and carried away. The dire condition of St Pancras Cemetery, which was memorialized in Thomas Hood's poem, 'Jack Hall', made it a favourite with body snatchers. As Jack lies dying, with twelve doctors hovering round for his body, he confesses that:

> *I sold it thrice,*
> *forgive my crimes!*
> *In short I have received its price*
> *A dozen times.*[17]

Deterrents against body snatching included iron coffins, and a series of cage-like devices, such as the one discovered in the crypt of St Bride's, Fleet Street, which could be placed over the fresh grave to prevent the casket being tampered with. In 1819, a Mr Gilbert attempted to have his wife buried in St Andrew's Burial Ground, Gray's Inn Road, in an iron coffin, as he had 'a great dread that her remains might be despoiled'. When the vestry demanded a £10 fee, a legal battle ensued, on the grounds that iron coffins, being durable, required a longer lease of the ground. Gilbert won his case on a technicality, but it was over a year before the remains of Mrs Gilbert, which had been placed in the St Andrew's charnel house, were safely interred.[18]

A less dramatic method of body snatching involved women posing as relatives and claiming the bodies of paupers from workhouses and hospitals. The latter, which had their own burial grounds, were convenient for body snatchers, and anyone else who needed to procure a fresh corpse for an anatomy demonstration at short notice. Laurence Sterne, buried in a pauper's grave at St George's, Hanover Square in 1768, allegedly turned up on the anatomist's slab at Cambridge University two days later, only for the surgeon, Dr Charles Collignon, to recognize the author of *Tristram Shandy* and release the body for a second, permanent burial.

In the fourth of his series of engravings, *The Stages of Cruelty*, Hogarth gives us a vivid depiction of a public dissection at the

'Company of Surgeons'. The anti-hero, a murderer, lies on the table, grimacing as if in pain. The noose is still round his neck, while one student pokes a scalpel in his eye, another knifes his chest and a third teases his intestines into a pail.

By 1828, a 'Bill to prevent unlawful disinterment and to regulate schools of anatomy' was proposed. Eminent surgeon Sir Astley Cooper informed the Committee that there were 700 anatomy students in London, but only 450 bodies supplied officially. This number was inadequate, as each student needed to dissect between four and twelve. The eventual legislation allowed anatomists to use the bodies of anyone who was not claimed within forty-eight hours. This meant that paupers from hospitals, asylums and workhouses regularly ended up on the table.

Burke and Hare, the legendary Edinburgh body snatchers (who actually murdered their victims, rather than disinterring them), supplied Dr Robert Knox (1791–1862), a pioneering anatomist who fled Scotland in disgrace and was eventually buried at Brookwood Necropolis after a second career as a consultant pathologist at the Royal Marsden Hospital.

The last celebrated body-snatching incident in London concerned Messrs Bishop, Williams and May, from Bethnal Green, who, in 1831, attempted to sell the body of a fourteen-year-old boy. At King's College, a suspicious demonstrator concluded that the body gave the appearance of an unnatural death and tipped off the police. The gang was remanded, and the boy provisionally identified as one Carlo Ferrari from Piedmont, with the crime being dubbed 'The Italian Boy Murder'. However, the gang later admitted that the lad was from Lincolnshire, and had been driving cattle to market at Smithfield when they kidnapped him. At Newgate, Bishop and Williams were sent to the gallows for their crime; their corpses – splendid specimens, apparently – went straight to the anatomists' table.

The disgusting state of the existing burial grounds, lingering fears of body snatchers, and the atrocity of Enon Chapel should have been enough to bring about a change in the burial laws. But it took another, even more terrible event, to effect reform. Two centuries after the Great Plague, London was terrorized by a series of epidemics.

In the days of my youth, the world was shaken with the dread of a new and terrible plague which was desolating all lands as it passed through them, and so regular was its march that men could tell where next it would appear and almost the day when it might be expected. It was the cholera, which for the first time appeared in Western Europe. Its bitter strange kiss, and man's want of experience or knowledge of its nature, or how best to resist its attacks, added, if anything, to its horrors.

This account by Mrs Stoker, in a letter to her son Bram, also demonstrates where the author of *Dracula* derived his chilling turn of phrase.

Asiatic cholera spread across Europe from the Far East, first reaching England in 1831. Helpless, the Government did nothing beyond calling a day of national prayer and fasting, while clerics declared that the epidemic was a vengeance from God for London's wickedness. By autumn, 5,000 people had died from the epidemic, but still no counter measures were taken. A second outbreak in 1848 compounded the already grisly condition of the burial grounds. Over 14,000 people died in London alone.

As with the Great Plague, it was the poor who bore the brunt of this epidemic. Thomas Miller, who lived in 'the land of Death' – Stoke Newington – referred to cholera as 'the dreadful disease which caused almost every street in the metropolis to be hung in mourning'.[19] At Fore Street in Lambeth, the residents 'looked more like ghouls and maniacs than human beings'. At high tide, their doorways had to be blocked with boards to stop the river getting in, and the surgeon would make his way to patients along planks laid over two feet of water. At the Tooting 'child farm', 180 out of nearly 1400 pauper children were wiped out within days, undermined by starvation, impetigo and scrofula.[20]

Cholera is a silent killer. One of its most terrifying aspects is its stealth. Early symptoms, including mild fever and gastric upset, seem inconsequential, but the disease can prove fatal within hours. Cholera takes its name from the Ancient Greek word for roof gutter. The violent diarrhoea which characterizes the disease was likened to the effects of a powerful rainstorm. People died swiftly and in terrible pain. Regulars shook hands outside the pub, went home, and were never seen again. The aspiring paterfamilias moved into the bigger house he and his wife had dreamed of, only to find that Death moved in with them, and the family was plunged into penury overnight. Small children, scarcely old enough to walk, found themselves dressed in black and trying to understand why their father had been carried away in a box and their mother would never wake up. Orphaned and penniless, they were destined for the workhouse. In some houses, everybody died. After the building had been closed a few days, other tenants moved in, and they perished too, since the mercenary landlords never divulged the fate of their predecessors. The dead were removed at night; sometimes twenty people were buried in one grave.

The medical profession was defenceless against cholera, with doctors clinging to the theory of 'miasma', the conviction that disease broke out when the air became polluted with waste. As rubbish rotted in the street during the long hot summers, it gave off a strong smell, which they believed caused the disease. Chadwick himself subscribed to this theory, maintaining that 'all smell is disease'.

Far from eliminating the outbreak, sanitation only made conditions worse. Water companies such as The Chelsea Waterworks Company, incorporated in 1723, 'for the better supplying the city and liberties of Westminster and parts adjacent with water' sourced their product direct from the Thames. In 1827, Sir Francis Burdett complained to the House of Lords that:

> The water taken from the River Thames at Chelsea, being charged with the contents of the great common sewers, the drainings from dunghills, the refuse of hospitals, slaughter-houses, colour, lead and soap works, and with all sorts of decomposed animal and vegetable substances, rendering the said water offensive and destructive to health, ought no longer to be taken up by any of the water companies from so foul a source.[21]

An artist recalled that the view from his Chelsea studio was marred by the corpse of a dead dog, thrown up every day by the tide, each time in a more advanced stage of decomposition. The wit Sydney Smith noted that, 'He who drinks a tumbler of London water has literally in his stomach more animated beings than there are men, women and children on the face of the globe.' And a cartoon of the day, entitled *Monster Soup*, shows a horrified woman looking down a microscope to discover the pullulating fiends breeding in a drop of Thames water.[22]

The development of piped water led to the popularity of flushing water closets, which emptied directly into the Thames. Instead of going into cesspits, human waste was being recycled in drinking water. There was also an element of sleaze involved: many MPs were reluctant to see the private water companies closed down since they had shares in them.

Although medical experts, such as George Walker, were aware of the relationship between pollution and disease, it was not until 1854 that the pioneering investigator Dr John Snow (1813–58) finally established the link between cholera and contaminated water. Snow observed that he had attended many patients, but never caught the disease himself. He also noted that cholera seemed to affect the alimentary canal before the patient began to feel ill – and concluded that it must be swallowed in some way. His *Mode of*

*Communication of Cholera* was published in 1849, but it was not until the particularly virulent epidemic of 1854 that his theories were vindicated, and he was able to prove that one outbreak of cholera had been spread by a common pump in Broad Street, Soho, poisoned by sewer water.

During the cholera epidemics, London's burial grounds became even more of a threat to public health. There was a general outcry that the churchyards were too full and that there was no longer any room for the dead. The expert on death and the Victorians, James Stevens Curl, notes that during epidemics, churchyards became 'scenes of the most appalling horror, where bones would be heaped on bones, and partially rotted bodies would be disinterred to make way for a multitude of corpses'.[23] In an effort to contain the disease, coffins were filled with lime, and the shrouds dipped in coal tar.[24] However, the authorities, admitting at last that there was a correlation between outbreaks of disease and the state of the burial grounds, drew up plans to burn the bodies of cholera victims directly after death – but this had to be abandoned after angry mobs opposed the suggestion.

Finally, spurred on by a combination of the cholera epidemics and the scandal of Enon Chapel in particular and London's graveyards in general, Walker and Chadwick were able to make their case before the Commons. In 1842, a Royal Commission was sitting on the question of the Health of Towns and the Sanitary Condition of the Labouring Classes, and a Select Committee had been convened to 'consider the expediency of framing some legislative enactments to remedy the evils arising from the interment of bodies within the precincts of large towns, or of places densely populated'.[25]

Chaired by Sir William MacKinnon, MP for Lymington, the committee sat from 17 March to 5 May 1842, and conducted sixty-five examinations. Witnesses included clergymen, the Bishop of London (C. J. Blomfield) and Sir Benjamin Brodie, President of the

Royal College of Surgeons. Dissenting ministers, doctors, sextons and gravediggers would testify to the appalling conditions which led one commentator to observe that: 'The dead are killing off the living.' The burial reformers had waited a long time for this moment.

With his killer details and incisive turn of phrase, George Walker was a star witness. Although some of his reports appeared to be exaggerated, and were criticized by opponents to closure who had their own agenda, Walker's message got through. As part of his evidence, Walker circulated a pamphlet on Spa Fields, Clerkenwell. While some Anglican ministers still conducted funerals there, Spa Fields had become so repellent that the Bishop of London refused to consecrate it. Eventually, Spa Fields was purchased by a Lady Huntingdon, who employed one of her own chaplains, enhancing the ground's snob appeal. This ground was, said Walker, '. . . saturated with the dead. No undertaker can explain it, excepting by a shrug of the shoulders. I can confirm, from frequent personal observation, that enormous numbers of dead have been deposited here.' It emerged that bodies were burned behind a brick enclosure, and gravestones moved about to give an appearance of emptiness in certain parts of the ground. Spa Fields was designed to hold 1,000 bodies. Walker calculated that, by burning coffins, mutilating remains, and using vast quantities of quicklime, at least 80,000 corpses had been buried there.[26]

William Chamberlain, a gravedigger at St Clement Dane's, testified that the ground was so full that he could not make a new grave without cutting into old ones. The bodies were so perfect he could distinguish the men from the women, and they had to be chopped up, and thrown behind the boards which were placed to keep the ground up where the mourners were standing. Once the mourners had departed, the flesh was thrown in and jammed down.

Chamberlain's assistant said that on one occasion, he found his colleague chopping off the head of his own father. Another admitted: 'One day I was trying the length of a grave to see if it was long and wide enough, and while I was there, the ground gave way, and a body turned right over, and the two arms came and clasped me round the neck!'

Quite apart from the public health consequences of overflowing graveyards, Walker was also concerned about the working conditions of gravediggers. They literally took their lives in their hands. Walker collected details of many deaths and illnesses directly attributable to contact with human remains in a state of putrefaction. The more experienced, when they opened a coffin, immediately fled to a safe distance, and stayed there until the corpse gas had been sufficiently dispersed to allow them to continue their unpleasant work in comparative safety. Another custom was to burn paper or straw in graves and vaults, while some men swore by a mouthful of garlic. Gravediggers suffered from bad health and alcoholism: notoriously heavy drinkers, it was claimed they couldn't perform their grisly task without spirits.

A transcript of the proceedings records the gravedigger William Miller bearing witness to conditions at Globe Fields burial ground in Mile End:

*Chairman:* What is your occupation?

*Miller:* A jobbing, labouring man, when I can get anything to do.

*Chairman:* Have you been a gravedigger in Globe Fields, Mile End?

*Miller:* Yes.

*Chairman:* Have many pits been dug in it for the depositing of bodies previously interred?

*Miller:* Yes.

*Chairman:* Where did they come from? Out of the coffins which were emptied for others to go into the graves? Were the coffins chucked in with them?

*Miller:* No, they were broken up and burned.

*Chairman:* Were they bones, or bodies, that were interred?

*Miller:* Yes; the bones and bodies as well.

*Chairman:* Were they entire, or in a state of decomposition?

*Miller:* Some were dry bones, and some were perfect.

*Chairman:* What did you do with them?

*Miller:* Chucked them into the pit.

*Chairman:* What sort of pit?

*Miller:* A deep, square pit, about four feet wide and seven or eight feet deep.

*Chairman:* How many bodies did you chuck in?

*Miller:* I cannot say, there were so numerous; each pit would hold about a dozen.

*Chairman:* How many of these pits did you dig?

*Miller:* I suppose I dug a matter of twenty myself.

*Chairman:* How near to the surface of the earth did these dead bodies or bones come?

*Miller:* Within about two feet.

*Chairman:* What is the size of this ground?

*Miller:* It is rather better than half an acre.

*Chairman:* How many bodies are buried in that ground within a year?

*Miller:* I cannot say; I suppose there are fourteen thousand have been buried in that ground.

*Chairman:* How long has it been open?

*Miller:* Since the year 1820.

*Chairman:* Do you recollect any circumstance which occurred there about the month of October, 1839?

*Miller:* Some boys were at work there; a policeman on the railroad happened to see them in the act of taking some bones out of baskets, and got a policeman in the police force of the metropolis, and sent him in and seized the boys with a bag of nails and plates off the coffins, going away to sell them, and going to sell the bones.

*Chairman:* To what purpose are the bones applied?

*Miller:* I do not know.

*Chairman:* What is done with the wood of the coffins?

*Miller:* Burned for their own private use.

*Chairman:* By whom?

*Miller:* By the sexton.

*Mr Cowper:* Is it burned in the sexton's house?

*Miller:* Yes.

*Sir William Clay:* What was done with the iron or metal handles of the coffins?

*Miller:* They were burned on the coffins when I was there, and were thrown out among the ashes about the ground anywhere.

*Mr Ainsworth:* Were you in the habit of performing this grave digging without the use of spirits?

*Miller:* No; we were obliged to be half groggy to do it, and we cheered one another and sang to one another.

*Mr Ainsworth:* You found the work so disgusting you were obliged to be half drunk?

*Miller:* Yes.[27]

Other evidence included a gruesome account of events at Church Passage, Aldgate, in 1838, when a gravedigger, John Oakes, was found lying at the bottom of a twenty-foot grave. A crowd gathered, and one young man, Edward Luddett, a fishmonger, volunteered to help. Ropes and a ladder were produced, and Luddett clambered down into the grave, intending to place the ropes under the gravedigger's arms so that he could be winched to safety. But the instant Luddett stooped to raise Oakes's head, he staggered as if struck with a cannon ball, collapsed and died. Another gravedigger, William King, made two or three ineffectual attempts to descend, but the air was so foul that he had to be drawn up again, and it was half an hour before the two dead bodies were brought to the surface with a hook attached to a rope.

At the coroner's inquest, Dr Jones, a local surgeon, testified that every effort had been made to recover the bodies. It emerged that this lethal pit was a paupers' grave, and that graves such as these were kept open until there were seventeen or eighteen bodies interred in them. The court heard that, on this occasion, the only occupant was the body of a still-born infant. It was not the custom to put any earth between the coffins in those graves, except in cases where the persons died of contagious diseases, and in that case some slaked lime and a thin layer of earth were put down to separate them. The practice of digging deep graves had been adopted by order of the churchwardens five or six years ago. There had been instances whereby gravediggers could not go down a grave, owing to the foulness of the air, but the churchwardens had never been told of this. On such occasions, Oakes, and his predecessor King, were in the habit of burning straw, and using other means to dispel the impure air, before descending.

According to Dr Jones, the cause of death was suffocation, resulting from the poor air quality in the grave, composed of carbonic acid gas, generated from decayed animal matter. When asked his opinion as to the effect of keeping a grave open a couple of months, the doctor replied that the noxious effluvia from it must be very injurious to health and he hoped something would be done about it. The jury returned a verdict of Accidental Death in both cases.[28]

The burial reformers faced considerable objections from the clergy, both Anglican and Dissenting, who made money from burials and turned a blind eye to the horrific consequences. In response, Walker condemned the apathy of the established Church, remarking that 'the sight of gold acts as an open sesame to the marble floors of our cathedrals and churches'.[29] Walker's critics accused him of being in cahoots with the private cemetery companies, while the cemetery companies condemned him for attacking their livelihoods. On more than one occasion, members of the medical establishment were wheeled in to give evidence against him. Dr Bentley Todd, Fellow of the Royal College of Physicians and the Royal Society, told the Select Committee that the Portugal Street burial ground, damned by Walker as 'a mass of putrefaction' caused no inconvenience to King's College Hospital, which overlooked the cemetery.

By May 1842, the Committee concluded that:

> The Nuisance of Interments in large Towns, and the injury arising to the Health of the Community from the practice, are fully proved . . . No time ought to be lost by the Legislative in applying a remedy. The Evidence has also exhibited the singular instance of the most wealthy, moral and civilised community in the world tolerating a practice and an abuse which has been corrected for years by nearly all other civilised nations in every part of the globe.[30]

There followed resolutions on the provision of cemeteries for parishes, either single or amalgamated; the fees which should be charged; respect for those who wished to be buried in unconsecrated ground, such as Dissenters; and exceptions in the cases of family vaults, such as St Paul's Cathedral and Westminster Abbey.

In summing up, Sir William MacKinnon concluded: 'That the duty of framing and introducing a Bill on the principles set forth in the foregoing Resolutions, would be most efficiently discharged by Her Majesty's Government, and that it is earnestly recommended to them by the Committee.'[31]

But legislation is time-consuming, and it was to be another ten years before a Bill against interment in towns was introduced. The Act to Amend the Laws Concerning the Burial of the Dead in the Metropolis, commonly known as the Burials Act, 15 and 16 Victoria, was finally passed in 1851. After that, notices were issued for the termination of interments in vaults and graveyards all over London. The list printed on 1 January 1855, of graveyards remaining open, was a short one – and in many cases, only vaults could be used. The Home Secretary was inundated with letters from London residents, begging for the Act to be enforced in their neighbourhoods, along with applications to open cemeteries on the outskirts of the town. Predictably, there were objections to closures by the investors who stood to make money out of burial grounds, but the environment eventually began to improve.

Thomas Miller, the journalist who had lived through the cholera epidemics, noted:

> The streets were no longer darkened with funerals; you no longer saw men running in every direction with coffins on their heads, knocking at doors, and delivering them with no more ceremony or feeling than the postman delivers his letters. The solemn hearse and the dark mourning-coach now moved slowly along, and the dead were borne away to green and peaceful cemeteries, far removed from the dwellings of the living.[32]

The closure of the inner-city burial grounds was just one factor in London's sanitary reform. The city reeked for nearly another decade. It was not until the problem was literally under the Government's nose that real action was taken. During the 'Great Stink' of June 1858, the stench arising from the Thames forced the House to adjourn. The stench was so overpowering that the curtains of the Commons were soaked in chloride of lime in a vain attempt to protect the sensitivities of MPs. Disraeli referred to the river as a 'Stygian pool' and tons of lime were dumped in it every day.

The House had been reviewing the Metropolitan Board of Works proposal for a system that would prevent sewage passing into the Thames in or near the Metropolis for the previous three years. The arrival of the Great Stink saw the Bill rushed through Parliament in eighteen days. The scheme had been created by Joseph Bazalgette (1819–91), one of the most distinguished civil engineers of the period. After considerable experience on railway projects, he was appointed Chief Engineer of the Metropolitan Board of Works in 1855. The Great Stink was the start of the sewer system as we know it today. Bazelgette built eighty-three miles of pipes that prevented raw sewage running into the Thames and took it to the east of London, where it joined the river with minimal effect on the population.

Following the closure of the inner-city burial grounds, and the founding of Thomas Miller's 'green and peaceful cemeteries' in the outlying suburbs, Londoners were now burying their dead beyond the city walls, just as the Romans had. This did not resolve the problem for long, however. Although space was allocated for common graves, the majority of plots were restricted to those affluent enough to afford them. But it is these Victorian Valhallas, as much as the 'pestiferous graveyards', which define the nature of death and burial in nineteenth-century London.

# 7: VICTORIAN VALHALLAS

*The Development of London's Cemeteries*

The great cemeteries of the nineteenth century demonstrate the sheer inventiveness of the Victorians, who could confront the issues of death and the disposal of the dead, and produce such innovative solutions as the coffin lift and the well-designed catacomb. John Claudius Loudon, Stephen Geary, Francis Goodwin and Benjamin Baud represented a triumph in the combined disciplines of architecture, landscape gardening and engineering. Falling eagerly upon all sorts of architectural styles, from Greek to Gothic, these engineers and designers created the quintessential London graveyard, wherein Egyptian pyramids jostle with weeping angels and Grecian urns stand alongside Celtic crosses.

The entrepreneurial Victorian spirit, coupled with genuine concerns over public health, led to the development of seven magnificent cemeteries, all within a six-mile radius of Central London; they surround the city like figures on a clock.

The legislation which permitted the first, Kensal Green, to open in 1833, paved the way for Norwood (1837), Highgate (1839), Abney Park (1840), Brompton (1840), Nunhead (1840) and Tower

Hamlets (1841). Of these, Highgate remains the most spectacular, although the sheer scale of Kensal Green is awe-inspiring.

Whilst Chadwick and Walker were lobbying to 'remove burial from populous places', entrepreneurs had already seized on the opportunity to invest in death. The lack of adequate burial space within London led inevitably to the founding of new cemeteries on the outskirts of town. It was only a matter of time before the outrageous fantasies of a giant pyramid in Primrose Hill or a British Père Lachaise achieved some form of reality, in the hands of astute property speculators.

In May 1830, a letter from the gifted inventor and landscape gardener John Claudius Loudon appeared in the *Morning Advertiser:*

*Sir,*

*Observing by the reports from the Commons House in this day's paper, that the above subject is likely to soon undergo discussion, allow me to suggest that there should be several burial grounds, all, as far as practicable, equidistant from each other, and from what may be considered the centre of the metropolis; that they be regularly laid out and planted with every sort of hardy trees and shrubs; and that in interring, the ground be used on a plan similar to that adopted in the burial grounds of Munich, and not left to chance like Père Lachaise. These and every other burial ground in the country might be made, at no expense whatever, botanic gardens; for, were nurserymen and gardeners invited, I am certain they would supply, everyone to his own parish, gratis, as many hardy trees and shrubs, and herbaceous plants, as room could be found for. It would be for the clergy and the vestries to be at the expense of rearing these trees if they choose, which I think they ought to do, if they get them for nothing.*

*The burial places of the metropolis ought to be made sufficiently large to serve at the same time as breathing places, and most churchyards in the country are now too small for the increasing population. To accomplish the above and other metropolitan improvements*

*properly, there ought to be a standing commission, for the purpose of*
*taking into consideration whatever might be suggested for the general*
*improvement, not only of London, but also of the environs.*[1]

Architects and planners were quick to take note of Loudon's suggestion. Joint stock companies devoted to the foundation of new
cemeteries sprang into being. Joint stock companies were limited
liability enterprises, comprising a number of individual members or
shareholders who each held a stock in the company. Cemeteries had
become a form of property development.

To meet the demand for out-of-town burial, enterprising individuals, often architects and engineers, purchased suitable tracts
of land, sold shares to finance the layout of new ground and the
erection of chapel and office buildings, then sold plots at a profit
and reinvested the capital, to the benefit of the shareholders. The
success of the ventures was a reflection of the general investment
mania that flourished between 1820 and 1840, and saw massive
investment in domestic enterprises such as banking, life assurance,
mining, railways and steam navigation.

Private cemeteries also represented a general drive towards civic
adornment in the form of municipal buildings, schools, churches,
parks, which was characteristic of the age and was reflected
throughout Victorian Britain, in cities such as Glasgow, Manchester,
Nottingham and Leeds.[2]

Although his previous scheme for a British Père Lachaise had
been turned down in 1824, the barrister and burial reformer George
Frederick Carden established the provisional committee of a
General Cemetery Company in 1830, which would result in the creation of Kensal Green Cemetary. Among the architects represented
were Thomas Willson, who had designed the failed giant pyramid
in Primrose Hill, and the Gothic Revivalist Augustus Pugin. The
scheme began when the investor John Dean Paul purchased fifty-
four acres of land, part of the Fillingham Estate, between the
Harrow Road and the Grand Union Canal in north-west London;

he paid John Nicoll, a local landowner, the sum of £9,500 for it. At that time, Kensal Green was in the country; sheep had to be driven from their pastures for building work to proceed.

The Act of Parliament to establish a 'General Cemetery Company for the interment of the Dead in the Neighbourhood of the Metropolis' received Royal Assent in July 1832, at the height of an early cholera epidemic. This Act provided the template for the other private cemetery companies which would be formed over the next twenty years. It contained a vital clause providing for the compensation of Anglican clergy, who would lose out to the new cemetery on burial fees, at a rate of between 1s 6d and 5s a time, depending on the type of burial.

The General Cemetery Company published a prospectus, inviting investors to take out shares at £25 each in order to raise the £45,000 needed to build the cemetery. A violent disagreement broke out over its proposed design. This was a notorious example of the 'Battle of the Styles' – an ongoing war of taste between Neo-classical architects such as John Nash, who was responsible for London's elegant Regent's Street, and the Gothic-Revival contingent.

The architectural historian John Winter has described the Battle of the Styles as the consequence of a period of architectural confusion, when the Palladian National Gallery could be built at the same time as the Houses of Parliament. At times of architectural change, the imagination can run faster than the more prosaic skills of planning and constructing a building. In the 1830s, designers wanted buildings that *looked* Gothic, but they had no real understanding of the planning and construction behind it. This dichotomy is evident in Charles Barry's Houses of Parliament: Gothic topdressing on an essentially Classical building. (Passing the Houses of Parliament one day, Augustus Welby Pugin commented: 'All Grecian, sir. Tudor details on a Classic body.'[3])

According to John Betjeman, 'If you wanted to rise in your profession you would join, if you were an architect, the Gothic side in the Battle of the Styles. The influential men favoured Gothic. They believed with Pugin that the pointed arch was the sign of Christianity, and that Gothic was the only honest style.'[4]

Gothic Revival was essentially a return to the building styles of the Middle Ages. Popular throughout Europe, it became a sensation in England. Early examples include Strawberry Hill (1770), Horace Walpole's remodelled house, and Fonthill, home of the Gothic novelist William Beckford. In England, the style reached its apotheosis under Augustus Welby Pugin, whose achievements include designs for the interior of the House of Commons; MPs still gather for refreshment in the Pugin Room, with its overwhelming wallpaper. Pugin maintained that the mediaeval aesthetic, in its way of life and art, was superior to the modern and should be emulated, using authentic methods to create the same level of craftsmanship.

Although Gothic Revivalists clashed with Neo-classicists, many architects, such as Sir Charles Barry, worked in both. On a sectarian level, Gothic Revival was associated with Roman Catholicism or 'Popery'. The Spanish Inquisition continued to strike terror into the Anglican heart. To gain some insight into the Establishment's horror of Rome, one need only repeat the art historian Kenneth Clark's anecdote: 'A lady alone with Pugin in a railway carriage saw him cross himself, and cried: "You are a Catholic, sir! Guard, guard, let me out – I must get into another carriage!"'[5]

To resolve the dispute over the cemetery's design, a competition was launched in November 1831. The challenge was to design a chapel on a budget of £10,000, and a gateway for £3,000. The prize was one hundred guineas (£105) for the winner. There were forty-six entries and Henry Edward Kendall (1776–1875) won first prize for his Gothic-Revival plans, uncompromisingly mediaeval and reminiscent of King's College Chapel, Cambridge. The plans included a splendid water gate, allowing coffins to be brought to the cemetery via the Grand Union Canal. However, the Board of Directors found Kendall's designs suspiciously 'Popish'. On a more practical level, Gothic Revival was high maintenance. The *Gentleman's Magazine* declared the plans to be '. . . a rather florid style of architecture. The slender proportions as well as the number of Mr Kendall's spires and pinnacles seem to us to be at variance with the sepulchral character of the edifice.'[6]

The General Cemetery Company aspired to the carriage trade, the majority of whom would be Anglican, and tended to support the Classicists in the Battle of the Styles. John Griffith of Finsbury (1796–1888), was subsequently awarded the post of Chief Architect on the project for his austere Greek-Revival plans, while Carden, a Gothic enthusiast, found himself voted off the board. Griffith's chapels, gateway and lodges were completed four years after the cemetery opened, by 1837, in a prostyle (having a row of columns in front) tetrastyle design of Portland stone and Roman cement. The Anglican Chapel is Doric, whilst the Dissenters' Chapel is Ionic. Both have colonnades and brick catacombs with enough space for over 10,000 bodies including approximately 4,000 below the Anglican Chapel and a maximum of 1,000 below the Dissenters' Chapel. The gateway, on the Harrow Road, is Doric, with a triumphal arch, and the Anglican chapel had the first coffin lift in Britain, invented by 'Mr Smith, Engineer, Prince's Street, Leicester Square' and costing £400. As one might have expected, the *Quarterly Review* disapproved:

> We should be very scrupulous as to the admission of every new-fangled and patented contrivance into the sepulchral pale. King Death's is a very ancient monarchy, and quite of the old regime. The lowering therefore of the coffin from the chapel into the crypt by means of Bramah's hydraulic press, so highly extolled for its solemnity in some of the cemeteries, has too much of the trick of the theatre about it for the stern realities of the grave.[7]

This was not the only problem. The relatively primitive manufacturing processes of the 1830s meant that this apparatus was far from reliable, and there were complaints of noise and occasional complete malfunction. An entry in the minute book of the General Cemetery

Company dated Wednesday, 24 April 1839, refers to an irate letter to Mr Smith, demanding that the current malfunction be rectified within a fortnight, 'or else!'[8] In December 1844, the coffin lift was replaced by a new one, installed by Bramah & Robinson at a cost of £200. The new model worked on the hydraulic principle, with the considerable advantage that it operated silently.

Landscaped by Pugin senior, and a Mr Liddell, a former pupil of Nash, the grounds of Kensal Green Cemetery were as elegant as a London park and observed strict social divisions between the forty-seven acres of consecrated ground for Anglicans and the seven others allocated to Dissenters.

'The left-hand road leads to the abodes of the Turks, Jews, Infidels, Heretics and "unbaptised folk", and the right-hand, after passing among the beautiful and consecrated graves of the faithful, leads to the Episcopal Chapel. This Chapel is a beautifully executed work, in the same style as the entrance buildings and is fitted up in excellent taste.'[9]

According to *Mogg's New Picture of London and Visitor's Guide to its Sights* (1844) as 'an elegant and beautiful sight, at a distance of three miles from Oxford Street', the cemetery was surrounded on three sides by a massive wall and on the fourth by a handsome iron railing, which allowed a view of the surrounding countryside and the Surrey Hills. The area was 'planted and laid out in walks, after the manner of Père Lachaise at Paris'.

The Bishop of London consecrated the forty-seven acres of the Anglican part of Kensal Green on 24 January 1833, a temporary chapel having been erected in the grounds until Griffith's designs had been completed. The cemetery was an immediate success with the rich and famous, after the lavish burial of George III's son, Augustus Frederick, Duke of Sussex, on 6 April 1843. Appalled by the scenes at his brother William IV's interment at the Royal Chapel, Windsor, the Duke had left strict instructions that he did not wish to be buried in 'that stinking hole'. William IV's ceremony had been a travesty. The diarist Greville described 'a wretched mockery, with a long tedious service miserably read by the Dean of Windsor; people of all ranks loitered around, chattering and sniggering', while Hobhouse 'did not see a tear in any eye: only the guardsmen, holding tapers and torches, looked solemn'. Instead, the Duke received a suitably uplifting send-off, and an imposing monument at Kensal Green.

When his sister, Princess Sophia, was buried opposite him in 1848, she lay beneath a sarcophagus designed by Prince Albert's architect, Professor Ludwig Grüner.

*The funeral of the Duke of Sussex made Kensal Green the 'Belgravia of Death'.*

Families anxious to secure a plot in this 'Belgravia of Death' besieged the General Cemetery Company. By 1850, it was described as the only one of the suburban cemeteries yielding a good dividend to the proprietors. This was not just because of its middle-class clientèle. There was money to be made from paupers, too. The Annual Report of 1842 records that: 'It has been found that seven acres will contain about 133,550 graves; each grave will receive ten coffins; thus accommodation may be provided for 1,335,000 deceased paupers.'[10]

Kensal Green was an immediate success, attracting the crème de la crème. The central drive and the area around the chapels, the most expensive parts of the cemetery, boast appropriately lavish tombs, large mausolea in a variety of architectural styles. These include the towering Gothic confections containing the remains of John Gibson (1892) and the Molyneux family (1864); Classical *telemones* (crouching male figures) (Sir William Casement, 1844), temples (John St John Long, 1834), and huge obelisks such as the one which celebrates the first head of the Metropolitan police (Sir Richard Mayne, 1868).

One of the most spectacular monuments is the £3,000 tomb of Andrew Ducrow, an Egyptian extravaganza that *The Builder* dismissed as 'ponderous coxcombry'. Ducrow (1793–1842) was a showman, 'the Colossus of Equestrians', who wrestled with lions, re-enacted scenes from Napoleonic battles, and could lift four or five children using nothing more than his teeth. Also buried here are Isambard Kingdom Brunel, Sydney Smith, and novelists William Makepeace Thackeray and Anthony Trollope. W. H. Smith lies, appropriately enough, beneath a stone book.

In 1842, the social commentator Samuel Laman Blanchard was overwhelmed by this 'beautiful garden of death' which had sprung up so quickly. 'It is scarcely ten years since the sheep were driven from their pasture, and already there have been about 6,000 interments.'[11] Kensal Green provided a wonderful alternative to the inner-London funeral, taking place to an accompaniment of rattling wheels and hoarse cries, enveloped by a yellow fog. Fulfilling John

Claudius Loudon's brief, it permitted escape from the choked charnel house to Blanchard's 'verdant wild expanse, studded with white tombs of infinite shapes, and stone-marked graves covered with flowers of every brilliant dye!' Kensal Green was truly an 'Asylum of the Dead'.

The decade between 1830 and 1840 constituted a golden age for the joint stock cemeteries. As they were constructed, the cemeteries came to resemble a jet necklace around the throat of London. The next big venture, the South Metropolitan Cemetery at West Norwood in Surrey, was consecrated on 6 December 1837 by the Bishop of Winchester. Sited on a hill, and designed by Sir William Tite, Norwood featured broad, sweeping paths, which led up to two chapels in Perpendicular Gothic.

One famous burial at Norwood was that of Baron Julius de Reuter (1816–99), originally Israel Beer Josaphat, who, as a humble bank clerk, founded a pigeon-post service which bridged a gap in the telegraph line between Aachen, Germany, and Verviers, Belgium. Arriving in England in 1851, Josaphat opened a news office in London, and in 1858 he persuaded English newspapers to publish his foreign telegrams, thereby changing the face of newsgathering forever by his founding of Reuter's.

Norwood was also the last resting-place of Mrs Isabella Beeton, the original domestic goddess, and Hiram Maxim (1840–1916), inventor of the machine gun. However, impressive though they might be, Kensal Green and Norwood had competition. High above North London, on a noted beauty spot, a rival was taking shape . . .

All cemeteries are places of reflection, but Highgate is unique, with a spirit all its own. A fusion of brooding Neo-gothic architecture and ivy-shrouded masonry, it lies 400 feet above St Paul's, looking out over one of the most mysterious and fascinating cities in the world. Perhaps there is something about the very location of Highgate which contributes to the cemetery's magical atmosphere. Even today, it is full of hidden beauty and eccentricity, a haven from the strange disease of modern life. In his introduction to a collection of essays, John Betjeman refers to Highgate as the Victorian cemetery *par excellence,* the 'Victorian Valhalla'. This is a wonderful description, combining as it does the pagan imagery and Dickensian atmosphere of Highgate.

This place was once a country meadow. 'Highgate means High Gate, and nothing more', a contemporary guidebook informs us bluntly. The name dates back to mediaeval times, when the Bishop of London erected a tollgate to extort payment for travellers riding north from the forests of Islington. The little village gained a mention in August 1485, when the victorious Henry Tudor – soon to be Henry VII – picked up a crowd of supporters that grew exponentially as he advanced towards London, after defeating and slaying Richard III at the Battle of Bosworth Field. The Lord Mayor and Aldermen received Henry in scarlet robes, with 'a great number of citizens on horseback'.

It was on West Hill, near what is now the Whittington Hospital but was then a leper colony, that Dick Whittington heard the bells prophesy that if he turned back, he would become Lord Mayor of London.

Highgate had always been considered a healthy spot, removed from the pollution of London. In 1661, the Spanish Ambassador, Count Gondomar, excused his absence from the English Court pleading that he had retreated to Highgate to 'take the fresh aire'. This was a popular remedy. A guidebook of the time notes that 'divers who have been long visited with sicknesse not curable by physicke, have in a short time repaired their health by that sweet salutary air'.

It was in Highgate that Guy Fawkes conspired to 'blow up King and Parliament, with Jehu and Powdire!' – the seventeenth-century equivalent of driving an ammunition truck onto St Stephen's Green. Unaware that their leader was already captured, Fawkes's confederates gathered on Highgate Hill to witness the atrocity.

Andrew Marvell, poet and spy, lived in Highgate, right opposite a house owned by Oliver Cromwell. Nell Gwynne was a resident during her affair with Charles II. And it was at the bottom of

Highgate Hill that the eminent sixteenth-century scientist, Francis Bacon, wagered King James I's physician that he could preserve food by freezing it. Bacon left the carriage, bought a dead hen from a nearby house, and stuffed the bird with snow. Sadly, Bacon died days later, at nearby Arundel House, annihilated by pneumonia 400 years before his concept of frozen food was vindicated.

This land high above the rooftops of London has always appealed to writers. Long before the cemetery was consecrated in 1839, Coleridge, Leigh Hunt and Byron would stroll along Swain's Lane, talking philosophy, poetry, women. According to the American writer Bartlett, Keats was making his way up the hill one morning in June, wondering whether to confide to his friends the true nature of his recent illness. As a medical student, Keats knew the implications of his symptoms. But before he could confess his fears that he had contracted tuberculosis, a wild-eyed Shelley bounded up, hallucinating on laudanum. Stopping to gaze upon the lovely scene spread out before him, tears streamed down his face as he exclaimed: 'I have seen this all before! In the past – in some previous existence – where? Where?'[12]

For Shelley, this insight seemed a profound revelation. But there is something about Highgate, standing there, gazing out over the city, that inspires these reactions, even now.

Less than three years later Keats was dead, buried under a pyramid in the Protestant Cemetery at Rome. In 'Adonais', Shelley paid tribute with an exercise in Graveyard Gothic, which is equally appropriate to Highgate:

> *Where, like an infant's smile, over the dead*
> *A light of laughing flowers along the grass is spread;*
> *And gray walls moulder round, on which dull Time*
> *Feeds, like a slow fire upon a hoary brand;*
> *And one keen pyramid with wedge sublime,*
> *Pavilioning the dust of him who planned*
> *This refuge for his memory . . .*[13]

As Shelley observed in his Preface to 'Adonais', 'It might make one in love with death, to think that one should be buried in so sweet a place.'[14] A year later, Shelley himself was gone – drowned and cremated on a faraway beach.

The spot where Highgate Cemetery now stands, halfway up Swain's Lane, was once the orchard of Ashurst House, built for Sir William Ashurst MP, Lord Mayor of London in 1694, on the Ashurst Estate. This in its turn was built on the remains of an earlier structure – the Banqueting House – first mentioned in 1647. An engraving of *A Prospect of the Seat of Sir William Ashurst at Highgate*, dating from 1710, shows an impressive Palladian mansion, with grounds laid out in the formal style, featuring avenues of trees, a fountain and terraces overlooking the Thames Valley to the distant horizons of Surrey and Kent. Beyond its walls, cattle graze on the slopes stretching down Swain's Lane and Highgate Hill.[15]

After Sir William Ashurst died in 1720, the house became the Highgate Mansion School for Young Gentlemen. By the 1780s, the gardens had deteriorated to such an extent they were used for grazing, and by 1830, the house was a ruin. That year, the then owner, Sarah Otway Cave, sold what was left of the house to HM Commissioners for Building New Churches, who demolished it so that a new church could be built. The Church Commissioners invited the Neo-gothic architect Lewis Vulliamy (1791–1871) to build a new place of worship. Consecrated in 1832, the resulting Church of St Michael in its new white brick and stone was well built, spacious and lofty, with clerestory, buttresses, crocked pinnacles, and pierced parapet, and at the west end a tower and octagonal stone spire. The style was impure Perpendicular. It occupied the highest point on Highgate Hill and its tall spire was conspicuous for miles around. But St Michael's lacked one essential thing – a churchyard.

Highgate was already fashionable – a trendy spot for promenading Londoners. A purpose-built cemetery adjacent to the new church on the west side of Swain's Lane and in such a sought-after part of London, was inevitable – and in 1839 it became a reality.

In 1836, Stephen Geary (1797–1854) founded the London Cemetery Company. An entrepreneur, architect and surveyor, Geary had turned his attention to cemetery design after witnessing the success of the General Cemetery Company at Kensal Green. A private Act of Parliament empowered the company to construct three cemeteries, not exceeding a total of 150 acres, in Surrey, Kent and Middlesex. The capital of the Company was limited to £100,000, consisting of 5,000 shares at £20 each. The newly incorporated London Cemetery Company opened an office at 22 Moorgate Street, London, and appointed Richard Cuttill as Managing Director.

Geary was born on 31 August 1797 to Stephen and Ann Geary of Dean's Yard, Westminster. Geary Senior ran a coffee-shop for the boys of Westminster School. Geary Junior was apprenticed at fourteen to Thomas Leverton, an architect and surveyor in St Pancras. A great Victorian inventor and entrepreneur, Geary subsequently took out patents for artificial fuel, waterworks, street-paving and a prototype fire escape – identical to those still used on New York brownstones. Geary also designed one of London's first public houses – the Bell in Pentonville Road – and London's first 'gin palace', which opened near Aldgate in 1830. With their handsome plates of ground glass, blazing gaslight, shiny mahogany counters and buzz of activity reflected in glittering mirrors, this British institution appears the antithesis of a cemetery. However, in terms of scale and influence, the gin palace performed a similar function, dominating the land of the living, particularly London, as surely as the cemetery set a precedent for the burial of the dead. In architectural terms, the gin palace and the elaborate Neo-gothic graveyard had much in common. One marked a gathering place for the living, the other, a gathering place for the dead. Later in life, Geary became a militant teetotaller, remorseful for contributing to the misery of alcoholism.

Geary's move into cemetery design was timely. For all his

inventiveness and creativity, he lacked a sound business sense and had come to grief over two previous commissions. The first had been for a prototype shopping mall, dubbed the 'Royal Panarmonion'. The specification included pleasure gardens, billiard rooms and a theatre, all crammed into a site near the Gray's Inn Road, with a projected cost of £50,000. The prospectus, published in 1829, stated that £20,000 would be raised from the sale of bonds, and the project would receive royal support from the Prince Regent, George IV – which lent a certain cachet to the scheme. But within two years the Panarmonion foundered, the uncompleted structure was demolished and Geary was made bankrupt.

Geary's next move was a new police station at Battle Bridge, near Euston Road. St Pancras was not the most salubrious of districts, so the idea of a police station was welcome. However, this was to be no ordinary police station. It was to support a huge monument, forty feet high, representing St George killing the dragon. Already approved by the Metropolitan Commissioners for Roads and the Metropolitan Police, the building would be called St George's Cross, in honour of the Prince Regent. Unfortunately, George IV died long before the monument was completed and the project was re-named King's Cross in honour of William IV.

Situated slap bang in the middle of an important junction of the roads now known as Euston, Pentonville and Gray's Inn, the monument was a constant hazard to traffic. The Vestry of St Pancras threatened demolition if it was not lit properly. By 1835, the building was already too small to be an efficient police station and, George IV having been dead five years, there was still no statue of him on top. As a result of his bankruptcy, Geary's project was not seen as a sound investment, so he was short of funds to complete it. The eventual statue was a pathetic, eleven-foot-high concrete echo of what might have been. Then the police moved out, and the lower section of the monument became a beer shop. After complaints that this represented a public nuisance, with scenes of binge-drinking and anti-social behaviour, seventy local residents petitioned for the shop's closure. The monument was unceremoniously demolished in February, 1845. The best that can be said of this unfortunate episode is that Geary's legacy lives on in the name he gave to the district: King's Cross. The success of the London Cemetery Company must have been a considerable comfort in the context of such ignominious failure.[16]

Geary's partner, James Bunstone Bunning (1802–63), had also played his part in creating the very fabric of Victorian London. As well as being surveyor to the London Cemetery Company, he was also responsible for Holloway Prison (1852) and Billingsgate Market (1853). Bunning was also surveyor of the Foundling Hospital Estates and a member of the Board of the Foundling Hospital in Coram Fields. Many of the young children from the hospital were buried in Highgate, their grave markers bearing only initials.[17]

The London Cemetery Company soon acquired the first plot of land at Highgate. The remaining twenty acres of the Ashurst Estate were purchased for £3,500. Allowing for verges and decent space between each grave, there would be room for 30,000 graves. Each grave, on average, contained three bodies. Sold at the lowest figure of £2 10s per body, the gross yield would be at least £225,000. The LCC was offering 'luxury burial' in a prime spot.

In June 1836, at the first meeting of the shareholders of the London Cemetery Company, Stephen Geary announced to cheers that Highgate would not only rival all other cemeteries but, as a suburban ornament, would be an honour to the whole country.[18] Geary's main competitor was Kensal Green and he knew from the outset that Highgate had to be different. The sloping expanses of the old orchard must have winding walks and different levels. There should be outstanding features that made Highgate unique, something spectacular that would persuade the well-to-do to invest.

In his capacity as founder, chairman and architect of the London Cemetery Company, Geary could act as his own client. His task was to design the cemetery, and he did so in his own idiosyncratic way. While he may have been inspired by the *commercial* success of Kensal Green, Geary was determined to use the most progressive architectural style of the day – which he then imposed on a Classical model. Two chapels flank a gateway on Swain's Lane, which bears the words LONDON CEMETERY and features impressive iron gates. The twin chapels (one for Anglicans, one for Dissenters), situated on either side of the entrance, comply with the Classical rules of symmetrical design. The curved walls enclose the entrance forecourt in the same way as those at Blenheim and Castle Howard. However, once the Classical layout was *in situ*, Geary was free to play around with his own interpretation of Gothic Revival, one which can only be described as 'Tudorbethan'. The octagonal chapels feature spiral staircases, stained-glass bay windows, lancet windows (as used by archers to repel invaders), steep gables and bristling pinnacles.[19]

Geary's original plans incorporated St Michael's Church, with an entrance leading directly from the church grounds into the cemetery. The Dissenters' Chapel was situated in the centre of the grounds, connected by a tunnel to the entrance path in the foreground. 'Dwellings for officers' and a terrace with catacombs also featured. The plan was abandoned when David Ramsay was appointed landscape gardener. Together, he and Geary created a picturesque landscape of avenues and plantations intersected by winding gravel paths, reminiscent of those at Père Lachaise, ingeniously leading from one level to the next without any need for steps, thus performing the dual function of allowing easy access to the graves, while also creating an illusion of spaciousness in the cemetery's twenty acres. The architectural historian Niklaus Pevsner praised Ramsay's 'remarkably successful landscaping, the circuitous roads winding about the acclivity'. Another entrance was built adjoining St Michael's, but it was not authorized by the Church, and the Bishop of London ordered it to be closed.

Geary now created a magnificent series of features intended to confirm Highgate's reputation as London's principal cemetery. The first of these, the Egyptian Avenue, pandered to the craze for Egyptiana inspired by the funereal specimens brought back to the

British Museum by nineteenth-century explorers such as Giovanni Battista Belzoni (1778–1823), a circus Strong Man turned tomb raider. Belzoni was an adventurer, motivated by profit, whose destructive methods of excavation horrified genuine antiquaries. His treasures went to the British Museum, courtesy of Consul General, Henry Salt. In 1821, his finds were exhibited in Piccadilly to a gawping public, and made a dramatic impact on all aspects of fashion. Sèvres created an entire 'Egyptian' dinner service, while Thomas De Quincey, in an opium-induced trance, dreamed of meeting Isis and Osiris and being 'buried for a thousand years in stone coffins, with mummies and sphinxes, in narrow chambers at the heart of eternal pyramids'.[20] Egyptiana offered magnificent potential for memorial art. It seems appropriate that the Victorians, with their fascination with mortality, should turn for inspiration to another culture that was equally obsessed by death, and incorporate the pagan symbolism of Egypt into the familiar rituals of Anglican burial.

The Egyptian Avenue is essentially a street of the dead, created by excavating twelve feet deep into the steepest part of the hillside. One enters beneath a colossal arch, flanked by columns featuring a lotus-bud motif and leading to a tunnel. The dead were interred in a line of sixteen family vaults, which resemble a street of terraced houses. Each vault was brick-lined, with enough shelf-room for twelve coffins. In front of each door was an inverted torch – the symbol of life extinguished. 'As we enter the massive portals', wrote William Justyne in his *Guide to Highgate*, 1865 '. . . and hear the echo of our footsteps intruding on the awful silence of this cold, stony, death-palace, we might also fancy ourselves treading through the mysterious corridors of an Egyptian temple.'

Beyond the Egyptian Avenue stood a huge Cedar of Lebanon, an original feature of the Ashurst garden, already over 150 years old when Geary was planning the cemetery. He constructed a circle of twenty catacombs around the tree, each with an Egyptian-style pediment. These were so popular that forty years later an outer circle of sixteen was constructed facing into the circle.

Above the Circle of Lebanon was Highgate's third great feature, the Terrace catacombs, which consisted of an underground gallery beneath the terrace; it was more than 80 yards long and contained 840 recesses, each big enough to take a single coffin. Known as *loculi*, the catacombs were roofed with asphalt and featured glass apertures, which admitted light into the tombs below.[21]

The London Cemetery Company's North London or Highgate Cemetery was consecrated to St James on Monday, 20 May 1839 by the Right Reverend Charles James Bloomfield, Lord Bishop of London. In accordance with the London Cemetery Act of 1836, several acres were left unconsecrated for the burial of Dissenters. Unlike Kensal Green, the Dissenters were not singled out as second-class citizens, but discreetly screened by a row of chestnut trees.

The establishment of a cemetery at Highgate was strongly opposed by local residents, who did not welcome this 'great garden of sleep' in their midst. The development was viewed with distaste by a community anxious to maintain its distance from the Modern Babylon creeping up the hill. But, once they had seen the flowers, trees, and 'quiet seclusion', residents applied to purchase keys, which conferred the privilege of walking in the cemetery whenever they pleased.[22]

Soon Highgate Cemetery was a tourist attraction in its own right:

No cemetery near London can boast so many natural beauties. The irregularity of the ground, rising in terraces, the winding paths leading through long avenues of cool shrubbery and marble monuments . . . In the genial summertime, when the birds are singing blithely in their leafy recesses, and the well-cared-for graves are dazzling with the varied hues of beautiful flowers, there is a holy loveliness upon this place of death.[23]

In 1855, fifteen years after the consecration of Nunhead, its second cemetery, in south-east London, the London Cemetery Company opened its third, and last, cemetery. This was not in East London, as originally planned, but consisted of a nineteen-acre extension to Highgate on the eastern side of Swain's Lane.

The New Ground originally formed part of the estate of Harry Chester, President of the Highgate Literary and Scientific Institution and a leading light of Highgate. The New Ground, or Eastern Cemetery, was enclosed and laid out with winding lanes, and connected with the Old Ground, or Western Cemetery, by a tunnel running beneath Swain's Lane. A coffin lift meant that caskets could be lowered from the chapels down into the tunnel and conveyed to the New Ground across the road.

Although part of the cemetery was set aside for foundlings, Highgate was never a cemetery for the poor. One of Mayhew's Spitalfields tailors, earning one penny an hour in the 1850s, would have found it impossible to pay £2 10s for a common grave, or £21 for a family-sized brick grave, accommodating twelve coffins.

Evidence of the cemetery's profitability is revealed in the St Pancras Vestry Minutes of 1839, when the London Cemetery Company appealed against the rateable assessment. The company said the eventual value of the plots, vaults and catacombs could be £150,000; however, their income to date was only £1,000. The LCC maintained that it was not the *owner* of the sold plots – the occupiers and their families were – and therefore the LCC could not be rated on them, only on the profits. The LCC won its appeal.[24]

Famous residents of Highgate Cemetery include Julius Beer, a German immigrant who made a fortune on the London Stock Exchange and became proprietor of the *Observer*. As a tradesman and a Jew, although he converted to Anglicanism, Beer was never accepted in elitist London society. However, his monument, which dominates Highgate Cemetery, delivers a colossal rebuff. Four years before his death, Beer purchased the plot for £800, stumping up a further £5,000 for a mausoleum designed by George Oldrid Scott, who had taken over the practice of his father, George Gilbert Scott.

Built by a team of Italian masons, the mausoleum contains a

life-sized white Carrara marble sculpture of young Ada Beer, the daughter who predeceased him aged eight years, being raised to her feet by a tall angel, stooping gracefully beneath the weight of its wings. Beer's wife and brother are also buried here, as is his son Frederick, a depressive, who married Rachel Sassoon, cousin of Siegfried. Rachel owned the *Sunday Times* and was devoted to the melancholy Frederick, even going to the length of having the family crest clipped into the coat of his favourite poodle in an effort to entertain him – to no avail.[25]

A reclusive Duke, an Australian claimant, a missing fortune and an exhumation: these sound like the elements of a classic Sherlock Holmes story, but are all factors in the real-life affair of the Druce Scandal, which rocked British society for over a decade. This bizarre sequence of events began in 1864, when a Mrs Anna Maria Druce, of Baker Street, London, claimed that if her husband's coffin at Highgate Cemetery were opened, it would be found to be empty. Anna, widow of Mr Thomas Charles Druce, had become convinced that her husband, far from being the former proprietor of the Baker Street Bazaar furniture store, was in fact none other than William John Cavendish Bentinck Scott, the late 5th Duke of Portland.

The Duke was an eccentric aristocrat who spent most of his time hiding away on his Nottinghamshire estate, Welbeck, which featured fifteen miles of secret tunnels and an underground ballroom. The Duke only travelled to London in strictest secrecy, leaving Welbeck by an underground tunnel, in a black carriage which was loaded onto the railway train at Worksop Station, and unloaded again in London so that he could be driven to his house in Cavendish Square.

Backed up by Druce's daughter-in-law and a grandson from Australia, Mrs Druce claimed that the Duke had embarked on a secret double life as a shopkeeper, reaching Baker Street by way of a secret passageway between his house in Cavendish Square and the furniture store. Tiring of the strategy, he had faked the death of his alter-ego, Druce, and returned to Nottinghamshire. Anna maintained that Druce was not dead after all, and that the coffin would be filled with lead.

When the Duke died in 1879, Anna Druce laid claim to the title and lands of the Portland family for herself and her son. The dispute raged for years, until the body was finally exhumed in 1907. The coffin contained 'a shrouded human figure, which proved to be that of an aged, bearded man'. This was good enough for the Home Office. The claimants were not legally liable, although two witnesses were sued for perjury and a third fled abroad. It also emerged that Anna Druce had been confined to an asylum since 1904.

Dante Gabriel Rossetti (1828–82), the Pre-Raphaelite artist and poet, buried his wife Lizzie Siddal at Highgate in 1862. Lizzie's story is one of the many tragic tales which give the cemetery its unique character. After their daughter was stillborn, Lizzie fell into a state of profound depression and overdosed on laudanum. Rossetti buried a notebook of his own unpublished poetry with her, only to regret the decision two years later. Already in a state of profound depression, Rossetti was walking in Scotland with a friend when they encountered a small bird, a chaffinch, on the path. The bird did not fly away, but remained still, even when Rossetti picked it up. 'What is the meaning of this?' he asked, shaking with emotion. His friend, George Scott, suggested with characteristic Caledonian logic that it was a tame bird which had escaped.

'Nonsense,' Rossetti replied. 'I can tell you what it is. It is the spirit of my wife – the soul of her has taken this shape. Something is going to happen to me!'[26]

When they returned to the house, the men were told that someone had rung the great bell at the door, but when it was answered, there was nobody there. Scott, about to venture another rational explanation, was astonished when Rossetti turned a ferocious look on him and rushed upstairs to pack. Within hours, he was heading back to London, determined to retrieve the notebook. Rossetti had already persuaded the Home Secretary, a fan, to waive the exhumation order. He stayed at home in a state of agonized suspense while his friends went to the cemetery. They had been told what to look for: 'the book in question is bound in rough grey calf and has red edges to the leaves. This will distinguish it from the Bible, also there as I told you'.

A fire was built near the family grave, the coffin raised to the surface, and the book removed. A doctor was on hand to ensure that it was saturated with disinfectant, and he dried it carefully, leaf by leaf. Lizzie's body looked quite perfect by the glow of the fire. When the book was lifted, there came away with it a strand of red-gold hair.

Tom Sayers (1826–65), the celebrated bare-knuckle fighter, has a tomb bearing the image of his famous dog, Lion. Born into poverty in Brighton, Sayers left home at thirteen and arrived in London eager to learn a trade. Apprenticed to a bricklayer, he was noted for his speed and dexterity and worked on the new London and North Western stations of King's Cross and St Pancras. According to his biographer, Alan Lloyd, his first big fight was against an Irishman of six foot three, whom he had antagonized on the building site. With a crowd of supporters, they met on Wandsworth Common to settle the argument, with Tom fighting barefoot. The Irishman's boots becoming clogged with mud, he slowed down and Tom slipped under his guard. Bricklaying had toughened his hands, and his large knuckles were exceptionally sharp. After two and a half hours he laid the Irishman out with a classic upper-cut to the jaw.

This was the start of a career as a prize fighter, which included a clash with Heenan, another Irishman. The fight lasted forty-two rounds and over two hours. Sayers was only five foot eight and weighed in at eleven stone. He was already suffering from tuberculosis when he engaged in this bitter bout on 17 April 1860, in a field in Farnborough, watched by a crowd of 12,000. But nobody ever beat Tom. Sayers retired only when his supporters got up a petition and raised £3,000 for him, on the condition that he never fought again. A national hero, he was the subject of Staffordshire figurines and ballads. In 1865, 100,000 mourners followed Sayers's funeral cortège, when he succumbed to tuberculosis at the age of thirty-nine. Lion headed the procession, black crêpe tied around his collar. Behind him trundled the carriages of the aristocracy, after which, one observer noted, came the 'slow-eyed, great-jawed multitude from the East, clattering over the gravel walks, trampling with their clinkered boots over delicate marble slabs, and playing leap-frog with every sepulchral monument of a convenient height in their way'. Later in the day, the proceedings degenerated into scenes of 'riotous behaviour'.[27]

Such was the public reaction to Sayers's death that cheap mementos went into mass production. Even *The Times* mourned the passing of 'the Ultimus Romanorum of the prize ring'. A campaign to build a huge marble statue to his memory was announced on the front page – which was quite something, considering the authorities were trying to suppress prizefighting at the time.

Sadly, the plans came to nothing, and Tom had to wait until 2002 to receive official recognition, when his former home at 257 Camden High Road finally got its Blue Plaque, unveiled by Henry Cooper, Britain's most famous heavyweight boxer.

There is another lion at Highgate: Nero, the stone lion lazing above the tomb of George Wombell, a Victorian menagerist who began his career importing snakeskin for bags and shoes before realizing he could make far more money from exhibiting exotic animals to a fascinated public.

Long after Keats and Shelley roamed Swain's Lane, Highgate Cemetery continued to be associated with writers. Charles Dickens's wife and daughter were buried here, as were Leslie Stephen, father of Virginia Woolf, and George Eliot (Mary Ann Evans), who earned the disapproval of Christina Rossetti (younger sister of Dante Gabriel), for living openly with a married man. A tortured soul, who never lived with any man, married or single, Christina Rossetti devoted her life to charitable work at Highgate Penitentiary, campaigning to raise the age of consent to sixteen to protect against child prostitution. In 'Remember' (1862) she was also responsible for some of the most haunting lyrics in Victorian poetry, lines appropriate to the elegant melancholy of Highgate Cemetery:

> *Remember me when I am gone away,*
> *Gone far away into the silent land;*
> *When you can no more hold me by the hand,*
> *Nor I half turn to go, yet turning stay.*
> *Remember me when no more day by day*
> *You tell me of your future that you plann'd:*
> *Only remember me; you understand*
> *It will be late to counsel then or pray.*
> *Yet if you should forget me for a while*
> *And afterwards remember, do not grieve:*
> *For if the darkness and corruption leave*
> *A vestige of the thoughts that once I had,*
> *Better by far you should forget and smile*
> *Than that you should remember and be sad.*[28]

Another literary name is that of Mrs Henry Wood, a Victorian popular novelist who, once the object of derision for the immortal line: 'Dead! . . . and never called me mother!' is now regarded in critical circles as a prototype feminist. Born Ellen Price in 1814, the daughter of a Shropshire glovemaker, Wood was a semi-invalid, confined to bed with curvature of the spine for most of her life. After an unhappy marriage to Sir Henry Wood and an abortive attempt to emigrate to Australia, Wood supported her family through journalism, sending twenty-four short stories to *Ainsworth's* magazine and receiving little payment in return. Then, following a mystery illness during which she was convinced she was going to die, Mrs Wood completed her first novel, *East Lynne*. The magazine editor Harrison Ainsworth hated it, but in 1861, *East Lynne* made Wood a best-selling author at the age of forty-six. A prolific writer, she completed over forty novels, although she was far from politically correct. An anti-trades' union novel, *A Life's Secret*, caused riots, with protesters storming her publisher's offices in Paternoster Row and threatening to put the windows out. According to her son, Wood predicted her own death, telling the family: 'My work is almost done. It is certain I can write no more.' And then, apparently, she laid down her pen.

At her own insistence, Wood died alone in the early hours of 10 February 1887, while her family waited anxiously in the next room. Crowds of readers turned up to the funeral at St Stephen's Church, St John's Wood. Her son described the day as 'bright and beautiful, one of the finest and warmest days that ever dawned in February. The day itself was soft, sunny and seemed a reflection of the brightest spirit who was ever laid to rest.'

Wood had a sixteen-carriage cortège, headed up by an open carriage drawn by four black horses. The coffin was piled with snow-white wreaths of hothouse flowers. Wood was buried beside her husband, with a headstone of red Aberdeen granite modelled on the tomb of Scipio Africanus and engraved with the words: THE LORD GIVETH WISDOM. 'If one was allowed to pursue one's former occupation in heaven,' she had said, 'I want to go on writing books forever in the next world!'

Derided as an author of sensationalist potboilers, Wood received grudging respect from one obituarist. After remarking that she was a careless writer and incorrigibly inaccurate both grammatically and legally, he admitted that Wood provided a 'faithful, realistic rendition of middle-class life, free from the pretensions of social superiority and the intellectual disdain that characterizes the middle-class portraiture in *Middlemarch*'. As to that famous, much-derided quotation? Wood never wrote it. The exclamation 'Dead! – and never called me mother!' appeared in a dramatized version of *East Lynne*, but not in the novel itself.

Another best-selling author lies buried at Highgate. Fresh flowers continue to mark the catacomb where gay icon Radclyffe Hall, author of *The Well of Loneliness*, lies buried with her partner, Mabel

Batten. Born Marguerite, Hall (1880–1943) named herself John from childhood, and preferred to dress as a boy. She idolized her father, 'Rat', a cheerful philanderer, but hated her drunken, violent mother, who beat her when she found 'John' in bed with one of the maids. Hall's first affair was with Mabel Batten, a former mistress of Edward VII, immortalized by John Singer Sargent in his 1897 portrait 'Mrs George Batten Singing', now in Glasgow's Art Gallery at Kelvingrove. Hall later took up with Mabel's cousin, Lady Una Troubridge.

When *The Well of Loneliness* was published by Cape in 1928, the novel was banned within days by the Director of Public Prosecutions, Sir George Stephenson, under the Obscene Publications Act, a move authorized by the Prime Minister, Stanley Baldwin. It was deemed that the book would 'tend to corrupt the minds of young persons if it fell into their hands, and its sale is undesirable'. Sir Chartres Biron, Chief Magistrate at Bow Street Magistrates Court, condemned the book for describing 'unnatural practices between women of the most horrible and disgusting kind', while the *Sunday Express* went one better and declared: 'I would rather give a healthy boy or girl a phial of prussic acid than this book!' An attempt to publish the title in New York met with a similar response, although the ban was eventually lifted after an appeal.

Hall died in 1943, and was buried alongside Mabel, who predeceased her in 1916. The tomb, in the Lebanon Circle, bears an inscription from Una: 'And if God choose, I shall but love thee better after Death.' Una planned to join Hall and Mabel in the tomb, but was buried in Rome, in 1963, before her desire to be buried in Highgate was known.[29]

Highgate Cemetery's most famous inhabitant is Karl Marx, who managed to cause controversy long after his death. Demonstrations arranged to mark the centenary of his birth in 1918 were banned by the Home Office, and only those carrying wreaths were admitted. In 1924, the Russian Communist Party petitioned the Home Office to remove his remains to Russia. This was opposed by the British

Communist Party, which claimed Marx belonged to the world, not just to Russia. Marx's grave was moved from the south of the New Ground in 1954, and the distinctive grizzled head was sculpted by Lawrence Bradshaw and unveiled in 1956.[30]

Of course, Highgate Cemetery is also home to legions of the mundane people who, in the words of George Eliot, 'rest in unvisited tombs'. John Galsworthy, who chronicled the fortunes of an upper-middle-class family in his *Forsyte* sequence, described a typical scene:

> From that high and sacred field, where thousands of the upper middle classes lay in their last sleep, the eyes of the Forsytes travelled across the flocks of graves. There, spreading in the distance, lay London with no sun over it, mourning the loss of its daughter, mourning with this family, so dear, the loss of her who was mother and guardian. A hundred thousand spires and houses, blurred in the great grey web of property, lay there like prostrate worshippers before the grave of this, the oldest Forsyte of them all. Soon, perhaps, someone else would be wanting an inscription.[31]

Back in 1839, the London Cemetery Company had acquired 130 acres of land in south London from Richard Edmonds and William Warlters. Fifty-three acres were set aside for a cemetery, with a new road planned between Queen's Road, Peckham, and Nunhead Lane. Located on a hill, 200 feet above sea level, the cemetery afforded magnificent views of London and the surrounding countryside. In those days, Nunhead was an Arcadian retreat; the name refers to the Nun's Head Tavern, 'favourite resort of smoke-dried London artisans' which gives the district its name.[32]

Consecrated on 29 July 1840, the Cemetery of All Saints, Nunhead, featured cemetery lodges and gates designed by James Bunstone Bunning. Thomas Little (1802–59) won the design competition with his Gothic chapels (which were wrongly attributed to

Bunning by Pevsner). The Anglican Chapel was octagonal, with a short nave and transepts with a crypt beneath. Despite achieving 'the balance of nature and architect' that Loudon had advocated, with luxurious planting and the gradual addition of some fine tombs, Nunhead was slow to attract custom, perhaps as a result of its proximity to the South Metropolitan Cemetery at Norwood. Only nine burials were recorded at Nunhead in the first six months, and only one hundred and thirteen in the first full year, several of which were in communal graves. This dip in trade was much to the delight of George Collison, a founder of the rival Abney Park Cemetery. Collison had opposed the Act of Parliament that permitted the London Cemetery Company to operate more than one cemetery in the metropolitan area. But trade improved, and Nunhead Cemetery prospered for twenty-five years, with an average of two hundred burials a year.

Stephen Geary, whose vision contributed so much to the success of the London Cemetery Company, was just fifty-six when he died, in 1854, a victim of London's final cholera epidemic. Of all the cemeteries he had been engaged on, including Nunhead, Brompton and Brighton, Geary chose to be buried at Highgate. And, like Highgate itself, Geary too became a victim of neglect. The relentless ivy engulfed many graves after the Second World War, his own included. It was only during conservation work, in the 1970s, that Geary's flattened tombstone was recovered. When the dirt had been scraped away, it revealed the inscription: STEPHEN GEARY ESQRE, ARCHITECT AND FOUNDER OF THIS CEMETERY, HAD DEPARTED THIS LIFE IN 1854.

# 8: GREAT GARDENS OF SLEEP

*Death Moves to the Suburbs*

*A sketch of Highgate Cemetery,* Illustrated London News, *1849.*

Stephen Geary's demise was merciful: he did not live to witness the scandal which threatened to engulf the London Cemetery Company. On 5 July 1865, Edward Buxton, Secretary and Registrar of the London Cemetery Company, collapsed and died. Described as 'respected and trusted', the forty-nine-year-old Buxton had complained of feeling unwell earlier in the day, when he attended a

Board meeting. A few days later, the clerk at the London Cemetery Company's head office in the City of London discovered a set of ledgers in Buxton's office. Under careful scrutiny, it was established that Buxton had systematically embezzled the company over a period of many years. The late secretary had kept two sets of books, and those placed on the table at Board meetings were bogus.

The Chairman and directors called in their solicitors and accountants. Buxton's Will, bequeathing his estate to his wife and child, was found to be invalid. Mrs Buxton was left destitute as a result of her husband's dishonesty. The distraught widow was persuaded to abandon any claim she might have had on the estate, and eventually settled for a meagre payment from the Board: one pound a week for ten years.[1]

With cemeteries established in north and south London, speculators soon saw the importance of similar enterprises in the East End. Abney Park, Stoke Newington, was founded in 1840 by the Abney Park Cemetery Company (which later constructed Chingford Mount, Greenford Park and Hendon Park) on land donated by Lady Abney, a celebrated philanthropist. The Abney Park Cemetery Company headquarters were accommodated in magnificent Egyptian lodges at the entrance on Stoke Newington High Street, featuring hieroglyphs reading THE GATES OF THE ABODE OF THE MORTAL PART OF MAN.

Designed by William Hosking (1800–61) a professor of architecture and engineering, who was buried at Highgate, it covered thirty-two acres and was designed as an arboretum (literally, 'tree garden') as well as a burial ground, true to the spirit of Loudon's 'breathing spaces'. At its zenith, Abney Park fulfilled its brief as the lungs of London, eclipsing Kew Gardens with over 2,500 varieties of shrubs and trees, and over 1,000 species of rose bushes, laid out on a north-facing slope from an ancient track, now Stoke Newington Church Street, to Hackney Brook, later diverted into an underground sewer by Joseph Bazalgette.

Abney Park had another dimension: situated in one of the most militant parts of London, it was not consecrated, drawing a clientèle from the growing ranks of the Dissenters and radicals who demanded another form of burial ground, now that Bunhill Fields was filling up.

Instead of being consecrated, Abney Park Cemetery was opened by the Lord Mayor of London on 20 May 1840. As a result, it attracted burials from all denominations and was particularly popular with Dissenters from the Anglican Church, including Methodists, Wesleyans and Baptists. Dr Isaac Watts, a famous preacher and a friend of Lord and Lady Abney, who was actually buried in Bunhill Fields, had a memorial there, near a 'large and venerable oak' where he liked to lie in the grass and compose his well-known hymns.

> Lady Abney was very liberal in her religious views, and the cemetery is, with its church, open to all alike, and though its grounds were never consecrated, yet many rigid churchmen have been buried in it. There is no quieter burial spot within a dozen miles of London in any direction, and there are Cedars of Lebanon in it, wide lawns, and beautiful flowers. There is an old clergyman in the church, who is always ready to officiate for a small fee on funeral occasions. He is over eighty years old, his hair is like the snow, and he is a fit companion to such a solemn place.[2]

Mrs Isabella Holmes, our famous Victorian historian, observed that 'If the mantle of Bunhill Fields has fallen anywhere, I suppose that Abney Park Cemetery claims the distinction. It has always been the favourite cemetery of the Dissenters, there being no separating line to mark off a consecrated portion.'[3]

Abney Park also addressed another important issue: where to bury the poor once the inner-city grounds were closed in 1852. In the 1860s, lower-middle-class families and above formed 20 per cent of the population, and the families of skilled workers 10 per cent, leaving the unskilled labouring classes and the labouring poor, the agrarian and urban proletariat, to make up 70 per cent of the British people. According to the late Chris Brooks, an expert on Victorian cemeteries, the trustees of Abney Park Cemetery resisted the imposition of Anglican burial fees to mitigate the usually prohibitive costs of cemetery interment for working-class families.[4] The company's prospectus stated quite specifically that its object was to provide a cemetery which not only was available to all denominations, but 'which shall be open to all classes of the community'. Abney Park was successful in attracting labouring-class burials, which took place in common graves between the perimeter paths and the boundary walls – 'All decent enough,' remarks Brooks, 'even if firmly demarcated from the bodies of the better off.'

The penultimate great London cemetery of this era, Tower Hamlets, was consecrated in 1841, enabled by an Act which permitted the City of London and Tower Hamlets Cemetery Company 'to acquire land for the burial of the dead in St Dunstan, Stepney, and St Leonard, Bromley-by-Bow'. The Board included John Hammack, Chairman, surveyor and a local timber merchant, and Sir John Pirie, the Lord Mayor of London at that time. The company's capital was limited by the 1841 Act to £20,000 divided into £10 shares, and it soon earned a handsome interest. The first burial was conducted on 4 September 1841. Over 500 burials were recorded in 1845, and by 1889, approximately 250,000 people had been buried there, the majority interred in common graves at 25s each,[5] with 'excellent financial returns derived from a policy of filling common graves as full as possible and packing them together as densely as possible'.[6]

The chapels, designed in 1848 by Thomas Wyatt and David Brandon, were:

in the early decorated period, with a belfry at one angle in which are some nicely ornamental windows; and at the sides are

155

attached cloisters for the reception of mural tablets, so constructed as to afford an effectual screen from the weather. The
octagonal Dissenters' Chapel is in the Byzantine style . . . beneath
both chapels are dry and extensive catacombs.[7]

Famous residents included Charles Jamrach (1815–91), a well-known
East End personality who imported exotic animals – his shop on the
Ratcliff Highway (now The Highway running from the Tower to
Limehouse) was much like a zoo. He survived an encounter with an
escaped tiger in 1857, and on another occasion a brown bear escaped
and was later found being fed bread and honey by two small girls.
Also buried at Tower Hamlets was Hannah Purcell (died 1843),
described on her obelisk as 'relict of one of the last surviving officers
of the Mutiny of the Bounty', and Alfred Linnell, a Socialist campaigner. Linnell was attending a demonstration by the Law and
Liberty League on Sunday, 20 November 1887 – a protest against
Government proposals to restrain free speech – when he was tram-
pled by a police horse. Linnell died of his injuries a fortnight later, and
received a massive funeral, organized by noted radicals Annie Besant
and William Morris. Over 100,000 people followed his funeral procession, which stretched from Whitechapel to the cemetery.

Death was not always a successful source of investment. In one case,
the sheer expense of construction brought a private cemetery to the
brink of bankruptcy, from which it had to be rescued by the
Government. This cemetery, which, according to historian James
Stevens Curl, effectively destroyed one architect's career, was
Brompton. Consecrated on 15 June 1840, Brompton Cemetery was
created by the West of London and Westminster Cemetery
Company. It was opened as The West of London and Westminster
Cemetery and still bears this inscription over the north entrance.
Brompton covered just under thirty-nine acres of land between
Brompton Road and Fulham Road in West London, on land

purchased from Lord Kensington. The land had previously been a market garden and consisted of nothing more than a flat, treeless rectangle, half a mile long.

Stephen Geary was appointed architect on 20 July 1837. Geary's duties were the carrying out of all works ordered by the Board, his remuneration being 2½ per cent on work completed. Competitions were held for the best walls, chapels, catacombs and buildings, with one hundred guineas (£105) for the best design, fifty (£52.50) for the second and twenty-five (£26.25) for the third.

Benjamin Baud (1807–75), a pupil of Francis Goodwin, won First Prize for an imaginative design which exploited the linear nature of the site. Baud's design was that of an immense open-air cathedral with a central 'nave' running up to a high altar, symbolized by the domed Anglican Chapel. Other features included colonnades flanking the central avenue, and a Great Circle, beneath which were catacombs with impressive cast-iron doors. Baud's original plan was to have two 'transepts' on either side of the 300-foot Great Circle, inspired by the piazza of St Peter's, Rome. These transepts would have been formed by two additional chapels, one for Roman Catholics and one for Dissenters. The imposing North Gatehouse on Old Brompton Road was built to look like a triumphal arch and represents the 'great west door' of Baud's cathedral-inspired design. The cemetery's layout was completely symmetrical, with two pairs of 'aisles' running parallel to the central 'nave', which was to be planted with lime trees, backed with a taller line of pines.

Baud, who had worked on the Houses of Parliament, was assistant to Sir Jeffry Wyatville at Windsor Castle. As Wyatville headed the Committee of Taste which judged the Brompton competition, there was some speculation that he influenced the judges' decision. It was also suggested that it was inappropriate of Wyatville to have picked his own assistant as the winner!

John Claudius Loudon acted as a consultant and David Ramsay, who had already worked with Geary at Highgate, was appointed landscape gardener on 5 December 1837. Ramsay had a nursery business in Brompton and supplied plants and materials. Problems began to emerge before the cemetery had even opened. Stephen Geary resigned on 7 January 1839, already preoccupied with Highgate, and demanded payment for the contribution he had made to Brompton. At this, the Board claimed his calculations as to the size of the cemetery were inaccurate. Geary's solicitors demanded £498 4s, but the Board were only prepared to offer £100. Geary rejected this, and took the Board to court for £499, eventually being awarded £162 after considerable wrangling.

On 19 February 1839, Baud was appointed architect – but his designs were changed, building specifications altered, and Isaac Finnemore, another landscape gardener working on the project, resigned. There was also an argument between Baud and the builder, Philip Nowell, with the Board taking Nowell's side. Inevitably, building work was not completed in time for the consecration the following June, and 'a disorderly appearance, caused by the fact that the building work was being carried out in bits and pieces, discouraged the public from making use of the cemetery'. Baud had difficulty completing his scheme, and the proposed Roman Catholic and Dissenters' Chapels were never built.

In addition, Baud himself was becoming a victim of the Board's financial mis-management, as it could not afford to pay him. Eventually, Baud was sacked, only to suffer litigation from which he never recovered. Turning his back on architecture, Baud had some success as an artist, but at considerable loss to Victorian design.

Despite its financial problems, Brompton flourished, becoming the last resting-place of Emmeline Pankhurst, the prominent Suffragette, and Dr John Snow, who, by ascertaining the cause of cholera, had brought to an end the 'bitter strange kiss' of epidemics that had choked London's graveyards.

In 1852, Brompton became the first cemetery to be nationalized, when the Board of Health made it the subject of a Compulsory Purchase Order. The shareholders demanded £169,000 for the cemetery, but were only offered £41,000. Only after the matter went to arbitration did they receive a meagre £75,000. The Compulsory Purchase Order represented the Government's change in approach to burial. Ten years after Chadwick and Walker had appeared before the Select Committee of 1842, legislation had finally been passed to close the London burial grounds. One consequence of this was that Parliament was debating whether it was appropriate for cemeteries to be run by private companies. Sir Edwin Chadwick had always been opposed to the idea. He campaigned for municipal cemeteries and proposed a National Cemetery at Abbey Wood, to be run by the Government. The British public had developed a suspicion of 'investors in death' and the mood was one of further reform.

MacKinnon's Select Committee of 1842 had simply suggested that burial in towns should be banned, and that municipalities be empowered to set up cemeteries on the outskirts. Chadwick went one better. He wanted all cemeteries to be municipalized and all 'trading cemeteries' or private burial grounds abolished. Noting the frequency of child murders, he required the certification of death to be improved, with new legislation enforced, meaning doctors had to state the cause of death before burial could take place (a step which was later incorporated in the 1848 Public Health Bill).

Ultimately, it was Chadwick who rang the death toll for private cemetery companies. He proposed the Metropolitan Interments Act (1850), a scheme whereby funerals would be made a public service, interments in churchyards and burial grounds would cease, and the joint stock companies be closed down. With characteristic reforming zeal, Chadwick recommended nationalizing Kensal Green, turning it into the 'Great Western National Cemetery', while a 'Great Eastern Cemetery' would be founded on the other side of London at Abbey Wood. Ninety-six coffins a day would be floated down the Thames from eight depots or 'reception houses' in London, much as corpses were ferried from Venice to the island cemetery of San Michele.

Chadwick's extraordinary design for Abbey Wood included a stained-glass dome, encaustic tiles and a glazed section for wet weather.[8] However, this scheme was unsuccessful. The Treasury did not consider it financially viable, and it was also rejected on the grounds of miasma, the noxious fumes which Chadwick himself believed caused disease. Convinced that twelve-thirteenths of a decomposed corpse passed into the air, the authorities were aghast at the prospect of 62,000 decomposing corpses annually blowing over 3 million cubic feet of putrescent gases back towards London. If a national cemetery were to exist, it was calculated that it must be at least twenty-four miles away.

With the inner-city graveyards closed, London had again run out of space to bury its dead. Ingenious solutions such as Willson's Pyramid at Primrose Hill had been snubbed, although Sir Francis Seymour Haden FRCS (1818–1910) proposed using corpses as land-fill for the Thames Estuary. Observing that the ground level of city churchyards had risen over the years due to the practice of interring bodies one on top of the other, he mused:

> Is there no ground in the immediate neighbourhood of our own city that would be the better for this increase and for being thus raised? Along the course of our great river from London to the sea, for instance, have we not vast lowland tracts of rich alluvial soil deposited by that very river and capable of being drained, planted and beautified, in which, with equal benefit to the land and to ourselves, we may bury our dead for centuries? If, as we have seen, the surface of the Holborn Burial-ground was raised fifteen feet or eighteen feet by the interments within it of three centuries, why should not the lowlands of Kent and Essex be raised and reclaimed in the same way?[9]

To Haden's surprise, his body-farming scheme never caught on. But by suggesting burial further away from London, he anticipated a trend. It was generally agreed that out-of-town burial was the safest, most hygienic method of disposing of the dead. The suburban cemeteries of Highgate, West Norwood, Brompton and Kensal Green already conformed to this recommendation. But London was growing, spreading. Street after street of tall narrow brick houses climbed the high hills of Hampstead and Highgate, and sprawled outwards through Battersea and Clapham. The sheep were long gone from Kensal Green.

Burial grounds had to be further afield. The solution to this conundrum came from another great Victorian development: the railway. The time had come for Londoners to go to their last home far from the city itself – twenty-five miles away, to be precise, on the desolate heaths of Surrey. Chadwick's vision of a national cemetery was eventually to be realized, in 1849, in the form of the Brookwood Necropolis at Woking. The last great London cemetery was not in London at all, but it had a vital part to play in the disposal of the city's dead. The *Illustrated London News* approved:

> To enjoy these beauties there needs to be the golden sunlight of the spring or summer day. We leave the dense city, and reach the open country with the speed of the winds. We pass villages, and cottages, and farms, fields, and open tracts of country; we see in the distance woods and heathery uplands. If it be summer, rivulet and little river and sedgy pool lie silvered in the sunlight, and wild flowers waft to us their scent from hedgerow banks, from fields, from blossoming heaths. By-and-by, the scene becomes wilder and more solitary. The dun heath reaches us on either hand, and we seem, whether so or not, to toll up a rugged ascent, to break speed, make pauses; and then on, on our difficult way. This sense of ascent adds inconceivably to the coming effect. In an instant the funeral train is unlinked from the giant power which led it on, and glides gently down into the undulating plain, which has thus been made one of the great burial-places of mighty London.

The whole scene is most varied and extensive, though a

succession of encircling hills bound this extent, and lend the charm of peacefulness and solitude. To the west and south these hills are very striking. Those towards Hampshire lie as we can see, amidst wild and solitary heaths, and bear to their summits traces of rugged nature; while those to the south are fringed by woodlands, and softened, to some degree, by cultivation.[10]

How different this cemetery seemed from the overcrowded London graveyards it was designed to replace. At over 2,000 acres, Brookwood in Surrey was truly a 'City of the Dead', a mirror of the metropolis, designed to provide a last home for every Londoner. A desolate heath transformed into a great garden of sleep, Brookwood Cemetery was modelled on Mount Auburn. Even today, nearly 150 years after its construction, and after vandalism and neglect have taken their toll, Brookwood epitomizes Loudon's ideals. Laid out and planted by Robert Donald (1826–66), an admirer of Loudon, Brookwood is spacious, with decorous gaps between each grave and mausoleum. Pines tower 60 feet high; there are magnificent sequoias, slim birches and dense monkey puzzles. Carpets of beech mast and pine needles soften footfalls, but any movement sends skeletal twigs skittering eerily between the tombs.

In 1849, Sir Richard Broun and Mr Richard Sprye produced plans for the London Necropolis at Woking, in Surrey. It is difficult to imagine now, but in the 1840s, today's commuter-belt was open country. Far from London, but easily reached by train, the Necropolis would be on a cheap, greenfield site, with plenty of room for expansion. 'Devoted to the Continental usage of giving to each corpse a separate grave', making it the most beautiful garden in the world.

Featuring a National Mausoleum Church, and catering for every sect, the Necropolis would provide burial space for all London's parishes, and be large enough to contain 'not only the thousands of coffins now lying within our numerous Metropolitan Churches, but also the coffins of all such dying in London, in this and future generations'. This was an ambitious plan. In 1856, it was calculated that 1,200 acres would serve London (assuming a death rate of 60,000 per year) for ever. This worked on the principle of one body per grave, with the grave being reopened every ten years.[11]

Brookwood's tranquil setting belies the acrimonious takeover battles involved in setting up the company. The vision was not realized without great cost, and those who suffered most were the originators of the scheme, as John Clarke has described in his excellent history. Broun and Sprye did not reap the benefits of their proposal. They set up a provisional company with four trustees. Under 'a deed of agreement' they were due at least £20,000 for their scheme. But the trustees brought in their own men, negotiated with Lord Onslow for the acquisition of 2,200 acres of land on Woking Common, of which 500 acres were used for the Necropolis, and negotiated with the London South West Railway – then set up their own joint stock company, cutting Broun and Sprye out completely! Broun eventually confronted the promoters in public and claimed that their prospectus was full of inaccuracies and misrepresentations.[12]

When the Bill to incorporate the London Necropolis and National Mausoleum Company was introduced in 1852, Broun and Sprye opposed it on the grounds that their rights had been ignored and that the Bill was inconsistent with the original scheme. They raised these issues:

Clause XI of the Bill allowed the LNC to sell surplus land. MP for West Surrey Henry Drummond claimed this was 'a fraud on the public', as the company would buy up land in Woking then sell it off to building companies.

Broun and Sprye objected to the amount of compensation offered to the commoners of Woking in return for losing their turbary rights (turbary is the legal right to cut peat or turf for fuel from common land). They reckoned £1,000 was enough, but in fact the LNC was willing to give £22,000 – in the end it was £15,000. Henry Drummond felt that local people were insufficiently consulted about the prospect of having an enormous cemetery on their doorstep, while MP for Guildford, James Mangles, opposed it outright, as he felt that the people of Woking were losing every acre of common land. Lacking in clout, local residents had no means to fight the Bill. Broun and Sprye also maintained that the high railway fares cited in the Bill, plus fees for clergy, would add £47,000 to the funeral expenses of Londoners buried at Brookwood.

Their petition failed. For one thing, the right to sell off land if demand was lesser than anticipated was a standard clause for many railway companies. And company architect Henry Robert Abraham had prepared detailed plans of the whole site as a burial ground which were enough to satisfy the Parliamentary Select Committee. A clause was inserted, however, to forbid the selling of land for building purposes – ostensibly to avoid the poor losing their cottages and becoming homeless – and the railway fares stayed low. The LSWR anticipated £40,000 a year from the extra traffic – 10,000 bodies a year, plus mourners and visitors, on two or three trains in each direction, each day. With regard to clergy fees (required by the Cemetery Clauses Act), these were suggested at 6s 2d – or a single shilling in the case of pauper burials, which was lower than in many parts of London; this was a way of getting the clergy behind the Bill.

The Bill had its third reading in the Commons on 21 May 1852, partly because it offered a solution to the pressing problem of burial by creating a cemetery outside the metropolitan area. Henry Drummond MP was eventually satisfied with a clause protecting commoners' rights.

Sir Edwin Chadwick opposed the Bill, objecting that the scheme was the invention of 'vulgar projectors and a vulgar architect, a building speculation disguised as a public measure, which included amongst its proposals pit burial for paupers, the use of railway arches as mortuaries, and the transport of corpses in the common horse-boxes of the railway'. Chadwick also suggested that the Necropolis Bill was receiving favourable treatment because the

Solicitor General was involved in the project, 'his brother-in-law, Mr Abrahams, being the architect'.[13]

When the Bill reached the House of Lords, it was sympathetically received, again because it offered a solution to the problem of burial. There was just one objection, from Lord Ashley, who found in it further evidence of private speculation in the burial of the dead. His main objection was the storage of thousands of corpses near Waterloo Station, close to housing, before they were transported to Woking. He also demanded to know what would happen if there were not enough burials to meet the expense of setting up the new cemetery.

The LNC's private Act received Royal Assent on 30 June 1852, incorporating the company and outlining requirements for setting up the cemetery. But it was to be another eighteen months before it progressed. Twenty thousand pounds worth of shareholders' money was 'squandered' (according to Broun). Time was lost; public confidence failed; the architect's surveys turned out to be all wrong, and had to be done again. Rumours and suggestions abounded of double-dealing and rigged voting among shareholders. Eventually, angry shareholders rebelled and, in July 1853, a committee of enquiry was set up to enquire how far the directors had fulfilled their duties; to ascertain the present state of the company and its future prospects; and to decide whether an entire change of the executive body was necessary. These proceedings installed a new spirit of confidence. A list of shareholders was drawn up and twelve new directors appointed. The surveys recommenced, this time in the capable hands of LNC's consulting engineer, Sir William Cubitt (1785–1861), who set out to ring-fence the land and consult with the LSWR on the best connections for the existing railway line while taking into account the nearby road connections with Guildford and Pirbright.

By 1854, the company had leased land from the London South Western Railway near Westminster Bridge Road for the site of the private station, despite objections from local residents who were not best pleased at living next to a station for the dead. Adjacent to

LSWR's viaduct into Waterloo Station, this was designed by William Tite and William Cubitt, at a cost of £23,231 14s 4d.

In Woking, the LNC acquired 2,200 acres of land from Lord Onslow, and set about transforming 500 acres with an ambitious programme of landscaping and planning. The chapels were designed by Smirke, the Anglican Chapel being Tudor-style, with a small tower and spire, loop windows, open pointed roofs, and a Gothic pulpit. The floors were paved with blue and red Staffordshire tiles, which resembled a tessellated pavement.[14]

The London Necropolis opened on 13 November 1854. It was an ambitious project, since George Stephenson had only launched the first passenger train service in 1830. The first through train from Waterloo to Southampton did not take place until 1838, only six years before the London Necropolis Company opened its private station at Waterloo. There was considerable doubt as to whether the noise and clamour of a railway station was appropriate to Christian burial.

The LSWR carried coffins from the private station down the main line. There were separate hearse cars for Anglicans and Dissenters, and, in keeping with Victorian notions of social propriety, three classes of carriage for the living and the dead. A First Class corpse received a higher level of customer care and a nicely decorated carriage. Trains ran straight into the cemetery grounds. There were two stations, each for different parts of the cemetery, North for Dissenters and South for Anglicans, adjacent to the corresponding chapels. The South Station was licensed and in addition to catering for funeral parties, offered afternoon tea to visitors strolling in the cemetery; it also operated as a pub, which did much to reconcile the locals to the giant cemetery on their doorstep. Porters and their families lived here, with the porter's wife catering for upwards of 100 mourners, with tea, coffee, homemade sandwiches and cakes.[15]

Brookwood received the dead from overcrowded London parishes, in a series of subdivisions, many of which resemble old-fashioned churchyards with their hedges and lych-gates. St Anne's,

Soho; Bermondsey; Chiswick; St Margaret's, Westminster – all have cemeteries within a cemetery. Brookwood had fulfilled its promise to play a major part in alleviating the burial problem in the metropolis. Another part of its remit was to provide a home for members of different faiths. As well as accommodating Anglicans and Dissenters, Brookwood was one of the first cemeteries in Britain to offer burial facilities to Muslims and Sikhs. By contrast, London's Jewish community had long established their own burial grounds.

By the mid-nineteenth century, Jewish cemeteries were in an enviable condition compared with those of the churchyards. As a result of Judaic law, they were never overcrowded. The law states that burial must take place within twenty-four hours of death, that the body must be six feet from the surface, and that only one body is allowed in each grave. It is forbidden to place one coffin on top of another.

In the Middle Ages, English Jews had only been allowed one burial ground, known as the Jew's Garden, outside London Wall near Cripplegate. When the Jews were expelled from England in 1290, the land passed to the Dean of St Paul's. Milton lived there while writing *Paradise Lost*. The location's origins lived on its name, Jewin Street, until it was destroyed in the Blitz.

At the time that Brookwood was being established, there were a number of Jewish cemeteries across London, from Brady Street, Bethnal Green – wherein lie the remains of Nathan Mayer de Rothschild, founder of the great banking house – to Willesden, West Ham and Fulham. West Ham Cemetery is dominated by the magnificent Rothschild Mausoleum, built by the grieving Ferdinand for his wife Evelina, who died in childbirth less than a year after their marriage in 1865. Many of the inner-city grave-yards, such as the one at Fulham, have been closed for over a century, and are tucked away behind shops and offices. These little graveyards have kept their secrets, Jewish law ensuring that they remain undisturbed.

At sixteen and a half acres, the Jewish Cemetery at Hoop Lane near Golders Green (the only Sephardic cemetery now left in London), was the largest of London's Jewish cemeteries when it was built in 1895. The Lombardic redbrick architecture complements that of Golders Green Crematorium, opposite. Sephardic Jews (Jews of Mediterranean origin who arrived in England in the seventeenth century) place their gravestones flat, a tradition dating from the days when Sephardic cemeteries were often in swampy ground. It is not customary to plant flowers or foliage in Sephardic cemeteries, which lends a certain stark grandeur, particularly on a bleak winter's morning. Ultimately, this reflects a different attitude towards death and burial. According to Jewish law, burial takes place in a plain, unadorned coffin, whether one is a Rothschild or a pauper. THE BODY RETURNS TO THE EARTH, AND THE SOUL TO GOD WHO GAVE IT is a regular Hebrew inscription at the entrance to many Jewish cemeteries.

The Quakers, or the Society of Friends, also made a conscious effort to protect their dead. Reporting to a Parliamentary Committee on the standard of their burial grounds in 1843, the Quakers maintained that they still had plenty of room in their graveyards, and that their coffins were buried at least seven feet below the surface. In keeping with their religious principles, the Quakers maintained their own burial grounds, rather than allowing them to become commercial enterprises. The Quakers stood apart from the Victorian funeral tradition in other ways. In many cases, they dispensed with tombstones altogether; and when they did allow this custom, the stones were small, regular, and half the size of conventional ones; and bereaved families were discouraged from wearing mourning.[16]

With the exception of Bunhill Fields, Dissenters' burial grounds did not survive. According to Isabella Holmes:

> The East London Railway has swallowed up the graveyards by
> Rose Lane Chapel, Stepney, and the Sabbatarian or Seventh Day

Baptists' Chapel in Mill Yard, by Leman Street; the Medical School of Guy's Hospital is on the Mazepond Baptist Chapel ground; the site of one which adjoined the London Road Chapel, S. E. is now occupied by a tailor's shop . . . the Baptist Chapel and burial ground in Worship Street, Shoreditch, forms part of the goods depot of the London and North Western Railway; a similar one in Wapping is now a milkman's yard.[17]

St Pancras was particularly popular with Roman Catholics; the eastern end of the cemetery even became known as 'Catholic Pancras'. It was said that St Pancras was the last church in England after the Reformation whose bell still tolled for Mass, and that Roman Catholics were burned at the stake there during the reign of Elizabeth I. Many French Catholics who fled to London after the Revolution were buried at St Pancras, including bishops, aristocrats and, intriguingly, 'the Chevalier d'Eon, the unfortunate nobleman whose sex was a matter of so much dispute during the last century'.[18]

London's hospitals had their own burial plots, some dating back to the mediaeval period when they were founded. Conditions were so grim during the early nineteenth century that patients were expected to provide a sum towards funeral expenses on admission. Bart's demanded 17s 6d and Guy's £1, while Bethlem Hospital was the steepest, requiring an entrance fee of £100. Friends or relations of the deceased were expected to remove and bury the body, which often led to bitter feuds as competing relatives held out for the life insurance. Unclaimed bodies were buried at the hospital's expense and, of course, these unwanted corpses were easy pickings for the Resurrection Men.[19]

The London Hospital had its own burial ground, from 1849 until it was closed by order of the Council in 1854, although burials continued until about 1860, with porters acting as gravediggers. The Medical School, the Chaplain's House and the Nurses' Homes were built over the graveyards. The remaining part of the burial ground became a garden for nurses and medical students, complete with tennis court, 'where they are in the habit of capering about in their short times off-duty, and where it sometimes happens that the grass gives way beneath them – an ordinary occurrence when the subsoil is inhabited by coffins!'[20]

The Royal Hospital, Chelsea, a sanctuary for injured and retired soldiers founded by Charles II, had its own burial ground at Royal Hospital Road. While the majority of residents were male, including one Pensioner who lived to be one hundred and three, there were two female Chelsea Pensioners buried here, Christina Davis and Hannah Snell. Davis (1667–1739) was Irish, and joined the army to search for her husband. Captured by the French, she saw action at Blenheim, and was wounded at Ramillies, where her gender was discovered. Presented to Queen Anne in 1712, Davis was given a pension, and three volleys were fired at her funeral. Snell (1723–1807) alas, was not so fortunate. After serving in the Army and the Navy while searching for her husband, she published her memoirs in 1750 and took to the stage. Sadly, there was to be no distinguished retirement for Hannah, who 'died insane'.[21]

Criminals were buried with the minimum of ceremony. The social reformers Henry Mayhew and John Binny visited the burial ground of Millbank Penitentiary in 1862, where, in the cholera epidemic of 1848, 'so many corpses were interred that the authorities thought it unhealthy'. Prisoners were buried at Victoria Cemetery, Mile End, instead:

We entered the sad spot, and found the earth arranged in mounds, and planted all over with marigolds, the bright orange flowers of which studded the place, and seemed in the sunshine almost to spangle the surface. At one part were three tombstones, raised to the memory of some departed prison officers; but of the remains of the wretched convicts that lay buried there, not a single record was to be found. It was well that no stone chronicled their wretched fate, and yet it was most sad that men should leave the world in such a way.[22]

Mayhew and Binny also inspected the convicts' burial ground at Woolwich Arsenal.

We thought it was one of the dreariest spots we had ever seen . . . we could just trace the rough outline of disturbed ground at our feet. There was not even a number over the graves. The last, and it was only a month old, was disappearing . . . it is perhaps well to leave the names of the unfortunate men, whose bones lie in the clay of this dreary marsh, unregistered and unknown. But the feeling with which we look upon its desolation is irrepressible . . . As we walked along we were told that under our feet dead men's bones lay closely packed; the ridge could no longer contain a body, and that was the reason why, during the last five or six years, the lower ground had been taken.[23]

Ordinary convicts were buried anonymously – but there was a peculiar refinement for 'those who had paid the extreme penalty of the law'. Prisoners executed at Tyburn, a few yards west of Marble Arch, were buried on the spot. At Newgate, executed murderers were interred in a passageway that led between the prison and the Old Bailey. They were buried under the flagstones, their coffins filled with quicklime to speed up decomposition, and with no other memorial than their initials, carved into the wall.

Once the inner-city burial grounds had been closed in 1852, the question arose as to what to do with deceased prisoners. The following clause was inserted into one of the Burial Acts:

. . . in every case in which any order in Council has been or shall hereafter be issued for the discontinuation of burials in any churchyards or burial-ground, the Burial Board or Churchwarden, as the case may be, shall maintain such churchyard or burial-ground of any parish in decent order, and also do the necessary repair of the walls and other fences thereof.[24]

The *Book of Church Law*, 4th edition, ruled: 'By his induction into the real and corporeal possession of his benefice in general, a Rector or Vicar becomes invested with freehold rights in all the land and buildings, which are enclosed within the churchyard fence or well.'[25]

This meant that the vicar had exclusive access to the churchyard, but whatever power he had, it was up to the churchwardens to see that the churchyard was kept 'in decent order'. The new legislation made it illegal to build on any ground that had been set apart for interments, but 'a carriage and horses was frequently driven straight through this law'.[26] Some graveyards were sacrificed for new streets or even railways, leading to the popular novelist Captain Marryat's observation that, 'The sleepers of the railway are laid over sleepers in death,' and inspiring the music-hall song 'They're Moving Grandpa's Grave to Build a Sewer'.

Inevitably, the final remains of many Londoners went into the latest foundations of their great city. Labourers at Borough, SE1, incorporated the remains of the 'repulsive' Ewer Street burial ground into the foundations of a railway viaduct in 1840. At St Pancras, following legislation in 1864, the Midland Railway Company acquired part of the old St Pancras churchyard in order to build a tunnel connecting the line with King's Cross, digging a trench right across the churchyard, from which ten to fifteen thousand bodies were removed. These were reinterred in the new St Pancras Cemetery, opened in 1854 on eighty-eight acres of Horse Shoe Farm on Finchley Common. In 1877, another ninety-four acres were added, and it became the St Pancras & Islington Cemetery, the largest in London at the time.

However, the bodies faced further disruption: in 2004, over 5,000 graves had to be reopened during the construction of the Channel

Tunnel rail link. The coffins, including those of French émigrés the Archbishop of Narbonne and the Bishop of Avranches, provided fascinating research opportunities for archaeologists. All were later respectfully reinterred in a series of burial services conducted by the Bishop of Edmonton.[27]

A few burial grounds became builders' yards, with the headstones flattened and obliterated by a constant succession of carthorses. New Bunhill Fields, near New Kent Road, was converted into a timberyard, with the Chapel used as a sawmill. The City of London Ground, in Golden Lane, became the location of a carrier's cart business. At Gibraltar Walk burial ground, Bethnal Green Road, small slices of land were cut off and doled out as yards for the surrounding houses, while the burial ground itself became a neglected jungle, forming a private garden for the big house which opened on to it, where the owner of the ground lived.[28]

Charles Dickens relished the gothic appeal of these neglected burial grounds. In 'The City of Absent' which appears in *The Uncommercial Traveller*, he tells us that:

Such strange churchyards hide in the City of London; churchyards sometimes so entirely detached from churches, always so pressed upon by houses; so small, so rank, so silent, so forgotten, except by the few people who look down into them from their smoky windows. As I stand peeping in through the iron gates and rails, I can peel the rusty metal off, like bark from an old tree. The illegible tombstones are all lop-sided, the gravemounds lost their shape in the rains of a hundred years ago, the Lombardy Poplar or Plane-Tree that was once a drysalter's daughter and several common-councilmen, has withered like those worthies, and its departed leaves are dust beneath it. Contagion of slow ruin overhangs the place.[29]

These closed churchyards remained useless and dreary. Nobody went into them, and children gazed through the railings, while their parents used them as a tip. In 1878, the Rev. H. R. Hawies told his congregation at St James's, Westmoreland Street, that in a swift walk through their own parish burial ground, in Paddington Street, Marylebone, he had encountered: 'Orange peel, rotten eggs, cast-off hair plaits, oyster-shells, crockery, newspapers with bread and meat, twelve old kettles, two coal-scuttles, three old hats and an umbrella, eleven dead cats and five live ones!'[30]

The burial grounds had become grim and depressing places, and nobody wanted to venture inside. Back in 1843, Sir Edwin Chadwick had recommended that the space previously occupied by burial grounds should be made available for public use, and his sentiments were echoed now by other reformers, who suggested that they be reopened as parks.

An early example of this change of use was Bunhill Fields, closed in 1832 and re-opened with considerable ceremony in October 1869 as 'a public walk'. The *Illustrated London News* reported that 'this ancient City burial-place, laid out ornamentally and planted with trees and flowers, was formally reopened by the Lord Mayor of London on Thursday week'. Hundreds of well-dressed people, admitted on a ticket-only basis, greeted the Earl of Shaftsbury, the Rector of Bishopsgate and members of the Preservation Committee when they arrived at the ground. Charles Reed MP, Chairman of the Bunhill Fields Preservation Committee, reminded the crowd of the cemetery's long history and its famous residents:

Not the 'rude forefathers' are buried here, but the founders of families, the pious and learned pastors and teachers of every religious community, not divines alone but men distinguished in literature, science and art, whose names are household words in every clime; John Bunyan, Daniel Defoe and Isaac Watts are the property not of any nation but of all mankind.[31]

The preservation work, one of the first instances of cemetery restoration in London, was painstaking. Not a fragment of stone was taken away, or soil removed. Tombs had been raised, headstones set straight, illegible inscriptions deciphered and recut, hundreds of decayed tombs restored, paths laid and avenues planted. The committee saw their task as a sacred trust: 'Trimming, as it were, the beacon-light left to warn future generations to defend their religion, even unto their blood.'

Today, Bunhill Fields seems a gloomy place, with its iron railings and dripping trees. It is one of the last surviving inner-city burial grounds in London, and gives some indication of what these places must have been like in Dickens's day. With its vivid moss and green paintwork, Bunhill has an unearthly quality. It is obvious why it became a 'public walk', with one path leading straight through. The headstones are so close together it would be impossible to squeeze between them, even if they were not corralled by railings. These stones are as plain and unadorned as one would expect among Dissenters, with the occasional anthropoid grave (shaped like a mummy case) or pyramid.

The household names buried here, Bunyan, Defoe and William Blake, are giants of literature, representing three aspects of English writing. Bunyan and Defoe were both Dissidents, both imprisoned, although Defoe for his debts rather than his opinions. Bunyan's tomb was restored in 1862 by private subscription, a piece of the original stone now being in the Congregational Church at Highgate. The monument to Defoe was raised in 1870 by a subscription in the *Christian World*. William Blake, perhaps the most eccentric of this great trio, lies here with his wife, Catherine.

In 1882, the Metropolitan Public Gardens Association was founded, influencing public opinion on open spaces in London over the next twelve years. By the end of 1895, the Association had carried through over three hundred and twenty successful transformations, with another sixty in hand, under the auspices of the energetic Lord Brabazon, Earl of Meath, philanthropist and campaigner for London's green belt. The Association's activities led to new Acts of Parliament, such as the Disused Burial Grounds Act.

Clauses were inserted in the Open Spaces Acts, and several Bills threatening public spaces were opposed and extinguished. In another development, the Association secured the opening on Saturdays of over two hundred school recreation grounds, ensuring that children had a safe place to play at weekends.

The success of the Association was directly attributable to the efforts of Mrs Isabella Holmes, who was employed as a 'scout'. Like her namesake Sherlock Holmes, Mrs Holmes was a detective and an indefatigable researcher: she visited every disused burial ground in London. She was filled with a reforming zeal, believing that turning graveyards into gardens preserved them as public spaces in an overcrowded metropolis where even the poorest parts of Whitechapel were valued at over £30,000 per acre in the 1880s.

'There could be no better way of securing the preservation of a burial ground from encroachment or misuse, than by laying it out and handing it over to a public body to be maintained for the benefit of the public,' Holmes declared. 'Once given to the people, the people are not likely to give up an inch of it again without a struggle.'[32]

Holmes was cunning, versatile, and ready for anything. Armed with old maps of London gleaned from the British Museum, she set forth to document every burying ground in the capital. Shy at first, Holmes quickly gained confidence in her curious task, knocking on the doors of private houses and asking if she could look down into a nearby graveyard from one of the upper windows. This was not always successful. Anxious to see what had become of Butler's burial ground at Coxon's Place, Horsleydown, she followed directions to two small yards. One was a hooper's yard, full of barrels. The other a builder's, with BEWARE OF THE DOG on the gate. Doubtful of the existence of this dog, Mrs Holmes pushed open the gate: 'but he was there, in full vigour, and I speedily fled.'[33] On another occasion, she was pelted with mud in Cable Street.

Occasionally, contractors refused to admit that their yards had once been burial places – but Holmes could see why. Builder's merchants were anxious about the planning consequences. What if they wanted to put up a wall or build a shed, only to find they were thwarted by the enforcement of the Disused Burial Grounds Act of 1884, as amended by the Open Spaces Act of 1887? Mrs Holmes was not to be deterred. And she also learned the investigative journalist's tricks of the trade:

> If one asks to go into a burial ground, it is generally imagined that one wants to see a particular grave. I have been supposed to have 'some-one lyin' there' in all quarters of the metropolis, and in all sorts of funny little places. I have been hailed as a sister by the quietest of Quakeresses and the darkest of bewigged Jewesses, by the leanest and most clean-shaven of ritualistic Priests, and by the bearded and buxom Dissenter.[34]

But Holmes's efforts were rewarded. The Metropolitan Public Gardens Association was a popular cause. In 1894, with a smiling face and sinking heart, the Earl of Meath made a speech to the Mansion House Fund for the Employment of the Unemployed, asking for a donation. He said that if they could find enough labourers, the money would be used in wages. To his astonishment, the Mansion House Fund donated over £11,000. This generosity constituted an emergency for Holmes, who was called to the Association's Lancaster Gate headquarters and asked for a list of projects. Within a few weeks, 'hundreds of men were employed, and their food arranged for into the bargain'.[35] By 1896, there were over ninety burial grounds within the metropolitan area dedicated to the public as recreation grounds. To people who remembered those places before they were converted, the transformation was wonderful.

A change in the climate of public opinion meant that newly appointed clergymen were writing off to the Association begging them to take over their churchyards. The new Rector of Bethnal Green not only asked for the Association's help in laying out his churchyard, he made a Christmas present of it to the vestry!

Mrs Holmes was adamant that this was the most appropriate use of the land. The burial grounds were there, in the middle of London, 'whether we like them or no, and they become far more wholesome when fresh soil is imported, good gravel paths made, and the ground drained, and when grass, flowers, trees and shrubs take the place of rotting rubbish.'[36]

To those who criticized the Association for lack of reverence, Holmes retorted that anyone with an interest in particular tombstones had the right to stop them being moved, and that, in theory, inscriptions and positions should be recorded by the Registrar of the Diocese. In practice, once the Association had taken over many of these closed burial grounds, they found evidence of neglect. Tombstones had become illegible over the years, and no family members stepped forward to claim them. In some grounds, such as Spa Fields, not a single gravestone existed when it came into the hands of the Association.[37]

Spa Fields, formerly a horrific exhibit in George Walker's evidence to the Select Committee in 1842, was purchased from the Marquis of Northampton in 1885. The latter handed it over at a nominal rate for the purpose of a children's playground and added another half acre. The Association drained it and filled it with soil and gravel. A sepia photograph from 1897 shows a view of the swings, with the parish mortuary in the background, 'the presence of which does not seem to have any sobering effect on the children'.[38] Two little girls in white aprons sit on the swings; a toddler stands nearby in a tightly buttoned coat that echoes the uniform of the caretaker, in his smart peaked cap. Visiting the playground, Holmes observed that:

A playground such as Spa Fields is about as different from an ordinary village green, where country boys and girls romp and shout, as two things with the same purpose can be. But it is only necessary to have once seen the joy with which the children of our crowded cities hail the formation of such a playground, and the use to which they put it, to be convinced that the trouble of acquiring it, or the cost of laying it out, is amply repaid . . . And can the dead beneath the soil object to the little feet above them? I am sure they cannot . . . Such a space as Spa Fields may never have been consecrated for the use of the dead, but perchance the omission is in part redeemed by its dedication to the living.[39]

Another of the Association's achievements was to rescue the stinking burial ground of Russell Court, Drury Lane – featured in Dickens's novel *Bleak House* – which had become little more than a heap of decaying rubbish thrown from surrounding houses. The carcases of eighteen cats were removed immediately. By 1896, the houses had gone, and the graveyard had become an asphalted recreation ground, with children playing on the swings. Only the old iron gate, where tragic Lady Dedlock's life was brought to a close, remained.[40]

With hindsight, it is possible to accuse Holmes of a patronizing and philistine attitude towards London's graveyards. Holmes was certainly no admirer of funerary art or elaborate mausolea; she detested Kensal Green, for example:

There is a special interest attached to Kensal Green Cemetery from its having been the first, but I think it is also the worst. Mr Loftie describes it as 'the bleakest, dampest, most melancholy of all the burial grounds of London' . . . Kensal Green Cemetery is truly awful, with its catacombs, its huge mausoleums, family vaults, statues, broken pillars, weeping images, and oceans of tombstones.[41]

Mrs Holmes lamented the cost of 'these massive monuments'. As a reformer, she believed the money would have been better spent on building schools and hospitals. 'To what purpose is this waste? Can there be any more profitless mode of throwing away money than by erecting costly tombstones?'[42]

But Holmes's reforming zeal can be understood in the context of a rational attitude towards death and burial which emerged towards the middle and end of the nineteenth century, a response to the oppressive pomp of the Victorian funeral and the condition described by the historian of death, Philippe Ariès, as 'hysterical mourning'.

# 9: THE PEOPLE WHO INVENTED DEATH

*The Victorian Funeral*

In 1887, as French writers Villiers de l'Isle-Adam and Léon Bloy were passing the flower-sellers, monumental masons and shops specializing in funeral accessories near the Père Lachaise Cemetery, Villiers exclaimed in fury: 'Those are the people who invented death!'[1]

Villiers's observation was just as true of the funeral industry this side of the Channel. By the 1880s, Victorian mourning showed manufacturers exploiting the commercial possibilities of an inevitable event, in a culture where death was just another excuse for merchandizing and black crape made the fortune of Courtaulds. James Stevens Curl has, rightly, referred to this phenomenon as 'the Victorian celebration of death'.

By the standards of the twenty-first century, the High Victorian funeral possessed an air of pageantry which is quite alien to our culture, apart from notable exceptions such as the funeral of Diana, Princess of Wales in 1997.

Before we turn to the phenomenon of the Victorian funeral itself, we should first consider the Victorian attitude towards death. It seems obvious to us now that the Victorians had a different attitude towards dying. Nothing in one's life became one like the leaving of it. In cultural terms, a dichotomy existed between a 'good' death, and a 'bad' one.

Derived from the mediaeval concept of *ars moretori*, the Good Death refers to death as the right true end of a Christian life, with the promise of an Eternal one to follow. A Good Death meant dying peacefully in your own bed, surrounded by family and friends, with a clergyman on hand to administer the Last Rites and your children brought in to kiss you goodbye. Elaborate Victorian customs eased the transition from deathbed to the final resting-place of the grave, from natural sleep to the sleep of death. A Good Death meant the opportunity for famous last words. So compelling was this that anaesthesia was discouraged, to allow the patient enough lucidity for final pronouncements. The worst fate was to die alone.

The Victorian Good Death was enshrined in literature and the visual arts, from Dickens to children's picture books. In *The Old Curiosity Shop*, the heroine, Nell, finds a group of children playing in a cemetery:

> Some young children sported among the tombs, and hid from each other, with laughing faces. They had an infant with them, and had laid it down asleep upon a child's grave, in a little bed of leaves . . . Nell drew near and asked them whose grave it was. The child answered that that was not its name; it was a garden – his brother's. It was greener, he said, than all the other gardens, and the birds loved it better because he had been used to feed them.[2]

Far from being a place of terror, this country churchyard is a sanctuary for children who have already accepted the certainty of death and have nothing to fear. Nell herself is later buried in the nearby church, after a perfect example of a Good Death:

> Opening her eyes at last, from a very quiet sleep, she begged that they would kiss her once again. That done, she turned to the old

man with a lovely smile upon her face – such, they said, as they had never seen, and never could forget – and clung with both her arms about his neck. They did not know that she was dead, at first.[3]

In the Good Death, the dead are depicted as at peace, continuing the Romantic perception of death which inspired Shelley: 'How wonderful is Death, Death and his brother Sleep!'[4] Tennyson's Elaine hears death 'like a friend's voice from a distant field, approaching through the darkness'.[5] This idealized condition allowed no indication of corporeal decay. Just as Hawksmoor's mausoleum at Castle Howard was enough to make Horace Walpole long to be buried alive, Little Nell's demise is enough to make one want to die young and leave a beautiful corpse:

> She was dead. No sleep so beautiful and calm, so free from trace of pain, so fair to look upon . . . Her couch was dressed with here and there some winter berries and green leaves, gathered in a spot she had been used to favour. 'When I die, put near me something that has loved the light, and had the sky above it always.' Those were her words.[6]

It was an age of high infant mortality. Even picture books prepared children for the melancholy realities. One by Dent featured the tale of 'The Three Little Kittens':

> *In the morn, full of pride – in the evening they died;*
> *How sudden and shocking their fate!*
> *The three little kittens, who still wore their mittens,*
> *Were buried next morning in state!*

The rhyme is illustrated by a tabby cat on a rooftop, witnessing the cortège winding off into the sunset, followed by a procession of weeping felines, all in deep mourning.[7] Regular visits to the cemetery familiarized children with inscriptions such as that of *Dear Little Rosie* at Highgate:

> *Day by day we saw her fade*
> *And quietly pass away*
> *Though often in our hearts we prayed*
> *That she might longer stay.*

This awareness of mortality and vulnerability was inevitably reflected in the trappings of a child's funeral. A trade catalogue of shroud designs contains one illustration of an infant's grave clothes embroidered with the Biblical imperative: *Suffer Little Children To Come Unto Me*. On display at the Museum of London there is a little German doll dressed in pink, lying on her back in a box. The doll was presented to one Letitia Hawkins, aged eight, on 18 December

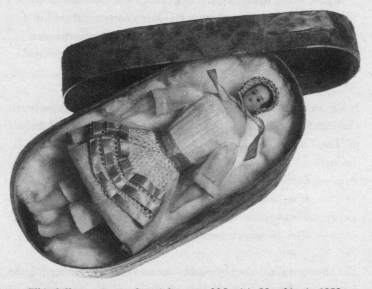

*This doll was presented to eight-year-old Letitia Hawkins in 1852,*
*the night before she died.*

1852, the night before she died. Perhaps the style of packaging is coincidental, but the box looks exactly like a coffin.

Reproductions of sentimental narrative paintings, hung in a million homes, reminded families that the Angel of Death was always hovering over London. *The Empty Cradle* depicted a mournful dog, head bowed over a vacant crib. Landseer's *The Old Shepherd's Chief Mourner* showed a grieving Border Collie, chin resting in devotion on his master's coffin. In *The Old Master*, labourers gather in a farmhouse to view the open coffin of their master and pay their last respects, while the aged widow looks mutely on. All these images represent a form of the Good Victorian Death.

London also offered many examples of the Bad Death. Prisoners, the poor, the lonely and the socially excluded expired in dismal circumstances, unmourned and unloved, from unbaptized babies to criminal suicides.

Socially excluded women were virtually guaranteed a Bad Death. The journalist James Greenwood recorded the fate of 'Poor Margaret', a nineteen-year-old girl who died in the workhouse in 1883, without so much as a surname. Poor Margaret went to her grave 'on the parish' in a box so cheap it had no handles, her passing marked by nothing more than a pencil crossing her name off a list.

In September 1888, the writer George Gissing (1857–1903) was called to a seedy lodging-house in Lambeth where his ex-wife, Nell Harris, had been found dead in the first-floor back bedroom. This 'wretched, wretched place' was a room so small he could scarcely turn round. Among the heaps of rags and medicine bottles were numerous pawn tickets. Even the bedclothes had gone. A former prostitute who had returned to the streets, Nell had spent every penny on drink. After an absence of three years, she had changed horribly. Gissing scarcely recognized her.

Gissing organized a six-guineas funeral through a Mr Stevens of Lambeth, who also ran a pub, and gave Nell's landlady three pounds to buy mourning clothes – a detail which illustrates the pervasive nature of Victorian mourning culture. It is doubtful that the proprietor was genuinely bereft. When Gissing returned for the funeral, Nell, in her coffin, had lost her frightening aspect and seemed more familiar. But there was one final humiliation. The landlady's daughter accompanied Gissing to the local pub, where they redeemed a pawned item for one shilling and ninepence – Nell's wedding ring.

Gissing blamed himself for Nell's death, although he had repeatedly tried to get treatment for her alcoholism. Theirs had been an unhappy marriage. However, her death also inspired him, in a strange kind of way, stirring his social conscience. 'As I stood beside that bed, I felt that my life henceforth had a firmer purpose. Henceforth I never cease to bear testimony against the accursed social order that brings about things of this kind!'[8]

The last category of Bad Death was, of course, suicide. No disgrace had attached to suicide in the Classical world. Indeed, to choose death before dishonour was regarded as perfectly acceptable. But the Church condemned suicide as a mortal sin, and it was illegal under English law, the act of suicide being referred to as *felo de se*.

As they had violated Christian morals, suicides were denied burial in consecrated ground and the usual observations of mourning. Instead, they were buried at night, often at a crossroads, their bodies ritually violated with a stake hammered through the heart, to anchor them down so that they could not return to haunt the living. The custom of burial at crossroads may have been to baffle the ghosts, as they would not know which direction to take. Another way to 'maze' or confuse the suicide's spirit consisted of ensuring that the funeral procession returned from the graveside by a different route, in order to make it more difficult for the departed shade to return and haunt the relatives.[9] The tradition of burying suicides at a crossroads was still observed in the early nineteenth century.

The 'funeral' of John Williams on 31 December 1811 became one of the most macabre spectacles in the history of London. Williams committed suicide after being accused of being 'the London Monster', perpetrator of the notorious Ratcliff Highway Murders of 1811, during which whole families had been bludgeoned to death. Williams's corpse was drawn through the streets on a cart with his weapons by his side: the bloodstained chisel and maul (sledgehammer) with which he had battered and ripped his victims to pieces, his face 'ghastly in the extreme'. The procession, which took place in daylight – presumably to up the attendance numbers – started at Coldbath Prison, Islington, where Williams had been found dead. Reinforced by several hundred police officers, it wound through the East End, pausing outside the victims' houses, followed by a crowd ten thousand strong. At last, the cart reached the junction of Cannon Street and Cable Street, where the body was crammed into the ground, and a stake driven through the heart with the same maul Williams had used to kill his victims. 'As the blood-stained maul thudded on the stake, the silence of the crowd was at last broken and the air became hideous with shouts and execrations.'[10] In 1866, remains thought to be those of Williams were discovered during excavations by a gas company. The skeleton came complete with stake.

Suicides were buried on the edge of town, far from the living, but, inevitably, many of these unhallowed spots have been swallowed up by the living. In St John's Wood, a tiny triangle of green opposite Lord's Cricket Ground marked the spot where John Mortland was buried with a stake through his heart in 1823, after murdering Sir Warwick Bampfylde, a poet, in Montague Square and then killing himself. This was probably the last case of crossroads burial. The tradition of burying suicides and murderers at a crossroads was abolished in 1823, when an Act was passed insisting that suicides should be buried in unconsecrated ground which was provided by law in all burial places, and specifying that burial take place between nine and twelve at night.

As well as being illegal, suicide was considered to bring the surviving family into disrepute. In Trollope's *The Prime Minister*, Emily Lopez's disreputable husband commits suicide by stepping into the path of the Euston to Inverness express and is 'knocked into bloody atoms'.[11] Emily's father ensures that Lopez does not receive a verdict of *felo de se* at the Coroner's Court, to preserve the family honour.

Victorian attitudes towards suicide demonstrate typical ambivalence, with the deed acceptably romantic in theory, as in Henry Wallis's 1865 narrative painting *The Death of Chatterton*, which featured poet George Meredith posing as the doomed forger, but unforgivable in real life. An eccentric carpenter, who killed himself with his own guillotine was decreed 'such a guilty wretch that he should be flung into a hole at night-time, with no more ceremony than attends the throwing a dead dog into a ditch'.[12] No wonder Dante Gabriel Rossetti was suspected of destroying a suicide note left by Lizzie Siddal.

The Victorian funeral was a major rite of passage. Many individuals had more money spent on them dead than alive, a tendency sustained by the aspirational middle and working classes, obliged to organize an elaborate send-off, whatever the ruinous expense. Families verging on destitution earmarked money for funeral expenses through burial clubs, unscrupulous organizations run by undertakers and the licensees of the pubs where the meetings were held. These clubs, which preyed upon the self-respect of working-class Londoners, induced them to contribute massive premiums towards future funeral expenses. Of the £24 million invested in savings banks, at least a quarter was earmarked for funeral expenses.

Investigating the high cost of dying, Sir Edwin Chadwick discovered that over 200 such clubs existed in Westminster, Marylebone, Finsbury and Tower Hamlets, with membership ranging from one to eight hundred, and deposits from around £90 to £1,000. The undertakers profited from the funeral orders, and the publicans got the custom. Chadwick even found stories of suspected infanticide: a child could be buried for £1, but it might be in four or five burial clubs, the multiple premiums adding up to ten times that amount. Up in Manchester, there was a common phrase: 'Aye, aye, that child will not live; it is for the burial club.'[13]

The bereaved were easy pickings for the unscrupulous undertaker. *Cassell's Household Guide* warned its readers to beware of 'the dismal trade':

> If there ever is a time when people find it painful to attend to any business, it is when oppressed with grief at the loss of someone who was both near and dear to them. This is especially the case when that business relates to the funeral of the one whom we have lost from earth for ever . . . The consequence is that he too often falls into the hands of persons who take advantage of his affliction . . . The only means of guarding against this is to obtain in time sufficient knowledge of this subject, so that, if death should suddenly visit the household, it may not find the mourner unprepared.[14]

Chadwick estimated that, in the 1840s, London saw over 100 deaths a day; with more than 250 undertakers competing for the bodies. This did not have the effect of driving down prices. Instead, the undertaker made it his business to find out how much insurance money was available, and tailor the funeral to fit. Bereaved families were scarcely in a position to haggle. Chadwick estimated that in London alone, nearly £1 million a year 'was thrown into the grave'.[15]

As a result, undertakers had not become any more popular since the trade was established in the late seventeenth century. A favourite music-hall song, performed by a leering ghoul in a crape-draped top hat, contained the enquiry: 'Would you care to view the body before we screw down?' His vocation made the undertaker a sinister figure, the personification of Death, little better than one of the dreaded Resurrection Men.

Dickens explores this theme in his caustic portrait of Mr Mould the undertaker in *Martin Chuzzlewit*. 'Why do people spend more money upon a death than upon a birth? I'll tell you why it is. It's because the laying out of money with a well-conducted establishment, where the thing is performed upon the very best scale, binds the broken heart, and sheds balm upon the wounded spirit.'[16]

Money, says Mould, can provide four horses to each vehicle, velvet trappings, drivers in cloth cloaks and top-boots; the plumage of the ostrich, dyed black; any number of walking attendants, dressed in the first style of funeral fashion, and carrying batons tipped with brass; it can give him a handsome tomb; it can give him a place in Westminster Abbey itself, if he choose to invest it in such a purchase.

In an earlier novel, *Oliver Twist*, the young orphan is apprenticed to an undertaker, who sports a snuffbox shaped like a coffin. One night, he is taken home to the shop:

Oliver, being left to himself in the undertaker's shop, set the lamp down on a workman's bench, and gazed timidly about him with a feeling of awe and dread, which many people a good deal older than he will be at no loss to understand. An unfinished coffin on black trestles, which stood in the middle of the shop, looked so gloomy and death-like that a cold tremble came over him, every time his eyes wandered in the direction of the dismal object; from which he almost expected to see some frightful form slowly rear its head, to drive him mad with terror. Against the wall were ranged, in regular array, a low row of elm boards cut into the same shape; looking, in the dim light, like high-shouldered ghosts with their hands in their breeches-pockets; coffin-plates, elm-chips, bright-headed nails, and shreds of black cloth, lay scattered on the floor; and the wall behind the counter was ornamented with a lively representation of two mutes in very stiff necklaces, on duty at a large private door, with a hearse drawn by four black steeds, approaching in the distance. The shop was close and hot. The atmosphere seemed tainted with the smell of coffins. The recess beneath the counter in which his flock mattress was thrust looked like a grave.[17]

Oliver's brief apprenticeship with the undertaker begins soon afterwards, with a shocking dose of reality when he accompanies his master to measure up the body of a woman who has starved to death, and whose demented husband refuses to part with the corpse.

Oliver's experience was very different from the top end of the trade. Funeral directors such as Banting, undertaker By Royal Appointment to the Crown, would organize the entire occasion. Their role was to ensure that a funeral was conducted with due propriety, that the hearse conveyed the body to the cemetery, that the ceremony passed off smoothly with a suitably uplifting interment, and that the weeping mourners were returned to their homes in the black funeral coaches. Funeral directors catered for all aspects of the event, as a description of Dottridge Brothers dating from 1878 illustrates:

The first room contained the funeral department, various palls, rich purple velvet. Bordered with gold fringe, interest with a text of scripture, HIS worked in gold thread in the centre . . . then the 'wareroom, with metal ornaments' including breastplates, handles, lid ornaments and crosses; then the drapery department with cloths, silks, cambrics, gloves, flannels, etc; then 'a mysterious department reserved for wicker baskets'; [biodegradable coffins pioneered by the originators of the natural burial movement] then the dipping room, where metals were oxidized to improve their appearance; the burnishing room, where electroplating, coppering, bronzing was carried out; the lacquering room and the japanning shop, where women worked; the Coventry room, where women sat at sewing machines and pinked, goffered and embroidered the shrouds; then the general metal working room for the draughtsmen, engravers, chasers, polishers, turners, etc; the stamping room, where presses of which the largest weighed three tons, embossed designs on tin and other metals.[18]

Dottridge Bros valued their 'solemnity' but boasted that they could have a coffin 'of the most artistic finish' ready for thirty shillings in seven minutes. And speed was of the essence. Embalming did not become commonplace until the 1920s, so funerals took place as soon as possible. Hence the mission statement in a coffin-plate manufacturer's catalogue:

PROMPT ATTENTION GIVEN TO URGENT FUNERAL ORDERS
PLATES ENGRAVED AND DESPATCHED BY THE FIRST POST

An elaborate funeral was a mark of respect, but the cost caused understandable resentment amongst all but the wealthiest of clients. It took strength of character verging on eccentricity to hold out against such conventions. Bertram S. Puckle, author of *Funeral Customs* noted that:

There is no doubt that many undertakers exploited their clients, despite their best efforts 'to break down these horrid conventions'. The scene of the following incident was a house in one of the 'best parts' of a well-known London suburb. A death had taken place in the family, and it had fallen to the lot of the eldest daughter to make the arrangements for the funeral. She asked for a plain elm coffin without any ornaments. 'Elm!' said the horrified undertaker. 'But you can't have anything but polished oak in a road like this!'[19]

There was more to organizing a funeral than buying a coffin. 'There are the coffin-furniture manufacturers, the funeral robe, sheet, and ruffle makers, the funeral-carriage masters, and funeral feather-men,' *Cassell's* reminds us. 'All these supply at first-hand the furnishing undertaker, who, in his turn, supplies the trade and the public.'[20]

The choice of coffin, and the type of funeral ceremony in which it featured, was dictated by price. *Cassell's* lists eight types of funeral, ranging from £3 5s to £53.

The cheapest bought a modest 'patent carriage, with one horse; smooth elm coffin, neatly finished, lined inside, with pillow &c. Use of pall, mourners' fittings, coachman with hatband; bearers &c.'

A funeral costing £4.14s included:

Hearse and pair of horses; a mourning coach and pair; fifteen plumes of black ostrich-feathers, and complete velvet covering for carriages and horses; stout elm coffin, with inner lid, covered with black cloth, set with two rows all round of best black nails; lead plate of inscription, lid ornaments, four pairs of handles and grips, all of the best improved jet and bright black; tufted mattress, lined and ruffled, and fine cambric winding-sheet; use of silk velvet pall; two mutes with 2 gowns, silk hatbands, and gloves, eight men as pages and coachmen, with truncheons and wands, crape hatbands, &c.

For £53, one could obtain a spectacular example of the Late-Victorian funeral:

Hearse and four horses, two mourning coaches with fours, twenty-three plumes of rich ostrich feathers, complete velvet covering for carriages and horses, and an esquire's plume of best feathers; strong elm shell, with tufted mattress, lined and ruffled with superfine cambric, and pillow; full worked glazed cambric winding-sheet, stout outside lead coffin, with inscription plate and solder complete; one and a half inch oak case, covered with black or crimson velvet, set with three rows round, and lid panelled with best brass nails; stout brass plate of inscription, richly

engraved four pairs of best brass handles and grips, lid ornaments to correspond; use of silk velvet pall; two mutes with
gowns, silk hatbands and gloves; fourteen men as pages, feath-
ermen, and coachmen, with truncheons and wands, silk
hatbands &c; use of mourners' fittings; and attendant with silk
hatband &c.

The amount of 'new goods' added much to the cost of a funeral. Kid
gloves, scarves, hatbands, most of which were retained by the
mourners, had to be bought new. The clergyman officiating at the
burial service required a fee, and then there was the cost of the grave:

> All orders for interments are to be given at the office of the ceme-
> tery company, and all fees and other charges are to be paid at the
> same time . . . It is usually required by the directors of most
> cemeteries that notice shall be given and fees paid at least thirty-
> six hours previous to interment . . . if a vault or brick grave is
> required, four clear days' notice must be given. Otherwise there
> is an additional charge for working at night.

Even the day upon which one was buried was an indicator of status.
Saturday was traditionally the 'aristocratic' day for funerals. And
although London's Victorian cemeteries are haunts of ancient peace
at present, in the mid-nineteenth century they were far from tranquil. Highgate alone saw over thirty funerals a day. Horseshoes
clattered across the cobbles; sextons grunted with effort as they sank
graves up to twenty feet deep in six foot-by-two foot shafts, without
shoring, in imminent danger of suffocation; hammers rang on
bronze as workmen set yet another pair of elegant bronze or copper
doors onto a newly-built mausoleum. Tennyson himself wrote to
Highgate Cemetery to complain bitterly about the noise levels
during his brother's funeral.

To be buried on a Sunday, the Christian day of rest, was regarded
as vulgar, although it was the only option for poor families, who

would be working for the remainder of the week. During a busy period, Sundays would see up to seventy funerals at London's biggest cemeteries, with teams of twenty gravediggers starting work at six o'clock in the morning. Sunday burials were not popular with undertakers. Frequently, there would be no hearse, and the coffin would simply be placed on the floor of a coach, beneath a pall. During cheap funerals, one horse would have to pull a coach bearing between eight and twelve people.

Interment in a brick vault is the most costly, and is only suited for those in comfortable circumstances. The price of such a vault at Highgate or Nunhead Cemeteries is £49 7s 6d; Brompton, £40 7s 6d; . . . for interments in the catacombs the lowest charges are, for Highgate or Nunhead, £17 10s; Brompton £12 12s . . . it must be remembered that additional expense attends interments in vaults and catacombs, owing to the regulations, which require lead coffins to be used.[21]

The hearse was the centre of the funeral procession. The term derives from a French word for 'harrow', a frame with metal teeth for breaking up the earth. Over the centuries, hearses became increasingly elaborate, with considerable craftsmanship expended on their construction. Once funeral processions had to travel considerable distances to the new burial grounds, some other form of transport was necessary. Bodies could no longer be 'chested' to the churchyard and borne through the lych-gate on the sturdy shoulders of family and friends. Instead, they had to be transported out of town by a special horse-drawn vehicle, with a series of carriages following at a stately pace. Once through the cemetery gates of a burial ground on the scale of Brompton or Kensal Green, there was a further distance to be covered to the cemetery chapel. By the 1860s, glass-sided hearses, with elaborately engraved patterns of flowers, became shop-windows for the undertaker's art, with the coffin clearly visible within.

Funeral coaches followed the hearse. In more prosperous families, it was common to send a funeral coach as a mark of respect. The number of coaches attending was indicative of the family's status. The black funeral horses, snorting and stamping, with the 'sable plumes of death' nodding as they tossed their heads, form one of the most iconic images of the Victorian funeral. Whatever the social status of the deceased, plumes were *de rigueur*. Even a £4.14s funeral ensured you fifteen black ostrich feathers.

The majority of horses used in 'the black job' or 'black coach' business were controlled by four proprietors, who were responsible for all the funeral vehicles in the city and could only be approached by undertakers. They provided hearses, mourning coaches, horses and drivers; no coach could be rented without a driver. The horses themselves, strong, handsome, blue-black animals, worth £50 each, were imported from Holland and Belgium. Traditionally, only 'entire' horses were used for funerals, never mares or geldings. Constantly in the public eye, they were always well groomed. A patch of grey would be painted out, a thinning mane or tail supplemented with hair from a deceased comrade. Mostly gentle and docile, they were sturdy animals; dragging heavy coaches for long distances, they had to be.[22]

Unlike hearses, which were specifically manufactured, mourning coaches were not built for funerals. Usually, these were old, previously fashionable chariots, once the pride of the West End, which were bought up, lacquered black, re-upholstered with black inside, and used for many years in their new incarnation, hired out at £35 a time.

In an attempt to solve the transport problem, Shillibeer introduced his Patent Funeral Omnibus in 1842. A combination of hearse and mourning coach, it seated up to six passengers. In a typically Victorian feat of engineering, the section containing the coffin could be packed away for the return journey. John Claudius Loudon was hugely impressed, regarding the invention as 'ingenious and most useful', but the omnibus failed to find popularity with the public. More significantly, it was not taken up by the trade, as undertakers wished to encourage mourners to hire as many coaches as possible.[23]

The act of attending a funeral was regarded as therapeutic, resulting in high moral uplift. William Justyne remarked of Highgate Cemetery that:

> The earthy smell, the sunless air, the sensation of the world shut out must indicate that this is a half-way house to the grave – a brief resting-place for death and sorrow. Could the visitor stand here, day after day, and watch coffin succeeding coffin and the black-robed mourners – could he hear the holy and breathless words of the burial service repeated and repeated before an ever-changing company of pale faces and troubled hearts, he would learn a grim, never to be forgotten lesson of the shadow side of human life.
>
> The hardest of men are humbled – the stoutest hearts will break here. The vanity of human life, the selfish and self-confident pursuit of worldly pleasure are here set aside, for a while at least; as the awful prospect of eternity is brought to us by a force of circumstance.[24]

While sentiment and uplift were regarded as an important outcome, funerals had their more vulgar side. Many found that the most effective way to staunch a flow of grief after the ceremony was a game of skittles at the nearest pub, accompanied by copious quantities of beer. James Greenwood was astonished to discover fifteen empty hearses and black coaches drawn up outside a pub near a great London cemetery. The big black horses required refreshment after a busy day, and so did the drivers and attendants. Undertakers lounged against the black wheels, with glasses of beer or gin in their hands and pipes in their mouths, laughing and joking as if they were on a day out in Epping Forest. Some even had white ribbons pinned to their hats, denoting the funeral of a baby or child.

The mourners, far from being outraged, plucking the pipes from their mouths, or spilling their drinks in the gutter, were doing exactly the same thing: drinking, smoking, even eating. The more decorous remained in their carriages, partaking of biscuits and ale, brandy and water, plates of cold beef and pickles, while the undertaker, with one black kid glove off and his weeper [black ribbon] askew bent in at the window and took their orders.

Inside, the pub was heaving, the bar four deep with men in black crape. Recently bereaved women, old and young, jostled in the narrow space, clamouring for their round of drinks and packs of tobacco. Forget the black crape and the widows' bonnets, said Greenwood, and it could be any Saturday night in Whitechapel. One costermonger was even challenging the slim young barman about the outrageous price of a pint. The more genteel mourners had taken refuge in the tea-garden. The majority of these were women, knocking back gin, some tearful, some defiant, preyed on by the undertakers, their fishy eyes blinking and noses glowing as the black hats slid off their heads.

These extraordinary scenes were a regular occurrence. After a funeral, the undertakers would pull up outside a quiet country pub, declaring that the horses needed watering, and respectfully suggesting that the mourners would care to stretch their legs. Few could resist, and so the undertakers got their skinful, and more, from a delighted landlord who was grateful for the business.[25]

Elaborate funerals were part of the rich panoply of nineteenth-century life. Horatio Nelson set the standard after he was mortally wounded by a sniper at the Battle of Trafalgar in 1805. Nelson's body was pickled in brandy, which was replaced with wine at Gibraltar, and brought back to England, amid macabre speculation that the Admiral's crew had drunk the embalming brandy in transit. Resting in a coffin made from the mainmast of the French flagship, *L'Orient*, Nelson's body lay in state in the Painted Hall at Greenwich for three days, before making the journey by barge to Whitehall, and thence to the Admiralty. Hundreds of thousands brought London to a standstill as they watched the body hauled through the streets to St Paul's in a magnificent funeral 'car', a copy of his ship, the *Victory*, complete with figurehead and a canopy topped with black plumes bearing the motto: *Hoste Devicto Requievit* – With the enemy conquered, he is at rest – and a pall which read simply: TRAFALGAR.

'When the coffin was brought of the admiralty, there seemed to be a general silence and every one appeared to feel for the death of so noble and such a good man,' wrote Nelson's nephew. Night had fallen by the time Nelson's coffin was lowered into the crypt. His crew, who had accompanied him on his final journey, ripped up the ensign covering the coffin and stuffed the fragments into their pockets.

Not to be outdone, Wellington's funeral, organized by Prince Albert in 1852, was a *pièce de résistance* fitting for a national hero.

When Arthur Wellesley, 1st Duke of Wellington (1769-1852), died on 14 September 1852, Queen Victoria declared him 'the greatest man this country has ever produced' and felt his loss as keenly as if it had been a death in the family. The Court went into mourning. Wellington, a Spartan type who favoured an iron bed and a hard pillow, had left no particular instructions, but the Government, led by the inexperienced Lord Derby (his first Tory cabinet were so young they were referred to as the Who? *Who?* Cabinet) considered that this was an opportunity for a spectacular state funeral for the war hero and former Tory Prime Minister. This would unite the people in mourning.

Immediately after his death, the Duke's coffin of oak, encased in lead went on display in a black-clad room at Walmer Castle. In the evening, it made the two-mile journey to Deal Station, where it was lifted onto a train, bound for London, and taken to Chelsea Hospital. Here it lay in state for three days, guarded by soldiers from the Duke's old regiment, in a hall hung with billowing black velvet decorated with silver cord and lit by dozens of tall candlesticks. A constant stream of mourners passed by the coffin. The first of these was Queen Victoria herself, accompanied by her children. Overcome with grief, 'she never got beyond the centre of the hall, where her feelings quite overcame her, and she was led, weeping bitterly, back to the carriage.'[26] On 12 November, a two-mile tail-back of carriages blocked the streets, and thousands of ticket-holders had to be turned away from the Private View when it closed at four. The following day, when the public were given admittance, the police were overwhelmed by the sheer weight of numbers, and two women were crushed to death.

Wellington's body was transferred to St James's Park, where it spent the night beneath a tent. The morning of the funeral was stormy and wild. Before daybreak, troops were assembled in St James's and Horse Guards Parade, their guns trimmed with black crape. At seven o'clock, a salute rang out – and then, with tremendous military ceremony, arms reversed and drums muffled, the enormous structure on which the body was carried rumbled through the streets to the sound of the 'Dead March from Saul' as the Duke began his final journey, to St Paul's Cathedral.

Wellington's coffin reposed in a magnificent 'funeral car', created by Richard Redgrave (1804–89) and Sir Charles Cockerell (1788–1863), designer of the Bank of England, and approved by Prince Albert. Twenty-seven feet long, ten feet broad, seventeen feet high, and weighing twelve tons, it was drawn by twelve black horses harnessed three abreast, embellished with nodding plumes of black ostrich feathers. Large bodies of troops representing every regiment in the British Army lined the route or followed in the procession.

According to *The Times*, the funeral car 'formed by far the most magnificent and interesting part of the procession. The whole lower part is of bronze. Above this rises a rich pediment of gilding, with a list of victories inscribed. On the sides, lofty coats of arms are surmounted by Ducal coronets and batons, topped by a velvet pall, embroidered with laurels in silver and the legend "Blessed are the Dead that die in the Lord"'.

Wellington's 'funeral car' was a good example of the transitional stage between the rudimentary horse drawn wagon of previous generations and the elaborate nineteenth-century hearse, designed to showcase the handiwork of the undertaker.

The streets of London presented a remarkable sight. A national day of mourning had been declared, and the Bank of England, Stock Exchange and Parliament suspended. Mourners had streamed into the capital from all over the country. In keeping with the Duke's Irish connections, special boats were laid on from Dublin. The newspapers were full of tickets for the big day (with the *Observer* estimating total sales of £80,000) and offers of accommodation. More than 200,000 seats were sold and 1,500,000 people were expected. Enormous crowds assembled hours before the ceremony, and every possible vantage point occupied, including the trees. The black-draped balconies of gentlemen's clubs such as the Athenaeum club and the Carlton were crammed with ladies, the traditional 'men only' policy having been abandoned for the day. People crowded onto the roof of the National Gallery; although the shops were officially shut, spectators who had paid for a place inside them squashed against the windows of the Strand. Everyone was dressed in deep mourning. Whatever the popular feeling towards Wellington during some periods of his life, there appeared to be heartfelt sorrow at his death. The crowd was mostly decorous, although one group, who had gathered to follow the procession near St Clement Dane's, were beaten back by police truncheons.

Although St Paul's had opened at eight in the morning, it was past noon by the time the cortège arrived at the Cathedral. It was a freezing cold day, with the wind whipping in through the open doors. The clergy tried to shelter their faces with their robes and the breeze rippled the feathers of the Duke's hat where it lay on his coffin, as if it were coming to life.

St Paul's had been closed for six weeks beforehand, while preparations were made for the expected 13,000 mourners. Banting's had draped heavy black cloth over the windows and the monuments, including that of Nelson. Light came from 7,000 gaslamps, hung under the Whispering Gallery. The service, featuring a choir 120 strong, lasted three hours. At three o'clock, bells tolled throughout the land and the Duke was lowered into his tomb. At this point, reality intervened. One mourner paused to glance into the burial chamber and turned away, retching. It was to be five years before Wellington's sarcophagus of Cornish porphyry was completed.

There are those who prefer to be different in every area of life, and death is no exception. In the eighteenth and nineteenth century, a small number of people chose not to be buried at all. The most famous case was that of Jeremy Bentham (1748–1832), the philosopher and jurist. Bentham left instructions in his Will that his body, dressed in his own clothes, be preserved and displayed at University College, London, as an 'auto icon', so that he could keep a watchful eye on proceedings at his own college. For years before his death, Bentham even carried around the glass eyes needed for the taxidermy process. In the event, his head deteriorated before it could be preserved and a wax one had to be substituted. The genuine head, so often a target for student pranks, eventually had to be locked away, after being found doing service in a football game, and, on another occasion, discovered in a locker at Aberdeen railway station.

While Mrs Holmes makes a tantalizing reference to a gentleman who left instructions that his body should be exhibited in a glass coffin on the roof of his Hyde Park mansion[27], one Martin Van Butchell (1735–1814), a dentist, kept the embalmed body of his first wife in a glass case in his drawing room.

Van Butchell, whose success as a surgeon was somewhat eclipsed by his unbridled eccentricity – he often rode through London on a white pony decorated with purple spots – had Maria Van Butchell's body embalmed by the pioneering anatomist Dr William Hunter when she died aged thirty-six. Hunter injected the vascular system with Oil of Turpentine and Camphorated Spirit of Wine, and introduced powdered nitre and camphor into the abdominal cavity. According to Dr Julian Litten, the entire procedure was documented by her widower, who then released a press statement announcing limited viewing of the results: 'VAN BUTCHELL (not willing to be unpleasantly circumstanced, and wishing to convince some good Minds they have been misinformed) acquaints the Curious, no Stranger can see his embalmed Wife, unless (by a Friend personally) introduced to himself, any Day, between Nine and One, *Sundays* excepted.'[28]

The procedure was also celebrated in a macabre and misogynistic poem, congratulating Van Butchell on the possession of a wife who never answered back. After Van Butchell died, his son presented Maria's body to the Royal College of Surgeons, where it went on display in the Hunterian Collection, devoted to medical curiosities. In 1857, one commentator noted:

What a wretched mockery of a once lovely woman it now appears, with its shrunken and rotten-looking bust, its hideous, mahogany-coloured face, and its remarkably fine set of teeth. Between the feet are the remains of a green parrot – whether immolated or not at the death of his mistress is uncertain – but it still retains its plumage. By the side of Mrs Van Butchell is the body of another woman, embalmed by a different process about the same period: she is even more ugly than her neighbour. As curiosities, these few loathsome relics are no doubt both valuable and interesting, but were there a heap of such dry rubbish, one would feel strongly disposed to make a bonfire of the whole, for it looks nothing fit for anything else.

His wish was granted: in 1941, Maria, the green parrot and her ugly neighbour were destroyed during an air raid. The 'ugly neighbour' was in fact one Sarah Stone, a medical artist who had been embalmed by her lover, a surgeon, back in 1774, after he had vowed that they would never be parted.[29]

Prince Albert, despite his elaborate plans for Wellington's funeral, had stipulated that, when the time came, he wanted an unassuming ceremony for himself. His wishes were respected, but the legacy of the Prince's sudden death, in December 1861, was a cult of extreme mourning, with his wife as the presiding genius.

# 10: THE VALE OF TEARS

*The Victorian Cult of Mourning*

Queen Victoria had been dealt a bitter blow by the death of her mother in March 1861, a cause of such 'unremitting grief' that it led to a nervous breakdown. The impact of Prince Albert's death nine months later was catastrophic. Victoria never recovered from her husband's sudden demise, ostensibly from typhoid. Although many commentators have suggested that the Queen's almost pathological grief should not be taken as representative, her bereavement was the defining moment of the Victorian attitude to death. Iconic in her grief, Queen Victoria became the presiding genius of mourning.

With the Prince's death, the Court was immediately plunged into mourning. The Lord Chamberlain's Office decreed, on 16 December 1861: 'The LADIES attending Court to wear black woollen stuffs, trimmed crape, plain linen, black shoes and gloves and crape fans. The GENTLEMEN attending Court to wear black Cloth, plain Linen, Crape Hatbands and black Swords and Buckles. Mourning to commence from the date of this Order.'[1]

Meanwhile, the Earl Marshall, whose role as organizer of royal funerals dated back to the thirteenth century, immediately ordered: 'A General Mourning for his late Royal Highness Prince Albert . . .

in pursuance of Her Majesty's commands, this is to give public notice that on the melancholy occasion of the death of His Royal Highness the Prince Consort, it is commanded that all persons do forthwith dress in decent mourning.'

In contrast to the elaborate ceremony he had organized for the Duke of Wellington, the Prince had left instructions for a modest ceremony, consisting of 'solemn but exceedingly simple obsequies'. The funeral took place at Windsor on 23 December 1861. As the Prince had requested:

> It was of a private character; but all the chief men of state attended the obsequies in the Royal Chapel. The weather was cold and damp, the sky dull and heavy. There was a procession of state carriages to St George's Chapel, at the door of which the Prince of Wales and other royal mourners were assembled to receive the coffin. Davey noted that 'the grief of the poor children was very affecting, with Prince Arthur especially sobbing as if his heart were breaking. When all was over, and the last of the long, lingering train of mourners had departed, the attendants descended into the vault with lights and moved the bier and coffin along the narrow passage to the royal vault. The day was observed throughout the realm as one of mourning.[2]

Bells tolled throughout the land, and in many churches special services were held. In the towns, shops were closed and window blinds in private residences were drawn down. No respectable people appeared abroad except in mourning, and in seaport towns the flags were hoisted half-mast high.

The Queen's mourning *was* extreme, even by Victorian standards. In the public realm, her display of grief reached its apotheosis in Sir George Scott's Albert Memorial, erected in Kensington Gardens in 1871. In private, Prince Albert's rooms were immaculately preserved, a shaving jug of hot water provided every day. The Queen was often to be found seated before a fire-screen bearing a picture of Albert's mausoleum at Frogmore, weeping into a hand-kerchief embroidered with black tears. And she continued to wear mourning dress, long, long after the statutory two-year period, creating her own trends among European royalty:

> When Her Majesty became a widow, she slightly modified the conventional English widow's cap, by indenting it over the fore-head à la Marie Stuart, thereby imparting to it a certain picturesqueness which was quite lacking in the former head-dress. This coiffure has not only been adopted by her subjects but also by the royal widows abroad. The etiquette of the Imperial House of Germany obliges the Empress Frederick to introduce into her costume two special features during the earlier twelve months of her widowhood. The first concerns the cap, which has both a Marie Stuart point in the centre of the forehead as well as a long veil of black crape falling like a mantle behind to the ground. The second peculiarity to this stately costume is that the orthodox white batiste collar has two narrow white bands falling straight from head to foot. This costume has been very slightly modified from the last three centuries ago when the Princess of the House of Hohenzollern lost her husband.[3]

Victorian widows had a template for bereavement in their Queen. By 1881, Victoria's legacy of grief had defined the mourning rituals of her subjects. A middle-class matron would be expected to conform to etiquette, whatever her personal reservations. Such a young woman would wear deep mourning for at least one year, consisting of black clothes made of a non-reflective fabric such as bombazine, Parramatta or black crape, evocatively described by Dickens as 'the breathless smell of warm black crape, I did not know what the smell was then, but I do now,' when orphaned David Copperfield is taken to the undertakers to be fitted with mourning for his young mother.[4] Matt black was felt to be appropriately lugubrious. Beneath the mourning ensemble, a widow wore funereal lingerie:

*The death of Prince Albert in 1861 inspired mourning fashions.*

white broderie anglaise, threaded with black ribbon. The under-
wear itself was not black, as the dye might wear off on a woman's
skin. Over her hair went a long black veil, reaching to her waist and
decorated with 'weepers' or black ribbons. The veil covered her face
whenever she left the house, to hide tears and deter the curious.
Originally made from crape, this oppressive garment frequently
afflicted wearers with asthma, catarrh and even cataracts as a result
of exposure to the black dyes. Towards the end of the nineteenth
century, 'nun's veiling' – a lighter material – was used.

When a young widow did venture out, which was not often, her
coat was trimmed with black fur, or sealskin, her only ornaments of
jet or bog oak (a thick dark wood) although she might wear an item
of mourning jewellery such as a brooch or locket containing a tress
of a loved one's hair, worked into the design of a willow tree, or
encased in glass and engraved with the motto *In Memoriam*. A sentimental attachment to locks of hair dates back to the Ancient
Greeks, who always cut the first hair of a child, the beard of a youth

and the hair of a young maiden, and offered them to the gods. On the death of a parent, children placed a lock of hair with the body.[5]

Black enamel jewellery was popular, containing a miniature painted on ivory, or an urn, with a figure weeping over a tombstone. Sometimes these were embellished with seed pearls, redolent of tears. There was a superstition that turquoise was affected by the ill-health of a person wearing it, and that it remained dull and leaden in appearance after death, until worn by a person in good health, when it would regain its distinctive colour.

Once a widow had completed her first year, she dressed in 'secondary mourning'. This had a less rigorous dress code, and white collars and cuffs, reminiscent of a nun's habit, were permitted. After nine months came 'ordinary mourning', a three-month stretch during which women were permitted to wear shiny fabrics such as silk and velvet, trimmed with lace or beads, and also gold and silver jewellery, with appropriately sombre precious stones like amethysts, garnets and opals. Finally, a widow entered the six months of 'half-mourning', when muted colours such as grey, purple and lilac were permissible. Black evening dress was accessorized with a black fan, trimmed with ostrich feathers, and, should she be deaf, a black Vulcanite mourning ear trumpet.

Children were expected to go into black too, although white was also acceptable for infants. Servants also adopted mourning, some dyeing their everyday garments in a laundry copper, with the attendant distinctive smell.

And God help the woman who would not, or could not, afford the best Courtaulds had to offer. 'This is a time for display, not for borrowing, and who knows better than a widow that a score of coldly criticizing eyes are watching events through broken Venetian blinds and dirty Nottingham lace curtains . . . one is left wondering where the money comes from to pay for the luxury of grief,' noted the writer Puckle, relating the sad fate of a young lady who chose to economize on mourning:

A superior servant, a girl, married a house painter. Within a year, the husband fell from a ladder and was killed. The poor little widow bought a cheap black dress and a very simple black straw hat to wear at the funeral. Her former employer, who had much commended this modest outlay, met the girl a few days later swathed in crape, her poor little face only half visible under a hideous widow's bonnet complete with streamers and a veil. Asked why she had made these purchases she explained that her neighbours and relations had made her life unbearable because she did not want to wear widow's weeds, and at last she had to give in. 'They said that if I would not wear a bonnet, it proved we were never married,' she sobbed.[6]

Puckle was a savage critic of mourning culture, but understood its oppressive nature, particularly among the poor. Among the wealthy, societal pressure was just as great.

Emily Lopez, in Trollope's *The Prime Minister*, is driven into widow's weeds after her husband's violent death. In deepest mourning, she becomes 'a monument of bereaved woe',[7] 'a black shade – something almost like a dark ghost.'[8] Emily observes all the formalities of Victorian mourning:

She herself had seen no visitor. She had hardly left the house except to go to church, and then had been enveloped in the deepest crape. Once or twice she had allowed herself to be driven out in a carriage, and, when she had done so, her father had always accompanied her. No widow, since the seclusion of widows was first ordained, had been more strict in maintaining the restraints of widowhood as enjoined.[9]

Even after attending a wedding, for which she dons half-mourning consisting of a grey silk gown, Emily reverts to full mourning as soon as the ceremony is over. But there is a twist to Emily's costume. Despite complying with Victorian etiquette, it is not her husband that Emily mourns. She feels 'disgraced and ashamed' for marrying Lopez in the first place, against the advice of her family. She takes personal responsibility for the families plunged into debt by Lopez's fraudulent conduct, and reimburses them. Weeping with loathing at her own shortcomings, Emily is in mourning for her own life. It is only when Arthur Fletcher, her devoted admirer, eventually persuades her to marry him that she can dispense with 'all the appurtenances of mourning which she usually wore' and embrace him: 'In a moment his arms were round her, and her veil was off, and his lips were pressed to hers.' Widow's veil ripped away, penance served, Emily permits herself to return to the land of the living.[10]

Just as an entire industry exists today around weddings and childbirth, with clothing and accessories for every contingency, high Victorian mourning demonstrated the ability of the Victorians to exploit an inevitable event. Victorian manufacturers seized upon the commercial possibilities of mourning with characteristic enterprise. There were no less than four mourning emporia in Regent Street including Peter Robinson's store. One of these later became Dickens & Jones, but the most famous was Jay's London General Mourning Warehouse, founded in 1841. A department store of death, Jay's developed from 'the *Magasin de Deuil* (Store of Mourning), an establishment exclusively devoted to the sale of mourning costumes and all the paraphernalia necessary for the funeral. Long regarded as French, this concept was actually 'a brilliant and elaborate adaptation of the old *mercerie de lutto* which existed for centuries and still exists in every Italian city, where people in the haste of grief can obtain in a few hours all that the etiquette of civilization requires for mourning in that country as the climate renders speedy interment absolutely necessary.'[11]

Black silks were a speciality of the house. The secret of Jay's success was to buy silks, cashmeres, crapes and tulles from recession-hit European mills at a competitive rate, and sell them to the customers for a small profit. The development of the sewing machine in the 1850s ushered in the era of mass-produced clothing, off the peg and

*An advertisement for Peter Robinson's Mourning Warehouse, 1885.*

made to measure, with dressmakers leaving the store to take fittings from the bereaved in their own homes. With mourning forever in fashion (demand soared with the death of Prince Albert), Jay's could never lose.

While the complex code of mourning remained virtually unchanged, new fabrics and styles provided endless variations. As with any fashion house, the buyers went to Europe every season, although in this case it was not to view the designer shows. Instead, they visited the principal silk manufacturers of Lyons, Genoa and Milan, and consulted the top Parisian designers. Grief was no time to be dowdy. Even in bereavement, women wanted to be stylish.

The store sold 'not only all that is necessary for mourning, but also departments devoted to dresses of a more general description, although the colours are confined to such as could be worn for either full or half mourning'. An advertisement from 1881 reads: 'Messrs Jay prepare for the season: a variety of black dresses which we can confidently recommend both for correctness of Fashion and Economy of Price.' The names of these dresses are intriguing. 'The Aesthetic', designed along Pre-Raphaelite lines, and 'The Houri', derived from the Arabic word for the beautiful nymphs who haunt paradise.

Widow's weeds are presented as anti-erotic in Emily's case, but in other spheres of Victorian society the appeal of a young woman dressed in black from head to toe was acknowledged. In Victorian popular culture, widows had two manifestations: the battleaxe and the man-eater, preying upon husbands and bachelors alike. Even today, an attractive, dark-haired person dressed all in black has vampiric connotations, as the novelist Alison Lurie has noted, 'so archetypally terrifying and thrilling, that any black-haired, pale-complexioned man or woman who appears clad in all black formal clothes projects a destructive eroticism, sometimes without conscious intention.'[12] The Victorian widow was a femme fatale, both seductive (widows had considerably more freedom than spinsters), and deadly.

On his visit to Jay's, social commentator Henry Mayhew was overwhelmed by the 'dazzling mirrors', and the 'bevy of bright-eyed fair damsels, clad in black silk', ready to do his bidding. At its zenith, Jay's employed over 200 shop assistants. With typical masculine amusement, he spots 'a wonderful assemblage of caps, which seem to range in density from the frosted spider-web to the petrified "trifle"'. One widow's cap, preserved in a glass case, is 'as light as thistledown, with long streamers like fairies' wings'. There is a variety of collars of white crape, black crape, tulle and muslin, collars dotted with black and edged with black. Writing up his observations, Mayhew quoted a sketch from a satirical magazine of the day:

*Shopman*: How deep would you choose to go, ma'am? Do you
   want to be very poignant?
*Lady*: Why, I suppose, crape and bombazine, unless they've gone
   out of fashion . . .
*Shopman*: We have a very extensive assortment, whether for
   family, court, or complimentary mourning; including the last

novelties from the Continent. Here is one, ma'am, just imported – a widow's silk – watered, as you perceive, to match the sentiment. It is called the 'Inconsolable', and is very much in vogue, in Paris, for matrimonial bereavements.

*Squire*: Looks rather flimsy though. Not likely to last long – eh, sir?

*Shopman*: Several new fabrics have been introduced to meet the demand for fashionable tribulation.

*Lady*: And all in the French style?

*Shopman*: Certainly. Of course, ma'am. They excel in the *funèbre*. Here, for instance, is an article for the deeply afflicted. A black crape, expressly adapted to the proposed style of mourning, makes up very sombre and interesting. Or, if you would prefer a velvet, ma'am . . .

*Lady*: Is it proper, sir, to mourn in velvet?

Shopman: Oh, quite! Certainly. Just coming in. Now here is a very rich one – real Genoa – and a splendid black. We call it 'The Luxury of Woe'. Only eighteen shillings a yard, and a superb quality – in short, fit for the handsomest style of domestic calamity. The mourning of the poor people is very coarse – very. Quite different from that of persons of quality – canvas to crape . . .

*Lady*: To be sure it is! And as to the change of dress, sir: I suppose you have a great variety of half-mourning?

*Shopman*: Oh, infinite! The largest stock in town. Full, and half, and quarter, and half-quarter, shaded off, if I may say so, like an India-ink drawing, from a grief *prononcé* to the slightest *nuance* of regret.[13]

These days, few of us choose to look at pictures of someone on their deathbed. Photographs of Diana dying in the wreckage of her Mercedes were deemed too shocking for general circulation; we are warned before terrorist atrocities are shown on a news bulletin. However, to the Victorians, memorializing the deathbed was part of the occasion. Like famous last words, famous last hours were recorded for posterity. For instance, an illustration depicting Alfred, Lord Tennyson, expiring peacefully among his pillows was the highlight of a special supplement of the *Black and White Magazine* in October 1892. The death of Prince Albert, surrounded by family and courtiers, was the subject of a famous painting by W. I. Walton, and appeared on numerous greeting cards; and many a Victorian lithograph depicted a weeping mother bidding farewell to her beautiful, dying daughter.

Henry Peach (1830–1901), a 'pictorialist photographer' and admirer of the Pre-Raphaelites, exhibited a tableau entitled *Fading Away* in 1858. This depicts a beautiful young girl dying of consumption, surrounded by her despairing family. Although stunted up by actors, the photograph was condemned as a foray into private grief, with one critic claiming that Peach had exploited 'the most painful sentiments which it is the lot of human beings to experience'. The censure originated from the fact that Peach's creation was a photograph, rather than a painting, and therefore uncomfortably realistic. Nevertheless, Prince Albert, a keen amateur photographer, was captivated, and ordered a copy; he went on to buy all Peach's subsequent work, including a portrait of a young girl reclining in a chair with her head on a pillow and eyes closed, presumably about to expire, and entitled *She Never Told Her Love*.

Photographs of people dying, or pretending to (Peach, was, after all, a photographic artist), were rare, but the Victorians did use the resources of photography to document their dead. Beyond the confines of the pathology lab or the battlefield (grim casualty photographs played a decisive part in the public perception of the American Civil War), post-mortem photography seems to us a grisly concept – but if photography allowed one to photograph the living, why not the dead? Yet again, one of the great nineteenth-century inventions played its part in the Victorian way of death. Post-mortem photography formed part of the Good Death, a means of preserving the memory of a loved one's dying minutes for those unable to attend, consolation for their absence from his or her deathbed. It was designed, not for public consumption, but for circulation within the family, and preservation in a memorial album. In an age of high infant mortality, post-mortem photography was also a way of preserving some lasting memory of children. When a newborn died, a photograph of an infant, apparently asleep in its cradle, was all that grieving parents had to remember their child by. Sometimes these bore an inscription, such as *A Last Sleep*, or devotional verses.

Louis Jacques Daguerre unveiled the Daguerreotype in 1839, but it was a time-consuming and costly procedure, with exposures taking up to fifteen minutes. This restricted post-mortem portraiture to the rich. The development of the ambrotype in the 1850s made photography cheaper. It consisted of imaging a negative on glass backed by a dark surface. Then came tintype, or ferrotype: positive photographs made directly onto iron plate and varnished with a thin sensitised film. The *carte de visite* method for producing multiple prints on a single plate meant that copies could be sent to all members of the family. American journalist David Bartlett visited the grave of one such subject at Stoke Newington.

Here, a few years ago, was buried a pretty, prattling girl whom I knew, and loved, and who often used to come and play among the flowers on our lawn. One day, very suddenly, she died of a heart disease. The suddenness of the stroke almost killed her father and mother. Her portrait was taken after death, and when she was arranged for the artist, I came in and looked at her. Never saw I so touching a sight. She was dressed as if alive, and was half reclining upon a sofa in the drawing room. Her cheeks were like the rose-leaves, and if her eyes had not been closed I should have believed her alive. The southern windows were thrown open – it was a June morn – and the odour of flowers came in with the songs of the birds. Her mother entered the room – the sight was too much for her and she fainted. The fair girl was buried in this sweet spot, but will never be forgotten by those who knew her.[14]

Beautiful in death, these creations are the apotheosis of the passive Victorian woman. In some quarters, the level of objectification suggests more than a hint of necrophilia, particularly among the Pre-Raphaelites and their admirers. The doomed Elizabeth Siddal modelled for Millais' *Ophelia*, dressed in a brocade gown, in a bath of water scattered with lilies. Siddal almost caught her death of cold when the candles which heated the bath from underneath went out, and was eventually recovered, shivering and blue. Atkinson Grimshaw's *Elaine* depicts the heroine's dead body borne downriver on a barge draped in black samite. The poem 'Consumption', by the forgotten poet Henry Kirk White, who succumbed to the disease himself at the age of twenty-five, gives the silent killer a sensual air, reminiscent of the *danse macabre*:

> *In the dismal night-air dressed*
> *I will creep into her breast*
> *Flush her cheek and blanch her skin,*
> *And feed on the vital fire within.*
> *Lover, do not trust her eyes*
> *When they sparkle most, she dies;*
> *Mother, do not trust her breath,*
> *Comfort she will breathe in death;*
> *Father, do not strive to save her,*
> *She is mine, and I must have her;*
> *The coffin must be her bridal bed,*
> *The winding sheet must wrap her head;*
> *The whispering winds must o'er her sigh,*
> *For soon in the grave the maid must lie;*
> *The worm it will riot on heavenly diet,*
> *When death has deflowered her eye.*[15]

The Victorians were half in love with death. Even Fallen Women, who did not meet a Good Death, seemed to undergo some form of redemption by drowning. Paintings such as *Found Drowned*, depicting the corpse of a prostitute, were regarded as salutary; the vogue was inspired by Thomas Hood's poem 'The Bridge of Sighs', which idealizes a drowned woman thus:

*Take her up tenderly*
*Lift her with care;*
*Fashion'd so slenderly*
*Young, and so fair!*
*Look at her garments*
*Clinging like cerements;*
*Whilst the wave constantly*
*Drips from her clothing.*[16]

Waterloo Bridge was particularly associated with the death of Fallen Women in the popular imagination, with the River Thames forming a last resting-place for the unfortunate, although it was the Serpentine, and the canals, in which the majority of suicides took place. (Shelley's first wife, Harriet, drowned herself in the Serpentine in 1816.[17]) In France and Germany, reproductions of the death mask of a beautiful woman found drowned in the Seine became a popular feature of French and German parlours. This, of course, was the romantic ideal: the reality consisted of the Dredgermen, who made their living dragging decomposed corpses out of the Thames and looting the bodies.

Monuments were integral to the Victorian cult of mourning. Visiting the grave to commune with the spirit of the dear departed was a practice which had developed over the previous 100 years, a consequence of the Romantic and sentimental sensibility. In 1809, William Godwin's *Essay on Sepulchres* had proposed the construction of simple monuments to commemorate notable historical figures whose remains had been lost in the mists of time. The *Essay* also revealed a changing attitude towards death and the treatment of the dead. Although a corpse itself was worthless (except to the Resurrection Men), a memorial, however simple, served to keep that person's memory alive. In physical terms, it occupied a space where survivors could mourn, and also commune with the dead person.

> When I meet the name of a great man inscribed in the cemetery, I would have my whole soul awakened to honour his memory . . . call his ghost from the tomb to communicate with me . . . I am not satisfied to converse only with the generation of men that now happens to subsist; I wish to live in intercourse with the illustrious Dead of all ages . . . I would say with Ezekiel, the Hebrew, 'Let these dry bones live!' as my friends, my philosophers, my instructors and my guides![18]

The journalist Samuel Laman Blanchard (1804–1845) developed this theme in his account of a trip to Kensal Green in 1842: 'With what a different impulse does memory revisit this Asylum of the Dead . . . Kneeling beside the bed of the Sleeper, the watcher Love has felt for a time that Death was but a dream, and Life little more. Affection has said, "Let these dry bones Live!" . . . the lost has been restored, and the separated have been joined.'[19]

In order to achieve this effect, the choice of monument was vital. In 1878 *The Builder* magazine decreed that: 'The principles of proportion and of harmony and grace and form which are required by a well-dressed woman in her costume are equally applicable when she comes to choose a tombstone for her husband.'[20]

Given the appropriate funds, the widow was not spoiled for choice. Monumental masons offered pattern books of designs; Stephen Geary published *Cemetery Designs for Tombs and Monuments* in 1840, a year after his partner Bunning had produced *Designs for Tombs and Monuments*. These books, and the stonemasons who executed the designs within, were a feature of every high street. At Highgate, the official mason was Millward in

Swain's Lane, and two statuary masons took over houses in South Grove there to meet the demand: Rebecca Bower in Russell House and Henry Daniel in Church House.[21]

Monuments became progressively bigger over the decades. They were comparatively simple in the 1830s and 1840s, shaped at the top in a manner suggestive of Classical origins with a pediment, until Pugin's Gothic Revival ushered in an era of crosses and pointed headstones. The Battle of the Styles raged on: not to be outdone, the Classicists began building entire temples.

Traditionally, materials consisted of Portland, Bath or York stone (Kensal Green was constructed from Portland stone). Granite became fashionable as the railway links made it possible to deliver the stone from remote areas of Britain. Although expensive, as it had to be polished and dressed, it was favoured for columns and obelisks. The most popular form – grey stone speckled with a 'salt and pepper appearance', came from Bodmin, Cornwall. Then there was pink Peterhead granite from Aberdeen, and Shap from Cumbria, which was red with large feldspar crystals. White Carrara marble, such as that used for the tomb of Julius Beer, was imported from Italy. Carrara is comparatively soft, and lends itself to figurative carving.

As well as the extraordinary diversity of shapes and styles, Victorian monuments possessed their own language of symbols, derived from religious imagery. Some are comparatively easy to decipher if we take into account the pervasive Christian iconography which inspired them. Three steps on a monument signify the three steps to heaven of the aspiring soul; trefoils indicate the Trinity; angels perform the role of guardian, and also that of mourner, harking back to the heraldic tradition of real people paid to weep at the tomb. Then there are the occupational symbols: anchors, scrolls, books. The Classical influence played its part, with broken columns signifying a life interrupted, and urns, derived from the funerary urn of Classical Antiquity. Urns draped with a cloth indicated that the deceased was head of the household, while pyramids, inspired by the Egyptian craze, were said to prevent the devil from lying on one's grave.

Monuments such as the four-poster bed of the Maple family and Tom Sayers's dog Lion at Highgate, and the extraordinary Ducrow Tomb at Kensal Green, contribute to the eclectic appearance of London's Victorian cemeteries, revealing a unique sense of the national character which has sadly been lost today. However, many nineteenth-century commentators were outraged by the flights of fancy to be found in the new cemeteries, considering them to be irreligious. Writing on Glasgow Necropolis in 1857, George Blair observed that the jumble of Doric, Corinthian, Egyptian and Italianate were elegant works of art, but had no religious significance. 'Erect them in any other locality, and their object would be difficult to divine.'[22] Pugin, champion of Gothic Revival in the Battle of the Styles, believed that such designs had no place in Christian burial: 'Surely the Cross must be the most appropriate emblem on the tombs of those who profess to believe in God crucified for the redemption of man?'[23] Pugin despised what he called 'that vile and pagan upstart, sepulchral Baroque', and was scathing on the subject of the new cemeteries, despite the fact that his chosen style had inspired so many of their architects:

> Most people's idea of a cemetery is something associated with great Egyptian lodges and little shabby flower-beds, joint stock companies and immortelles, dissent, infidelity, and speculation, the irreverences of Abney Park or the fripperies and frigidities of Père Lachaise.
>
> The entrance gateway is usually selected for the grand display of the company's enterprise and taste, as being well calculated from its position to induce persons to patronise the undertaking and by the purchase of shares or graves. This is generally Egyptian, probably from some association between the word catacombs, which occurs in the prospectus of the company, and the discoveries of Belzoni on the banks of the Nile; and nearly

opposite the Green Man and Dog public-house, in the centre of a
dead wall (which serves as a cheap medium of advertisement for
blacking and shaving-strop manufacturers); a cement caricature
of the entrance to an Egyptian temple, 2½ inches to the foot, is
erected, with convenient lodges for the policeman and his wife,
and a neat pair of cast iron hieroglyphical gates, which would
puzzle the most learned to decipher; while to prevent any mistake, some such words as 'New Economical Compressed Grave
Cemetery Company' are inscribed in Grecian capitals along the
frieze, interspersed with hawk-headed divinities, and surmounted by a huge representation of the winged Osiris bearing a
gas lamp.[24]

Despite these criticisms, elaborate monuments proved enormously
popular, and working-class families, who could least afford to, continued to lavish money on funerals and memorials. But, even at the
height of the cult of Victorian mourning, other outlooks were
beginning to emerge, which would eventually change attitudes to
death, bereavement and burial.

In 1855, less than ten years after Laman Blanchard's trip to Kensal
Green and his invocation to 'Let these dry bones live', Henry Bowler
exhibited a remarkable painting. It depicts a beautiful young woman
brooding over a tombstone in a country graveyard. Behind her is a
lych-gate; at her side, an ivy-covered church wall. At first glance the
scene is idyllic; sunlight filters through the green chestnut leaves; she
wears a bonnet trimmed with fresh flowers over her golden hair;
only the black shawl covering her red dress gives some indication
that she has, at some point, been in mourning. The tombstone reads:
*Sacred to the Memory of John Faithful 1711–1791* and bears a quotation from the Burial Service in the Anglican *Book of Common Prayer*:
'I am the Resurrection and the Life.' And then the eye is drawn to
the foot of the tombstone, the pile of horse chestnuts and the human
skeletal remains among the clumps of soil. The title of the painting
is: *Doubt – Can These Dry Bones Live? Can*, not *Let*.

Partially inspired by the evolutionary theories of Charles Darwin and Herbert Spencer (the latter was buried at Highgate), the growth of religious doubt led the educated public to challenge the old strictures, including the concept of physical resurrection on Judgement Day. This, in its turn, led to a less reverential, although not irreverent, attitude towards the disposal of the dead. This appeared first among the nobility, who followed the trend for modest funerals set by Prince Albert. Former Prime Minister Benjamin Disraeli requested burial in the chapel of his country house, Hughenden, rather than the interment in Westminster Abbey to which he was entitled. His wishes were observed in 1881. The Anglican Church's Campaign for Mourning Reform lobbied for a more enlightened approach to bereavement and the cost of burial.

In a letter to *The Times,* one member of the House of Lords demanded:

> How long are we to be subjected to the tyranny of custom and undertakers? How long are we to be smothered with overflowing hatbands, scarves, and mourning cloaks, mobbed and overpowered by mutes, ostrich feathers, &c? How long are we to continue to see the remains of some quiet old gentleman or lady, who perhaps never in his or her life sat behind anything more exalted than a small pony, drawn to their last home by four long-tailed black horses, or someone who, having lived unloved, dies unmourned, and is yet attended to his grave by half a dozen hired mourners at 5s per day and beer? Truly, it is all vanity and vexation of spirit – a mere mockery of woe.[25]

Having developed suburban cemeteries, which were more like parks, and railway cemeteries, which helped solve the London burial problem, the Victorians were moving towards another solution to the overcrowded necropolis: cremation.

# 11: UP IN SMOKE

## *The Development of Cremation*

The development of cremation almost completes the circle in the London experience of death. Just as their remote ancestors were immolated in pits outside the city walls, their cremains buried in urns, modern Londoners choose a similar method of burial. The United Kingdom has the sixth highest rate of cremation in the world – after Hong Kong, Singapore, the Czech Republic, Switzerland and Denmark. A number of factors contributed to the development and popularity of cremation, the foremost being the abiding shortage of burial space in and around London.

London's older cemeteries, those little gardens 'dotted as green spots all over the city', which had been closed by the Burial Acts of the 1850s, were disappearing beneath the railway and new buildings.[1] Extensions to the Bank of England, for example, swallowed up an entire parish. Within cemeteries, headstones were shuffled about like chess pieces, with monuments routinely smashed by contractors and the rubble used for foundations. Burial reformer William Robinson reported that broken pieces of monumental stones, some of them bearing names and dates, had been found scattered across a park in South Kensington in the 1860s, dumped by the Victorian equivalent of cowboy builders.

Despite the best efforts of reformers, many London cemeteries remained in a disgusting state. William Robinson, author of *God's Acre Beautiful*, argued that, given the massive profits of certain suburban cemeteries, the temptation to continue burial in them longer than decency or sanitary reasons would allow created a health hazard. 'At Highgate, for example, strong undertakers' men have been made seriously ill while at work by the underflowing drainage from the higher parts of the burial ground.'[2] A letter to the *Lancet* alleged that 'some of the cemeteries within the metropolitan district are rapidly becoming sources of peril not only to the neighbourhoods in which they are situated, but to the whole metropolis.'[3] Considering that the suburban cemeteries had been created to solve the problem of the overflowing city graveyards, the situation was somewhat ironic.

The development of secularism and the decline of organized religion was another important factor in the speed of cremation. Writing in 1896, Mrs Isabella Holmes demanded:

Are we ever to allow England to be divided like a chess-board into towns and burial-places? What we have to consider is how to dispose of the dead without taking so much valuable space from the living. In the metropolitan area alone we have almost filled (and in some places overfilled) twenty-four new cemeteries within sixty years, with an area of above six hundred acres; and this is nothing compared with the huge extent of land used for interments just outside the limits of the metropolis. If the cemeteries are not to expand indefinitely they must in time be built upon, or they must be used for burial over and over again, or the ground must revert to its original state as agricultural land, or we must turn our parks and commons into cemeteries, and let our cemeteries be our only recreation grounds – which Heaven forbid![4]

Mrs Holmes, an enthusiast for cremation as it freed up more land for her beloved public parks, did not find it impossible to reconcile the procedure with her religious beliefs:

> I fail to understand how any serious-minded person can harbour the idea that burning the body can be any stumbling-block in the way of its resurrection, for the body returns 'earth to earth, ashes to ashes, dust to dust' whether the process takes fifty years or fifty minutes.[5]

Being a realist, Mrs Holmes knew that cremation would not gain real credibility until religious leaders such as the Archbishop of Canterbury, the Chief Rabbi and the Head of the Roman Catholic Church in England gave it their blessing.

Ironically, although cremation was a controversial topic during the nineteenth century, the Roman practice of cremation had been well established in London by the first century AD; as we have already seen, Roman cremation practices were easily reconciled with existing British ones. Cremation eventually went out of favour under the influence of the Christian Church, and by AD 500, it was obsolete in Britain. There was a brief revival of interest in the sixteenth century, with the discovery of a series of burial urns near the Roman fort of Brannodunnum in Norfolk. It was this discovery, at what is now Brancaster, which inspired Sir Thomas Browne to metaphysical contemplation. Reflecting that: '*Pyramids, Arches, Obelisks*, were but the irregularities of vain-glory, and wilde enormities of ancient magnanimity,' Browne argues in favour of cremation, if only as an alternative to the disgusting consequences of putrefaction:

> In an Hydropicall body ten years buried in a Church-yard, we met with a fat concretion, where the nitre of the Earth, and the salt and lixivorous liquor of the body, had coagulated large lumps of fat, into the consistence of the hardest castle-soap.[6]

This refers to adipocere or 'grave wax' – the insoluble fatty acids left as a residue of the pre-existing fats of animals, and produced by the slow hydrolysis of the fats in the wet ground. This is generally regarded as Browne's one notable scientific discovery, well in advance of its rediscovery by Fourcroy in the eighteenth century.[7] For Browne, it was 'most natural to end in fire', to be consumed and purified by the most powerful of the elements, rather than undergo a 'visible degradation into worms' and suffer:

> the malice of enemies upon their buried bodies . . . Urnal enterrments, and burnt Reliques lye not in fear of worms, or to be an heritage for Serpents; In carnall sepulture, corruptions seem peculiar unto parts, and some speak of snakes out of the spinal marrow . . .[8]

Cremation was first seriously contemplated in 1664, when it featured in *Philosophical Discourses of the Virtuosi of France*, and had many advocates on the Continent. The first recorded cremation in Britain appears to be that of Honoretta or Henrietta Pratt, a society matron who died aged ninety-three, on 25 September 1769. Honoretta left instructions in her will that 'my Body be burnt upon the place where my late dear niece Ann Place lies buried', which was St George's Churchyard, Hanover Square. However, experts have argued that Honoretta's was likely to have been a 'chemical cremation', accomplished with quicklime rather than fire.[9] The *St James's Chronicle* recorded that 'her corpse was burnt to ashes in the grave by means of unslaked lime', but later records suggest her request was overruled.

In 1816, Joseph Taylor, author of *Danger of Premature Interment*, commended Honoretta as:

> An extraordinary female, whose mind was superior to the weaknesses of her sex, and to the prejudices of custom, being fully sensible, 'that the bodies of the dead might be offensive to the living'.[10]

One of the most famous (or infamous) cremations of the nineteenth century was that of Shelley, who was drowned off the Italian coast in 1822. Shelley's immolation was vividly described, with considerable poetic licence, by Edmund Trelawney in the latter's memoirs. Given the poet's flamboyant personality and atheistic views, one could be forgiven for assuming that Shelley had left instructions for this method of disposal as a dramatic ending to a romantic career, or that the Hellenophiliac Byron had been responsible for the funeral arrangements. In fact, Shelley was cremated in accordance with local by-laws designed to prevent the spread of plague, which ruled that anything washed up by the sea must be burned on the shore.

Shelley's cremains were eventually buried in the Protestant Cemetery at Rome, near the grave of Keats. A volume of Keats's poetry had been found in Shelley's pocket when the body was recovered, the pages doubled back, as though it had been thrust away in a hurry. When Mary Shelley died in 1851, his heart plucked from the flames of his pyre, according to Trelawney, was discovered among her possessions, wrapped in a page of 'Adonais', his lament for Keats.

Shelley was, perhaps, a romantic exception, and Trelawney's grisly account of the scene might not have done the cremation movement any favours. It was to be the middle of the nineteenth century, when Londoners were all too aware of the problems facing overcrowded burial grounds, before cremation received any serious consideration. Loudon had predicted the rise of cremation in 1843, when he observed that it: 'would soon account for the disposal of the great mass of the dead, much sooner than even most enlightened people predict. Every large town will have a funeral pire [sic] constructed on scientific principles, next to the cemetery; and ashes may be preserved in urns, or applied to the roots of a favourite plant.'[11]

By 1850, a paragraph in *The Builder* had noted that:

> ... an association has been formed at the City of London
> Mechanics Institution to promote the practice of decomposing

the dead by the agency of fire. The members propose to burn, with becoming solemnity, such of their dead as shall have left their remains at the dispersal of the Association.[12]

The year of 1869 marked a significant step forward in the acceptance of cremation, after a presentation at the Medical International Congress of Florence by Professors Coletti and Castiglioni 'in the name of public health and civilisation'. Further papers appeared in 1872, with a model of Professor Brunetti of Padua's cremating apparatus, the procedure being conducted in the open, going on display at the Vienna Exposition in 1873. The first serious experiments in early cremation had been carried out by Brunetti in Italy in 1869. Siemens later invented an indoor version. Germany was in the field early, erecting an apparatus in Gotha in 1878.

Between 1887 and 1906, nearly every country in Europe had a crematorium.[13] The French installed 'Gorini' furnaces, using them originally for the destruction of anatomical parts from hospitals and smallpox victims. The first, erected in Paris, disgusted a Parisian commentator, who said it looked like a sewage farm.

Brunetti's cremation apparatus at the Viennese exhibition attracted the attention of Sir Henry Thompson FRCS, surgeon to Queen Victoria, who returned home to become the chief promoter of cremation in England. In 1874, he published *The Treatment of the Body After Death*, in which he promoted cremation on public-health grounds, as 'a necessary sanitary precaution against the propagation of disease among a population daily growing larger in relation to the area it occupied'. He also maintained that cremation reduced funeral expenses, spared mourners from the weather during interments and prevented vandalism. As a further inducement, he suggested the ashes could be used as fertilizer, a pragmatic solution endorsed by Mrs Holmes:

The most advanced cremationists advocate the use of the few remaining ashes as manure for some kinds of farm lands. Sir

Henry Thompson, a cremationist worthy of every honour, has referred to the great increase there would be in the fish supply if burial at sea were generally practised, a plan approved of by some *anti*-cremationists.[14]

Sir Henry offered another incentive. Cremation, he suggested, was the ultimate solution to premature burial, a fate which filled many with genuine alarm. In 1816, Joseph Taylor published *Danger of Premature Interment*, a lurid, sensationalist little book stuffed with anecdotes and apocryphal accounts of people revived after being left for dead: 'proved from many REMARKABLE INSTANCES of People who have recovered after being laid out for dead, and of others entombed alive, for want of being properly exhumed prior to Interment.'

On the title page Taylor dwells with true Gothick relish on the horrors of this unlikely contingency:

To revive nailed up in a Coffin! A return to Life in Darkness, Distraction and Despair! The Brain can scarce sustain the reflection in our coolest moments. Amongst the most dreadful calamities incident to human nature, none sure is more horrid, nor can the thought be more appalling, than even *in idea* to be buried alive – the very soul sickens at the thought.[15]

So widespread was this anxiety that, at a cemetery near Frankfurt designed by Friedrich Rumpf (1795–1867), the architect planned in a mortuary chapel where bodies could be removed immediately after death had presumably taken place, in order that they might be systematically observed until putrefaction had definitely set in. Precautions included placing a bell-rope in the hand of the corpse, so that the person could call for help if they returned to consciousness; and an official was in constant attendance, his duty being to inspect the bodies from time to time.[16]

In 1896, the Association for the Prevention of Premature Burial

*Henry Thompson's cremation method, 1874.*

was founded, designed to safeguard its members by arrangement with medical experts in various localities, who would scientifically certify death in accordance with certain tests laid down by the Association. Writing in support of this movement, Sir W.J. Collins MD, FRCS, said: 'It is morbid sentiment that precludes the adequate consideration of the subject in this country, while it is only too easy to dismiss it with ill-directed jest.'[17]

Collins invited us to 'suppose that a person has passed away'. He no longer breathes, his heart has stopped, and the doctor has pronounced life extinct. Perhaps some test has been applied, such as breathing on glass – a popular method – and there appears to be nothing to be done but arrange the funeral. It would be a shock, then, to be told on the authority of Dr Brouardel, an eminent French physician and former director of the Paris Morgue, that 'the moment of death cannot be assumed to be identical with cessation

231

of respiration' and that 'many persons who no longer breathe have been recalled to life by means of care and skill'. Brouardel recalled the case of a man, executed at Troyes, whose heart continued to beat for an hour after decapitation, the body being accompanied from the scaffold with two doctors who testified to this fact. Brouardel also quoted a case where he had 'exhumed at eight PM Philomele Jonetre, aged twenty-four, buried at five PM, in a grave six feet deep. Several persons heard her tap distinctly against the lid of the coffin.' After being brought round with ammonia, it was clear that the young lady was not dead, but 'like a candle, the flames of which had been extinguished, though the wick continues to glow. No definite sounds of the heart, but the eyelids moved in my presence.'[18]

Cremation, at least, ensured that nobody would 'return to life in Darkness, Distraction and Despair'.

On 13 January 1874, Sir Henry Thompson called a meeting at 35 Wimpole Street, and drew up the following declaration to mark the founding of the Cremation Society of Great Britain:

> We, the undersigned, disapprove the present custom of burying the dead, and we desire to substitute some mode which shall rapidly resolve the body into its component elements, by a process which cannot offend the living, and shall render the remains perfectly innocuous. Until some better method is devised we desire to adopt that generally known as cremation.[19]

Signatories included Ernest Hart, Editor of the *British Medical Journal*, the Pre-Raphaelite painter John Everett Millais, Anthony Trollope and William Robinson, author of *God's Acre Beautiful*. One of the Society's aims was to simplify funerals:

> It cannot be too clearly understood that it is most undesirable to convey the body in a heavy or costly coffin; a light pine shell is the best receptacle for the purpose of cremation. There is no reason why, for the funeral service, a simple shell should not suffice, but

it may be covered with a black cloth at very small expense, if preferred. There is a certain fixed but ample limit for the breadth and depths of this, which is not to be exceeded. When, however, it is intended to hold a funeral service in public, and with some degree of ceremony, before cremation, a more ornate coffin may be used if desired, but it should contain the shell described, which can afterwards be removed. When a funeral service is performed over the ashes after cremation, they should be placed in a casket suitable for the purpose.

A day's notice being given, Messrs Garstin & Sons, the well-known undertakers, of 5, Welbeck Street, Cavendish Square, will provide a shell and remove the body in a hearse from any house or station within the four-mile radius from Charing Cross, to the Society's crematory.[20]

By this simple act, the Cremation Society of England (subsequently of Great Britain) was formed. It was organized 'expressly for the purpose of obtaining and disseminating information on the subject, and for adopting the best method of performing the process, as soon as this could be determined, provided that the act was not contrary to Law.'

The first duty of the Council of the Cremation Society was to ascertain whether cremation was legal in the United Kingdom. After a favourable response from legal experts, the Society decided to buy an appropriate plot of land on which to build a crematorium. The Society was offered a plot in the Great Northern Cemetery (New Southgate), which had its own railway station via a branch line of the Great Northern Railway, and the building would have gone ahead but for the Bishop of Rochester, who forbade the establishment of a crematorium on consecrated land. Instead, a plot was purchased from the London Necropolis Company at Woking, which was ideal, as the Necropolis Company had already established a funeral train service for its own cemetery at Brookwood.

Italian expert Professor Gorini was invited to Britain to supervise the construction of a crematorium, assisted by William Eassie, Honorary Secretary of the Society. On 17 March 1879, the body of a horse was successfully cremated in less than two hours. When he saw how completely the horse had been reduced to ashes, Sir Henry Thompson observed that it indicated how swiftly a human body could be incinerated, without smoke escaping from the chimney.[21]

The residents of Woking, still reeling from the impact of the Brookwood Necropolis, were less than impressed by the idea of a crematorium on their doorstep, and a deputation, led by the vicar, lobbied the Home Secretary, Sir Richard Cross, to ban the development. The Home Secretary was not in a position to ban the construction of a crematorium, but he could threaten to prosecute the society if a cremation was carried out.

The cremationists also had another opponent in the form of Sir Francis Seymour Haden FRCS (1818–1910), inventor of the Earth-to-Earth coffin. Sir Francis was a consultant at the Chapel Royal and one of the founders of the Royal Hospital for Incurables. A stern critic of undertakers, Haden regarded coffins as a pernicious modern invention. It was better to rot.

Haden had proposed the Earth-to-Earth disposable coffin (cardboard or wicker), filled with aromatic herbs and grasses, which would break down quickly and allow the body to decompose faster, meaning the burial ground could be used again. Haden's invention appealed to the London Necropolis Company, since the gravelly soil of Brookwood was particularly suitable for disposable coffins, and the Patent Necropolis Earth-to-Earth Coffin went on display at trade fairs.

In 1885, *The Queen* magazine compared Haden's theories with the famous romantic story of Isabella. Immortalized by Keats, this is the tale of a romantic heroine who carries her dead lover's head around in a pot of basil. 'She might have conveyed her lover's head from place to place without suspicion or offence, for the earth would have converted it into food for the plant that she was so fondly cherishing.' *The Queen* also revealed that a 'sanitarian' had kept a dead dog in an open box in the middle of his sitting room. Covered with earth, within a few weeks the dog had resolved itself into carbolic acid and watery vapour without offence.[22]

Haden was virulently opposed to cremation. He believed it to be wasteful, expensive and polluting. In a series of letters to *The Times* in the 1870s, Haden condemned the proposal:

> to drive into vapour the bodies of the 3,000 people who die weekly in Greater London alone, at a needless cost, an infinite waste and with an effect on the respirable air of the city . . . not to mention the problems of finding somewhere to put 3,000 urns a week.[23]

Haden referred to crematoria as 'vomitaria' and, in *Cremation: An Incentive to Crime* (1892), even tried to argue that, as a result of cremation, murders would go undetected as there would be no body to exhume for a post mortem. Sir Henry Thompson responded to these anxieties with a novel solution. For every corpse that was to be cremated, two carboys (large glass bottles with wicker frames) would be provided, in which the stomach and intestines could be preserved in the event of a post-mortem examination for poison. Haden criticized this in turn, claiming the system was open to abuse and 'as to the sanitary side of the question – the less said about it the better . . .'[24]

From March 1879, the Cremation Society was restricted to lobbying activities, trying to change the public attitude to cremation. The Society received unexpected support from one member of the Anglican Church. Given that the Bishop of Rochester had forbidden the establishment of a crematorium on consecrated ground in Southgate, it was all the more surprising that the Bishop of Manchester advocated the practice in the same year. The Bishop had just consecrated a new Corporation cemetery on the south side of Manchester, but couldn't help thinking two things: first, that this was a long way for the poor to bring their dead; and secondly, 'here is another hundred acres of land withdrawn from the food-producing area of the country for ever.' Land should be for growing food, not burying corpses.

'I hold that the earth was not made for the dead, but for the living. Cemeteries are becoming not only a difficulty, an expense, and an inconvenience, but an actual danger.'[25]

Where Mrs Holmes campaigned for cremation on utilitarian principles, William Robinson, author of *God's Acre Beautiful* published in 1889, advocated 'urn burial' on aesthetic grounds, inviting us to imagine soft, green lawns; acres of ground disturbed only by the burial of ashes, not entire coffins; groves of trees instead of 'hideous vistas of crowded stones'. Cremation was cheap, practical, and did away with 'onerous charges', and the grim spectacle of the Victorian funeral.

Urn burial could be carried out in graveyards the size of the present, overcrowded ones, for hundreds of years without ill-effects to the living. And the result would be to create beautiful gardens, in an extension of Loudon's philosophy, with cemeteries truly becoming, as the Greek roots of the word suggest, sleeping places for the dead.[26]

Cremation also made burial in churches possible once more, without any of the revolting consequences of interring corpses beneath walls or in vaults. The great and the good could be buried at Westminster Abbey again, without it becoming a place of horror. In the unlikely event of a revolution, cremation would at least ensure that the English royal family escaped the fate of the French, as chronicled in the periodical *Vanity Fair*, where one Lord Ronald Gower describes the horrific desecration of the royal tombs at St Denis during the French revolution.[27] This clever piece of anti-Republican propaganda, recycled to endorse the benefits of cremation, is a typical example of modern historian Matthew Sweet's observation that the Victorians turned atrocity into entertainment.

The royal sepulchres of St Denis, located 17 kilometres north of

Paris, were the last resting-place of most of the kings and queens of France. The revolutionaries' 'work' – which consisted of smashing the tombs and throwing the remains into quicklime – commenced in October 1793 and lasted all month. The first corpse to be found was that of Henry IV, the once-beloved Henri de Navarre. Some curiosity, if not affection, for the old King seemed to have lingered among the body snatchers, for they propped him up against the church wall in his shroud, and he became something of an attraction. One of the Republican guards cut off the King's grey moustache and placed it on his own lip. Another man removed the King's beard, saying he would keep it as a souvenir. After this, the body was thrown into a huge pit of quicklime.

The following day, the corpses of Henri IV's wife, Marie de Medicis, his son, Louis XIII and his grandson, Louis XIV, went in to the pit. The body of the Sun King was as black as ink. Louis's wife, and his son, the Dauphin, followed.

Next day, the body of Louis XV's wife, Marie Leczinska, was torn from its resting-place, as were those of the Grand Dauphin, the Duke of Burgundy and his wife, and several other aristocrats, including the daughters of Louis XV. All the bodies were in a dreadful state of decomposition, and in spite of the use of gunpowder and vinegar the stench was so great that many of the workmen were overcome and others had to continue their gruesome task.

By a strange coincidence, on 16 October, the very day that Marie Antoinette was executed at the Place de la Révolution, the body of another unfortunate Queen saw the light of day. The corpse of Queen Henrietta Maria, who had died in 1669, was taken from its coffin and added to the 'ditch of the Valois' as the ghastly pit had been named. That of her daughter, once 'Belle Henriette', came next, and then, in quick succession, those of Philippe d'Orleans, his son, the notorious Regent; his daughter, the no less notorious Duchesse de Berri; her husband and half a dozen infants, from the same family.

That same day, another coffin was cautiously opened. It was

found at the entrance to the royal vault, the customary position for that containing the late deceased King, and contained the remains of Louis *le bien aimé*. The body snatchers hesitated before withdrawing the corpse from its enclosure, remembering that Louis had perished from a terrible illness, and that an undertaker had died as a result of placing the diseased corpse in its coffin. As a result, the body was only removed from its coffin on the brink of the ditch, and hastily rolled over the edge: but not without the precaution of discharging guns and burning powder, and even then the air was putrid far and near.

This was only the beginning. The Republic Resurrectionists, as Gower dubs them, began with the Bourbons and still had to disentomb all the Valois, and further back, up to the Capetian line, and would not be content until the legendary remains of Dagobert and Madame Dagobert reappeared. They continued with the grim work, the corpses appearing like the line of royal ghosts seen by Macbeth: Charles V, who died in 1380, whose well-preserved body was arrayed in royal robes, with a gilt crown and sceptre, still bright; his wife, Jeanne de Bourbon, who still held a decayed distaff of wood in her bony hand; Charles VI, with his Queen, Isabeau de Bavière; Charles VII and his wife, Marie d'Anjou; and then Blanche de Navarre, who died in 1391; Charles VIII, of whom nothing but dust remained; Henri II; Catherine de Medicis; Charles IX – and Henri III.

And so the work went on, till one tires even of the details of the preservation of this or that king and queen. Can anything be more shocking than to know that all the horrors of decay and decomposition will remain even after two or three centuries have passed over the lifeless form, and that, supposing one has the ill luck to be thus coffined and one's body removed, a black fluid emitting a noxious smell will run out from our last home, as was the case with those royal remains during that hot summer month at St Denis in 1793? Who, after reading such instances, can doubt that it is infinitely better that the dead should be quickly resolved into white and odourless ashes than subjected to insult and degradation even much less shocking than the cases mentioned in the foregoing pages?

Despite these arguments, it seemed as if cremation would never become acceptable in Britain. 'Cremation was regarded with repulsion by many, who knew it either mainly as a pagan method of disposing of corpses, or as a method of execution in former times for heretics, witches and female traitors, or as a means by which infanticides (of which there were very many in the nineteenth century) attempted to conceal the evidence of their crime.'[28]

But then, in 1882, the opportunity arrived to put the Society's resources into practice. A Captain Hanham of Blandford, Dorset, asked the Society to cremate two members of his family – his wife, Mrs Hanham, who had died of cancer in July 1876, and his mother, Lady Hanham, who had died in her ninetieth year in June 1877. Both had left specific instructions that they were to be cremated, their objection to burial deriving from grim scenes when coffins in the family mausoleum became waterlogged after flooding.[29]

Once again, the move was blocked by the Home Secretary. He repeated his previous objections and, unable to comply, the Society had no alternative but to decline the Captain's request. But Captain Hanham was not easily deterred. He promptly built his own crematorium on his estate, and proceeded to cremate his wife and mother on 8 and 9 October 1882. Since death, the bodies had remained in elm coffins, in lead shells, in the family mausoleum. When the time came, the coffins were placed in a simple and inexpensive furnace, on a platform of firebricks and iron, which allowed the flames to play freely, but without the ashes falling into the furnace. The elm coffins had to be burned first, requiring greater heat and more time than usual. The lead melted and ran through the furnace into the ashpits, and the white flames played round the strong elm shell, until that fell at a white heat over the body, of which, about an hour later, only the ashes remained.

Hanham wrote that the cremations were carried out:

without any nuisance to the neighbourhood and without the slightest unpleasantness to those who stood within two feet of the white flames which promptly resolved the bodies to their harmless elements ... the act was well and quickly done in each instance, nothing being left but perfectly calcinated bones. The fragments of the larger ones looked like frosted silver, and they broke at a touch. I gathered the ashes of each body and placed them in a large china bowl, in which they will remain until urns of an improved form are ready; then they will be moved to the mausoleum among the trees on the lawn.

Compared with the contents of such Roman and other urns as I have seen, the ashes are greater in amount and much more perfectly preserved. This was owing to complete and quick combustion, and to the body being kept from direct contact with the fire. Every part of the bony structure is represented in the ashes, but without any definite form which would make them recognizable to any but experts. In size the remains vary from pieces 1½ inch long to ashes and fine dust.[30]

A year later, the Captain died, and he too was cremated. Despite frenzied speculation in the press, the Home Secretary took no action.

However, events took an extraordinary turn twelve months later, when a Dr William Price, 'the Welsh Wizard', attempted to cremate the body of his five-month-old son, Jesu Grist Christ, high on a hill above Llantrisant, ten miles north-west of Cardiff.[31] Claiming to be a Druid, Price, aged eighty-three, performed the rites dressed in a white tunic. He placed the petrol-soaked body in a barrel and lit a fire, which was clearly visible from the road. Horrified onlookers summoned the police. One officer tipped the barrel over so that the body could be removed, and another man dragged it some twenty yards, where it could be covered with turf.

Dr Price went on trial at the Glamorgan Assizes in Cardiff, charged with cremating rather than burying his son. This was not

Price's first time before the Bench. An outspoken Welsh Nationalist and former Chartist, he was more than capable of holding his own in court.[32] Price was fortunate in his judge. Mr Justice Stephen, on his first circuit in Wales, had a progressive outlook and 'objected to the criminal law being used to crush opinion'.[33] In February 1884, Mr Justice Stephen made a groundbreaking pronouncement ruling that cremation was *legal*, provided no nuisance was caused to others in the process: 'The burning of the dead has never been formally forbidden, or even mentioned or referred to, so far as I know, in any part of our law.'

Dr Price was acquitted, much to Stephen's delight: 'He was the strangest old creature, calling himself a Druid and an Archpriest . . . I was quite glad to let the old man off. It would have been such a pity to interfere with the last of the Druids.'[34]

Price attempted to claim damages against the police for preventing his son's cremation, but was only awarded the nominal sum of one farthing.

Mr Justice Stephen's ruling was the development the Cremation Society had been waiting for. Fortified by the Cardiff judgment, the Council of the Cremation Society circulated a document, informing the public that it was now prepared to proceed with the cremation of anyone requesting it.

However, the Society could not leave itself open to criticism. Sir Henry drafted three legal forms which had to be completed before a body would be accepted for cremation at Woking; these were designed to prevent the cremation of anyone who might have died under suspicious circumstances. Despite these precautions, the Council of the Cremation Society appreciated that official regulation was desirable and, on 30 April 1884, Dr Charles Cameron, Member for Glasgow, introduced a Bill into the House of Commons 'to provide for the regulation of cremation and other means of disposal of the dead'. Dr Cameron was supported by Dr Farquharson, the Member for Aberdeen (another member of the Council), and the eminent surgeon Sir Lyon Playfair.

The Bill was opposed, however, not only by the Government but also the Leader of the Opposition. One hundred and forty-nine members voted against it, but the seventy-nine votes in favour were more than the promoters had dared hope for.

Meanwhile, the first cremation at Woking took place on 26 March 1885, using the Gorini furnace. According to Puckle:

> In its perfect state, a light pine shell is provided in which the body reposes wrapped in a flannel shroud. The coffin is placed on a platform during the funeral service, at the conclusion of which, a mechanism set in motion by a lever in the chapel, carries the coffin out of sight of those present on its way to the furnace, where coffin and body are soon reduced to ashes by the intensity of the heat. To burn a special form of furnace-coke in a forced draught is a very different and much less costly matter than the old method of burning wood, as used by the ancients. If a sufficient demand existed to keep the modern type of furnace at the proper temperature, the cost of a cremation need not exceed half a crown.[35]

A Mrs Pickersgill was the first of three cremations that year. Mr Charles William Carpenter was cremated on 19 October and, in December, the body of a fourteen-stone woman was cremated in just one and a half hours.

During 1888, when twenty-eight cremations were carried out, the Society appealed for funds to build a chapel, waiting rooms and other amenities at Woking. Despite a subscription list graced by the Dukes of Bedford and Westminster, the appeal raised only £1,500. At this point, the Duke of Bedford sponsored the construction of the buildings, the purchase of further land and the creation of a thirteenth-century Gothic-style chapel, which was completed in 1891. By 1892, 253 cremations had been carried out and the cremation movement had been successfully launched in Britain.

In 1892, a second English crematorium opened in Manchester,

with the next opening in Liverpool in 1896. Under an arrangement with the Necropolis Railway Company, up to fifty bodies a day were leaving Westminster Bridge Road for the final journey to Woking. However, Londoners still needed a crematorium closer to home.

In 1900, the Council of the Cremation Society purchased 12 acres of land adjacent to Hampstead Heath for £6,000. Backed by a £4,000 bank loan, the Council of the Society assisted in the formation of a company by taking 2,000 ordinary shares of £1. In October, 1900, the London Cremation Company was formed, with the object of establishing a crematorium on the new site.[36]

The design of the new crematorium offered an architectural and artistic challenge. Existing crematoria were either 'ecclesiastical or lamely Gothic'.[37] As the showcase of the cremation movement, Golders Green had to be as beautiful as the great Victorian cemeteries it would, in part, replace. 'Visitors would wish to take leave of their loved ones in appropriate surroundings, and the architectural style was of crucial importance in creating the ambience. While reassurance was important, so was grandeur and dignity; it was a delicate balance. While committed supporters of cremation looked for a dignified and glorious departure, sceptics might look for reassurance.'[38]

Sir Ernest George and Alfred Yeates were commissioned to design the buildings, which were constructed on a piecemeal basis as financial constraints allowed, i.e. a columbarium (a vault having niches for funeral urns) was built in 1911; a 240-foot cloister in 1914; a second columbarium in 1916 and a second chapel, in 1938. George's architectural style was the perfect solution to the design conundrum. George was a RIBA Gold Medal winner, 'one of the most prolific and respected of late-Victorian architects'.[39] He favoured the 'Lombardic' school, derived from an influential Northern Italian style characterized by rounded arches, warm red-brick, terracotta and marble. George had designed many country houses in this style, as well as townhouses in Kensington inspired by old Dutch and Flemish designs. Today, 'Lombardic' seems not so much Italianate as Londonish, in its slightly oppressive grandeur. The Italianate references are very different from those of Kensal Green or Highgate; there is no hint of Highgate's Graveyard Gothic or Kensal Green's Elysian Fields. Instead, the atmosphere is substantial, sombre, and as prosperous as a rose-red mansion block in a crescent behind Harrod's.

In practical terms, Lombardic offered the ideal way of incorporating the crematorium chimney into the design, an essential item 'which did not group happily with either Greek temples, Renaissance domes or Gothic chapels'.[40] Bells were even hung in the tower for a further note of authenticity.

William Robinson laid out the gardens according to the criteria of his book *God's Acre Beautiful*. His picturesque, Pre-Raphaelite gardening aesthetic favoured oaks, cedars and fir, with 'crematoria located away from the garden cemetery itself, tastefully designed, screened by trees, adorned with creeper, rose trellises, sweetbriar or honeysuckle'.[41]

In 1901, the first municipal crematorium in Great Britain was opened in Hull. This was a significant development for the Cremation Society. Hitherto, private individuals were, of their own accord or acting through the medium of the Society, responsible for combating prejudice against cremation, and for establishing existing crematoria. Now, for the first time, a local authority had acknowledged how important it was, both socially and economically, to provide cremation services for the community.

The following year saw an even more crucial event. In 1902, an Act of Parliament was passed, for the Regulation of Burning of Human Remains, and to Enable Burial Authorities to Establish Crematoria. Cremation had finally achieved governmental regulation and had become officially recognized in the highest quarters.[42]

In November of the same year, Golders Green Crematorium was officially opened by Sir Henry Thompson. The crematorium soon became a roll call of the great and good, and was particularly popular with progressive and artistic individuals, including George Bernard Shaw, H.G. Wells, (cremated here, but his ashes scattered at sea), Rudyard Kipling, Gustav Holst and Ralph Vaughan Williams, and scientists Sir Alexander Fleming and Lord Rutherford. Sir Henry himself, who died on 18 April 1904, was cremated here, and a statue erected to his memory in the chapel.

Golders Green is a remarkable architectural achievement, combining a timeless appearance with a modern function. As its architectural historian Hilary J. Grainger has written 'From the road, the crematorium looks like a collection of interesting buildings, behind a high wall, while, from the garden front it resembles a cloistered monastery, fitting into the landscape with all the natural ease of such buildings . . . the cloister recalls, appropriately, the monasteries which also aimed to provide space for contemplation and silent prayer for individuals and communities simultaneously.'[43]

In its extension of the Roman practice of cremation, and the imitation of the mediaeval cloister, Golders Green forms another link in the chain of London and the dead. Like the pagans and Romans, the dead are buried out of town, in urns, high on a hill, while the Italianate architecture recalls the role of the Church in burial during the Middle Ages. But, even as the magnificent cloister was being constructed in 1914, London's treatment of the dead, and the London way of death was to change for ever.

# 12: OUR DARKEST HOURS

*World War and the Decline of Mourning*

Looking back at the First World War from a distance of sixty years, art historian Gavin Stamp wrote:

> Over one million, one thousand members of the British Empire perished in the First World War; over eight million men died worldwide. The tropes and traditions of nineteenth-century mourning were inappropriate to a loss of such magnitude. It fell to the architects to put into tangible and symbolic form the sense of tragedy felt by survivors.[1]

One of the most painful aspects of the war was that the bereaved were left without a body to bury. Almost half the British dead were posted Missing, leaving their families with the agonized hope that they might one day return – alternating with the bitter knowledge that their remains were lost in the mud of France. Rupert Brooke's meditation from his poem 'The Soldier' (1914), *That there's some corner of a foreign field/That is forever England* was of little comfort to a grieving widow, left with no coffin to follow and no gravestone to visit. In many cases, when bodies *had* been identified, it would have been impossible to return them. Mutilated by shells, the dead were buried where they fell, often to be disinterred by further enemy action.

In previous campaigns, only the bodies of officers were returned for burial. The rank and file casualties of Waterloo and the Crimea had been interred in mass graves. It was not until the American Civil and Franco-Prussian wars that the concept of military cemeteries for all participants developed.

Another complication was a refusal by the British Government to allow families to disinter remains from France and bring them home for reburial. The official line was that such an action affected morale, and that all ranks – officers *and* men – should be buried together as comrades.

By 1915, it was already clear to the authorities that the sheer scale of casualties demanded an organized scheme of burial. The War Office created a Graves Registration Commission headed by Fabian Ware (1869–1948), a former colonial administrator, devoted to locating and burying the dead. Originally run by the Red Cross but later transferred to the Army, the Commission negotiated with the French and Belgian governments about the grant of land for cemeteries once the war ended. In 1917, the Imperial War Graves Commission was established to care for all the graves of members of the Imperial forces who died in conflict throughout the British Empire. Ware sent the British architects Sir Edwin Lutyens (1869–1944) and Sir Herbert Baker (1862–1946) to view the battle zone and make recommendations.

Lutyens, a humane and cultured man, was profoundly affected by what he found in France. In 1917, he wrote:

What humanity can endure, suffer, is beyond belief. The battle-fields – the obliteration of human endeavour, achievement, and the human achievement of destruction, is bettered by the poppies and the wild flowers – that are as friendly to an unexploded shell as they are to the leg of a garden seat in Surrey. It is all a sense of

wonderment how can such things be. The graveyards, haphaz-
ard from the needs of much to do and little time for thought –
and then a ribbon of isolated graves like a Milky Way across
miles of country, where men were tucked in where they fell –
Ribbons of little crosses each touching each other across a cemetery – set in a wilderness of annuals – and where one sort of
flower has grown the effect is charming, easy, and oh so pathetic,
that one thinks no other monument is needed.[2]

Given the scale of the carnage, a more permanent monument was
required than this charmingly pastoral Milky Way. As Gavin Stamp
has noted, although human life during the First World War seemed
as expendable as shells, each life was eventually to receive a permanent memorial in stone. Before the Great War, Britain had few
memorials compared with Germany and France. While Berlin and
France had numerous nineteenth-century military memorials,
London, wrote Stamp, 'merely has a square and a bridge named
after battles'. The First World War, however, inspired memorials
on a colossal scale, in the Neo-classical tradition of Inigo Jones and
Sir Christopher Wren and the Napoleonic monuments of France.
Even when the memorials incorporate the Christian symbol, as in
the Cross of Sacrifice – originally designed by Sir Reginald
Blomfield for the Commonwealth War Graves Commission and a
familiar sight at cemeteries – they are essentially pagan, marking
the cultural link between the heroes of the Ancient World and the
doomed youth of the First World War, sent to their deaths steeped
in the Classical ideal of sacrifice.

In his role of Principal Architect for France for the War Graves
Commission, Lutyens oversaw the creation of 126 cemeteries, and
designed the Great War Stone or Stone of Remembrance placed in
all cemeteries, with its quotation chosen by Kipling (who lost a son
in the war), from *Ecclesiasticus:*

*Their Name Liveth for Evermore.*

In Britain, Lutyens's most famous contribution was the Cenotaph. When the Prime Minister, Lloyd George, commissioned him to design a national memorial for the Peace celebrations in July 1919, the architect came up with the 'Cenotaph' or 'empty tomb'. Originally a wood and plaster construction, bearing the legend THE GLORIOUS DEAD, it was only intended to be temporary – but at its unveiling, it provoked such a strong response from the public that it was spontaneously covered in wreaths to the dead and missing. Lutyens recreated the Cenotaph in Portland stone in 1920, and it still forms the centre of the Remembrance Day Service, held on the Sunday closest to Armistice Day (11 November) every year, and attended by heads of state and representatives of the armed and auxiliary services who gave their lives in both world wars and other conflicts.

The following year, the funeral and burial of The Unknown Soldier represented one attempt to commemorate the millions who died unidentified and to assuage the grief of their families.[3] This extraordinary event harked back to the heraldic funeral in its sombre pomp and circumstance. On one level, it may be seen as an exercise in top-dressing – a cynical attempt to manipulate the sorrow and pain of the British public; but it was also unique in the annals of great London funerals in that it saw an unknown man suddenly elevated to the status of a war hero.

In 1916, the Reverend David Railton was serving as a chaplain to British forces at the Front, when in a garden at Armentières one day, he noticed a makeshift grave, marked by a rough cross, on which somebody had written: AN UNKNOWN BRITISH SOLDIER. He never forgot this sight and, four years later, wrote to the Dean of Westminster, Dean Ryle, describing the scene. As a result, the Dean decided that an unknown casualty should be buried in the nave of Westminster Abbey. Four bodies were disinterred from the four different battlefields of Aisne, the Somme, Arras and Ypres, and taken to St Pol in northern France on 7 November 1920. Brigadier General L.J. Wyatt, Commander of All British Troops in France and Flanders, entered the chapel where the bodies lay, each covered with a Union flag. He chose at random one casualty to become The Unknown Soldier of the Great War, and the body was placed in a coffin and sealed. The remaining bodies were reburied at a nearby military cemetery.

The following morning, a service was conducted to commemorate the sacrifice of The Unknown Soldier, officiated by Anglican, Roman Catholic and Non-conformist chaplains. The body was then escorted to Boulogne under a French honour guard, drawn by a wagon with six horses and followed by a mile-long procession. On 9 November 1920, the plain coffin was sealed inside another, constructed of oak from Hampton Court, and secured with a sixteenth-century Crusader's sword from the Tower of London. The coffin plate read: A BRITISH WARRIOR WHO FELL IN THE GREAT WAR 1914–1918 FOR KING AND COUNTRY.

Escorted by six warships, the coffin travelled to Dover on the HMS *Verdun*, and was greeted by a nineteen-gun salute. Six Warrant Officers from the Royal Navy, Royal Marines, Royal Air Force and the Army bore the coffin to be taken by train to Victoria Station, in London. Six barrels of Yprès soil accompanied The Unknown Soldier back to England, so that he might lie on the soil where so many of his comrades had lost their lives.

On the morning of 11 November 1920, Armistice Day, six black horses drew the carriage of The Unknown Soldier through the streets of London, pausing at the Mall, Whitehall, where King George V unveiled the new Cenotaph. The King, his three sons, members of the royal family and Ministers of State then followed the coffin through the streets to the north entrance of Westminster Abbey.

At the west end of the nave, The Unknown Soldier was laid to rest after passing through an honour guard that consisted of 100 recipients of the Victoria Cross. Following the hymn 'Lead, Kindly Light', George V sprinkled soil from the battlefield of Yprès. After the coffin had been lowered, the congregation sang 'Abide with Me' and Kipling's 'Recessional' ('Lest we forget, lest we forget'). Reveille and Last Post were sounded, and the grave covered with a silk funeral pall.

The tomb remained open for the next seven days, as thousands of mourners passed by to pay their last respects. According to the *Daily Mail*:

> *Most impressive of all was the night scene in Whitehall. The vast sweep of the road was almost silent save for the ceaseless murmur of footsteps. Under the brilliant glare of the lamps that were softened by the foggy air, the long, dark lines of people stretched from Trafalgar Square to the Cenotaph, from whose base they could be seen vanishing in the distance, two narrow lines of slowly moving people separated by a wide pathway on which stood here and there vague figures of policemen on horseback.*[4]

On 18 November, the tomb was sealed with a temporary stone bearing the words: A BRITISH WARRIOR WHO FELL IN THE GREAT WAR 1914–1918 FOR KING AND COUNTRY. GREATER LOVE HATH NO MAN THAN THIS. A year later, on 11 November 1921, the tomb was sealed forever with a slab of black Belgian marble.

During the First World War, over 3,305 merchant ships were lost, together with a total of over 17,000 lives. At Tower Hill, Lutyens's *Memorial* commemorates the '. . . men of the Merchant Navy and Fishing Fleets who gave their lives to preserve the life of the nation and have no grave but the sea.' It stands on the south side of the garden of Trinity Square. Built of Portland stone, it consists of a vaulted corridor, 21.5 metres long, 7 metres wide and 7 to 10 metres high, open at either end. The names of the dead are arranged alphabetically under their ships, with the name of Master or Skipper first. Unveiled by Queen Mary on 12 December 1928, it commemorates 11, 919 names and bears the following inscription:[5]

1914–1918
## TO THE GLORY OF GOD AND TO THE HONOUR OF TWELVE THOUSAND OF THE MERCHANT NAVY AND FISHING FLEETS WHO HAVE NO GRAVE BUT THE SEA

By the end of the war, every town, city and village in Britain had its war memorial, a collective expression of grief which replaced the individual graves that war had made impossible. In London, the cemeteries reflected the carnage of 1914–18. At Highgate, the Cross of Sacrifice of the Commonwealth War Graves Commission commemorates 310 dead from both world wars, of whom 95 have unmarked graves which are commemorated on the Screen Wall memorials; 53 graves are marked by Commission headstones and 162 are private memorials.[6]

In 1917, by arrangement with the Brookwood Necropolis Company and the War Office, an area of Brookwood Cemetery was set aside as a military cemetery for the burial of soldiers, sailors and nurses who died in the London Military District.

The design of Brookwood Military Cemetery is similar to that used by the Commonwealth War Grave Commission elsewhere in the world: the large Cross of Sacrifice, with its bronze Crusader's sword (designed by Sir Reginald Blomfield), and Lutyens's Stone of Remembrance. Brookwood, uniquely, contains two sets of these features. All headstones are of a uniform size and design. The top includes the national emblem or the service or regimental badge; this is followed by the rank, name, unit, date of death and age, if known. There appears the appropriate religious emblem, and, in many cases, an inscription chosen by relatives.[7]

As well as the United Kingdom (602 burials) men and women of the forces of the Commonwealth were buried here, as well as Americans who had died, many of battle wounds, in London. Siegfried Sassoon, who had witnessed the horrors of war at first hand, condemned war memorials as 'a pile of peace complacent stone, a sepulchre of crime'.[8] But, as Stamp argues, these memorials were not mere imperial bombast. There is nothing triumphalist here, among the silent acres of graves. Even on the brightest of spring days, Brookwood's military cemeteries are a sombre sight. The vista of plain white headstones lining up into the distance reflects the terrible nature of war, while individual accounts testify to heroism and sacrifice.

At the outset of the First World War, mourning traditions were still strictly upheld among the lower middle and working classes. The social anthropologist Geoffrey Gorer recalled that 'the parade of funerals – horsedrawn, of course, with black plumes and all the trimmings – was a consistent feature of street life; and we children had to keep an eye out for them and take off our hats or caps for the whole time that the funeral procession passed us; it was very *rude* not to.'[9] In 1915, Gorer's father had been killed on the *Lusitania*, heroically, after giving up first his seat in a lifeboat, and then his lifebelt, to two female passengers. Gorer had black crape armbands stitched to his sleeves, but, when his mother came to visit him at school, she was: 'A tragic, almost a frightening figure in the full panoply of widow's weeds and unrelieved black, a crape veil shrouding her (when it was not lifted) so that she was visibly withdrawn from the world.'[10] At first, Mrs Gorer was conspicuous in her widow's weeds – but not for long. By the summer of 1915, widows in mourning became increasingly numerous in the streets. 'Mother no longer stood out from the crowd.' Almost every family was affected by the death or wounding of a relative or friend; of the young men of every class, a generation disappeared for ever.

By 1918, a reporter for the *Illustrated London News* was lamenting the dress code at a private view of a Royal Academy Exhibition:

Over all social functions war has thrown its blight, and such 'fixtures' as continue are bereft of most of the oldtime glory . . . This year not one solitary costume was in any way remarkable. Where is there not a person who is not suffering family and financial losses that make display and frivolous expense seem folly . . . In the hall I met a peeress – one of the richest women in England – but a bereaved mother wearing an old-fashioned black satin dress made with a train to lie a few inches on the ground.[11]

The old traditions were being eroded by the war, which put civilians on the front line for the first time and made mourning dress expensive and impractical – particularly for women, who were being pressed into service in almost every occupation. With their lives in danger on the Home Front, they had little time for the Victorian paraphernalia of 'warm black crape'.

The first Zeppelin raid on London, on 31 May 1915, killed twenty-eight people and injured over sixty. By 1916, 550 Britons had been killed in Zeppelin raids. Propaganda posters urged:

IT IS FAR BETTER TO FACE THE BULLETS
THAN TO BE KILLED AT HOME BY A BOMB.
JOIN THE ARMY AT ONCE
AND HELP STOP AN AIR RAID.

On 26 August 1916, young Margaret McMillan and her sister Rachel were bombed by a Zeppelin in London. Margaret glanced out through her bedroom window to see 'something bright and sparkling in the sky'. While the girls stared, fascinated, their friends ran upstairs to warn them. 'It's a Zeppelin, dropping bombs!' As they rushed downstairs, the house was struck by a terrific blast, and an explosion shook the building to its foundations. Looking up, Margaret realized her sister was still upstairs. She called as Rachel appeared on the landing, carrying blankets. Rachel just had time to escape before a third crash blew out all the windows.

Proximity to such exciting, if terrifying events, made it clearer than ever that the majority of women would not shrink back into heavy Victorian mourning. As the war progressed, it became impossible to observe the niceties of traditional grief. Labour shortages caused by recruitment and conscription sent women out to work, many for the first time in their lives, in hitherto male bastions such as munitions factories, mines and railways, fire stations and the police. Others were nursing, or running charities. Geoffrey Gorer's widowed mother, for instance, trained as a physiotherapist.

This potential army of widows had no time for the archaic seclusion demanded by Victorian convention, and they were reluctant to act as if their lives were over for good. 'The holocaust of young men had created such an army of widows; it was no longer socially realistic for them all to act as though their emotional and sexual life were over for good, which was the underlying message of the ritual mourning.'[12]

For all its horror, the First World War brought women of all classes a degree of social and sartorial freedom which they would be reluctant to relinquish when Peace arrived. Clothing became practical, or 'mannish'; jewellery was military, with a trend for wearing the regimental badge of one's deceased husband or sweetheart as a mark of respect. Public morale was another issue: the last thing young men wanted to see, when they returned from the Front, was thousands of women swathed in black from head to foot. After 1919, the sales of Courtaulds black crape went into irreversible decline. The Great Victorian funeral suffered the same decline, as almost every available man, and horse, was sent to the Front. And the appearance of funerals had been changing before the war started. On 1 January 1914, the British Undertakers' Association was urging 'the trade' to discontinue the practice of placing plumes on horses' heads as it caused 'unnecessary suffering'.[13]

As the First World War drew to its close, and exhausted soldiers made their way home, the spirit of death still hovered above London. Another, even more terrible enemy emerged, deadlier than the cholera epidemics which had laid waste the city between 1832 and 1849.

The first symptoms – headaches, loss of appetite – had appeared in the trenches in early 1918, but most patients made a swift recovery within three days. Doctors referred to the virus as 'Three Day Fever', and the soldiers called it 'Spanish Flu', except in Spain, where it became 'French Flu'.[14] Its origins were vague, but it was commonly supposed to have started in China, India or the Middle East, the very spots where bubonic plague, with its variants of pneumonia and septicaemia, had originated, centuries earlier.

The Great War spread the virus around the globe. Soldiers from Britain, the United States, Canada and Australia arrived in France for the first time, and took it home with them. Cases began to appear in London, but patients quickly recovered.

However, in the summer of 1918, as families welcomed their sons home and victory celebrations broke out, 'flu patients succumbed to bronchial pneumonia or septicaemia. Others developed 'heliotrope cyanosis', a dusky blue-grey pallor indicating that they were suffocating from a build-up of fluid and cells in their lungs. They began to die.

The epidemic spread fast. In Germany, over 400,000 civilians died in 1918, dealing a critical blow to their war effort. The first cases arrived in Britain in May 1918, appearing first in Glasgow. Over the following months, 228,000 people died: the highest mortality rate since the cholera outbreak of 1849. London, still recovering from the disruption of the war, could not deal with the epidemic. Ship after ship arrived at the docks, bringing more victims. Hospitals overflowed, although doctors could do little to save their patients. One of the most shocking aspects of the Spanish Flu was that, like its predecessors the Black Death and the Plague, it struck with terrifying speed. Victims could be fine at breakfast and dead by teatime.

In desperate attempts to contain the virus, streets were sprayed with disinfectant, and some people started wearing medical masks. Factories encouraged their workers to smoke, on the grounds that it prevented infection. Eventually, the disease ran its course, but not before it had killed 30–40 million worldwide: more people than the First World War.

Exhausted by war and pestilence, the English were losing their faith. The certainties which had governed High Victorian mourning were gone. An entire generation had been swept away. Death was as random, and terrifying, as it had been in mediaeval London, but with none of the consolations of piety. It was no longer possible to believe that death was swallowed up in victory.

By the 1930s, elaborate funerals had fallen out of favour among the upper and middle classes. The Earl Marshall's orders on the death of King George V in 1936 shortened the official mourning period from one year to nine months, and *Vogue* magazine directed its readers to steer clear of ostentatious mourning dress for the King, unless they were directly connected with the royal family.

In the East End, however, the full pomp and pageantry of funerals was still very much alive, as the funeral of Charlie Brown demonstrated.[15] Charlie had been landlord of the most famous pub in the East End, the Railway Tavern, located on the corner of Garford Street in Limehouse, near the West India Dock. The pub was hugely popular with sailors and dockers, and Charlie Brown, 'the uncrowned King of Limehouse', was a larger-than-life character. According to East End historian Arthur Royall, Charlie was a flamboyant individual with a broken nose, a legacy from his boxing days. Always immaculately dressed, he was often seen out riding; unusually, for a pub landlord, he kept a stable of horses. Known for his charity work, and proud to be a Life Governor of the London Hospital, what really made Charlie famous was his passion for collecting. Displayed in his pub were Ming vases, carved ivory, mysterious medical monstrosities in glass jars, opium pipes and human skulls. Toffs and swells from Up West visited regularly to sample this slice of East End life.

When Charlie died at the age of seventy-two in 1932, his funeral was one of the most celebrated in the East End. The Church of St Peter, Garford Street, was standing room only. Mourners included the Mayor of Poplar and civic leaders. Outside, street vendors were selling pictures. Long before the cortège was due to set off at half-past two, thousands had gathered near the Railway Tavern. The local paper reported that: 'K Division supplied a large force of police, but their duties were light, as the crowds were orderly and respectful. All the neighbouring premises show signs of mourning in one way or another. Seldom is such a general manifestation of respect and regard shown.' People lined the pavements along the route to Tower Hamlets Cemetery six deep, with huge crowds at West India Dock Road and Burdett Road. Three coaches filled with flowers followed the hearse, along with three mourning coaches and dozens of private cars. The cortège took twenty minutes to pass the Eastern Hotel. In the cemetery, the path to the grave was packed with people, and the police had difficulty making room for the cortège.

This tradition was upheld nearly fifty years later by the Krays, one of the East End's most notorious gangster families. In October 2000, Reggie Kray's elaborate send-off had all the hallmarks of a great Victorian funeral. Local shops closed as a mark of respect. Over 100,000 mourners lined the route along Bethnal Green Road, with heads bowed, as six black-plumed horses drew his hearse, decked with flowers reading FREE AT LAST. Well-wishers gathered outside St Matthew's Church over two hours before the service, and the pavement was covered with wreaths. Afterwards, the cortège made its way to Chingford Mount Cemetery, where the coffin was placed in the family plot, alongside his twin, Ronnie, and their older brother, Charlie.

The good old-fashioned East End funeral appears to have survived the vicissitudes of time and fashion and become a national institution. At the end of 2005, a beloved matriarch in *EastEnders* specified just such a send-off, suggesting that, in some quarters at least, the Victorian funeral is alive and well.

If the First World War put civilian Londoners on the front line, it was nothing compared with the impact of World War Two. The first bomb to fall on London during the Second World War was dropped by accident. On 25 August 1940, the German pilots were aiming for aircraft factories in south London, but hit the City by mistake. The bomb landed near St Alban's Church in Wood Street, beside the Roman wall that had once formed part of London's ancient fortifications, sadly, it provided no defence against death from the air.

Although Londoners had endured Zeppelin raids during the First World War, nothing had prepared them for the Blitz (from the German, *Blitzkrieg* – 'lightning war') – an intense period of bombing which was to last for the next nine months. In July 1940, preparing to invade Britain, the Luftwaffe had bombed RAF airfields and radar stations. Then Hitler, forced to put his invasion plans on hold, and incensed by British raids on Berlin, resolved to destroy London.

'If you could knock out London, you could knock out England,' the historian Philip Ziegler once said. 'You could almost knock out Western Europe.'[16] Hitler believed destroying London would demoralize the population and force the British to surrender.

At 4 p.m. on 7 September 1940, 348 German bombers, escorted by 617 fighter planes, swarmed over London. Their mission was to hit hard and move on. They flew up the Thames, heading for the commercial and industrial districts of Docklands and the East End. The raid lasted until 6 p.m., and then, two hours later, guided by the burning buildings bombed on the first assault, a second group of raiders began another attack which lasted until 4.30 a.m. the following morning. Concentrated on the City and central London, the raid left 430 people dead. Woolwich Arsenal and the Docks were ablaze, with an intense smell of burning pepper, wheat and sugar coming from the warehouses, where cans of paint and barrels of rum exploded.

London was bombed day and night for the next fifty-seven days. In the worst single incident, 450 people were killed when a bomb destroyed a school being used as an air-raid shelter. The city blazed as it had not done since 1666. Churches, offices, entire rows of houses were ravaged by scores of fires which made nighttime bright as day. The sounds of whining sirens, booming explosions, crackling flames and grinding aircraft engines filled the air as batches of incendiary bombs fell in pinpoints of dazzling white. By mid-October, over 250,000 people had been made homeless.

On 29 December 1940, another raid devastated the City but, unlike 1666, St Paul's Cathedral escaped. 'If there was one building in London that symbolized the determination of a Londoner to stand fast, I think it was St Paul's,' said Philip Ziegler. 'The most dramatic of all the Blitz images is that wonderful picture of the dome of St Paul's silhouetted against a wall of flames.'[17] The scene was brilliantly described by the American war correspondent Ernie Pyle:

> St Paul's was surrounded by fire, but it came through. It stood there in its enormous proportions – growing slowly clearer and clearer, the way objects take shape at dawn; it was like a picture of some miraculous figure that appears before peace-hungry soldiers on a battlefield.
>
> The streets below us were semi-illuminated from the glow. Immediately above the fires the sky was red and angry, and overhead, making a ceiling in the vast heavens, there was a cloud of smoke all in pink, and up in that pink shrouding there were tiny, brilliant specks of flashing light-aircraft shells bursting . . . the barrage balloons were standing out as clearly as if it were daytime, but now they were pink instead of silver. And now and then through a hole in that pink shroud there twinkled, incongruously a permanent, genuine star – the old-fashioned kind that has always been there.[18]

Although St Paul's survived, the following famous buildings were damaged: the House of Commons, Westminster Abbey, the Law Courts, the Guildhall, the British Museum, the Royal Mint and the Tower of London, as were fourteen Wren churches. Parts of

London were simply wiped out. 'The East End and Docklands had been shattered. The great fire-bombs, in particular, had swept away whole streets, whole areas. All over London there were huge holes where formerly fine houses had stood.'[19] The writer Graham Greene recalled his shock at seeing a house in Woburn Square 'neatly sliced in half', where 'a grand piano cocked one leg over the abyss'; an approaching bomber was 'muttering like a witch in a child's dream, "Where are you? Where are you? Where are you?"' Greene's Queen Anne house in Clapham was destroyed, and the signed first editions of his own books looted; he later had to buy them back from Sotheby's.[20]

Returning to London in September 1940, Virginia Woolf found that a neighbour's house in Bloomsbury had been struck by a bomb and was 'still smouldering. That is a great pile of bricks. Underneath, all the people who had gone down to their shelter . . . the casual young men & women I used to see, from my window; the flat dwellers who used to have flower pots & sit on the balcony. All now blown to bits.'[21] The following month, she returned to find that her own house in Mecklenburgh Square had been hit: 'I cd just see a piece of my studio wall standing; otherwise rubble where I wrote so many books. Open air where we sat so many nights, gave so many parties.'[22]

A raid on the night of 8 March 1941 left 159 people dead. Among the victims were the revellers at the Café de Paris, a smart West End nightclub, which suffered a direct hit. Thirty-four people were killed. Ken 'Snakehips' Johnson and his entire West Indian dance band died. (Johnson was buried at St Pancras and Islington Cemetery.) Anthony Powell, in his sequence *A Dance to the Music of Time*, gave a vivid but unsentimental account of the tragedy. One character observes gruffly, of a dead socialite: 'Poor Bijou. I'm afraid it was her last party.'

On 16 April 1941, a Foeke 685 fighter bomber raid killed over 1,000 people, caused over 2,000 fires and destroyed many historic buildings. The terminus of the Necropolis Railway at Westminster

Bridge Road was among them. Berthed in its siding, the train was bombed; a photograph shows a burned-out wreck, tossed aside like a discarded toy atop a heap of rubble and twisted metal. The station's entrance, workshops, mortuary chapel and caretaker's flat were flattened. All that remained were the platforms and waiting rooms.

At Kensal Green Cemetery, where mechanical excavators were on standby in the event of mass civilian casualties, bombs falling on the nearby railway lines and gasworks blasted graves open, showering the cemetery with human remains that were quickly reburied. The catacombs doubled as air-raid shelters, as did the crypts of many churches – sometimes with fatal consequences. Eighty-four people sheltering in St Peter's, Walworth, died when it was bombed.

Although London had been a potential target since war broke out in 1939, with children evacuated to the country and gasmasks distributed, arrangements to protect civilians were woefully inadequate. The authorities banned people from using the Underground as a shelter, fearing they would never come out. But they had reckoned without the bloody-minded determination of the Cockney character. Faced with this new weapon of terror, Londoners took matters into their own hands. They bought halfpenny tickets, the cheapest available, and sat it out on the platforms until the raids were over. Closed lines were brought back into service. At Borough Station, a disused section of the former City and South London Railway's tunnel was reopened as an air-raid shelter. The C&SLR was the world's first electric underground railway and its deep-level tunnel provided accommodation for 8,000 people. A concrete floor was laid over the tracks, bunks installed and six entrances built for rapid access. It was subsequently resealed. Of course, not even Tube stations were immune to the Blitz. On 17 September 1940, seventeen people were killed when a bomb hit Marble Arch Underground Station. On 14 December of that year, Balham Station received a direct hit at street level, and sixty people, sheltering in the tunnel below, drowned when the bomb destroyed a water main. Bank Underground Station took a direct hit on 11 January 1941, and 117 people were killed.

Despite Hitler's plans to destroy national morale, Londoners developed a grim determination to carry on as normal, 'in spite of all terror'.

'The most noticeable point about Londoners' response to the air raids was that it was not very dramatic,' Philip Ziegler has said. 'They did not surge out and shake their fists at the skies or strike dramatic poses and say, "We will go on fighting until the end!" nor did they panic and hide in corners and scream. They just phlegmatically went on.'[23] At a popular level, this spirit manifested itself in lyrics such as Noel Coward's 'London Pride', while even Virginia Woolf, with Modernist distrust of patriotic fervour, revealed an intense love of London in her diary, recalling the circular walk at the Tower with its garden of hollyhocks and the portrait of a little girl.

> Odd how often I think with what is love I suppose of the City: of the walk to the Tower: that is my England; I mean, if a bomb destroyed one of those little alleys with the brass bound curtains & the river smell & the old woman reading I should feel – well, what the patriots feel.[24]

One of the worst civilian casualty incidents of the war occurred at Bethnal Green Underground Station.[25] By March 1943, the Blitz had been over for two years, but air raids were still an everyday occurrence for East Enders, since the docklands remained a key target for German bombers. Bethnal Green Underground Station, one of the few deep-level stations in the East End, was an obvious place for a huge public shelter. It could hold up to 7,000 people and contained 5,000 bunks. People would gather nearby when an air raid was due. They were expecting retaliation after a successful raid on Berlin on 1 March.

About 500 people were already in the shelter when the sirens went off at 8.17 p.m. Bombers had changed their tactics from slow, heavy aircraft to faster craft, so people had less time to get inside the shelter. Knowing this, the residents rushed out of cinemas and jumped off buses. They came from everywhere – and in less than ten minutes, an estimated 1,500 people had made their way into the entrance. Because of the blackout, they had only one 25-watt bulb to guide them. It had been raining, and the steps were wet. At 8.27 p.m., a nearby anti-aircraft battery fired off sixty rockets. It was a new gun, with an unfamiliar sound. Rumours were already circulating of deadly new flying bombs, and fear turned to panic.

As the crowd surged forward down the slippery steps, a woman holding a baby fell near the bottom of the first staircase. A man tripped over her, and a tragic human domino effect began. Hundreds of people fell within fifteen seconds. Unaware of what was happening, more people surged into the shelter. PC Thomas Penn, escorting his pregnant wife to the shelter, arrived as the disaster was unfolding. He crawled over the massed bodies to the bottom of the nineteen steps and found two hundred people in a space the size of a small room. He climbed back and called for help, before returning to try to extricate people.

Despite all that could be done, one hundred and seventy-three people died: twenty-seven men, eighty-four women and sixty-two children. A further sixty-two were taken to hospital. The woman who had originally fallen survived: her baby did not. One eyewitness, a boy whose father made a last-minute decision to head for another shelter, almost lost his sister: 'She came in late, thought the ground was very soft but she was on the top of bodies and the wardens pulled her from the top. In our class at school two brothers were both killed, their sister, their mum and dad and their gran. Three generations wiped out.' Like the direct hits at Bank and Balham, the disaster was hushed up by the authorities, for fear of damaging public morale.

One inevitable consequence of the war was the expansion of Brookwood's military cemeteries. The Commonwealth sections were extended, and French, Polish, Czechoslovakian, Russian, Belgian and Dutch plots created for the graves of Allied casualties. The Free French section, marked by two crosses of Lorraine, featured different styles of memorial which testified to the colonial elements of the French forces: as well as crosses, headstones bore the Star of David, and appeared in the form of a Moorish arch. There was a Moslem section, and plots for Italian and German prisoners of war, and a plot that commemorated fourteen members of the Turkish Air Force. By 1945, over 4, 220 casualties from both world wars were buried in the Commonwealth War Graves Commission section.

During the Second World War the cemetery was extended for the burial of members of the US armed forces who had died in England. Burials commenced in April 1942, and by August 1944, over 3,600 bodies had been laid to rest. An isolated plot behind the Chapel was used for the burial of nineteen American servicemen executed at Shepton Mallet prison for various offences during the Second World War. These graves were unmarked. After the war, the bodies were transferred to a 'dishonoured' plot in the American Military Cemetery at Oisne-Aisne in France.[26]

The Brookwood Memorial commemorates nearly 3,500 men and women of the forces of the British Commonwealth 'to whom the fortune of war denied a known and honoured Grave'. These include personnel who died at sea, in the campaign in Norway in 1940, as members of the raiding parties that set out from the United Kingdom or as special agents with Allied underground. Designed by Ralph Hobday, the memorial is made of Portland stone, and the names are carved on panels of green slate. These include Violette Szabo (1921–45), the first woman to be awarded the George Cross, whose life was immortalized in the film *Carve Her Name With Pride*. A Londoner, Violette volunteered for the Special Operations Executive after her French husband was killed in North Africa.

Parachuted into Occupied France, she did valuable work for the Resistance prior to D Day. Captured on her second mission, Violette was tortured by the Gestapo but refused to betray her comrades. In January 1945, she was shot. A year later, Violette's young daughter collected her posthumous George Cross from the Palace.

At Tower Hill, the memorial to the Merchant Seamen was extended. Nearly 4,786 merchant ships were lost during the Second World War. The number of merchant seamen who gave their lives totalled nearly 32,000. The Atlantic was the chief battleground. In the worst year, 1942, four-fifths of the total merchant-ships losses occurred in the North and South Atlantic. Conveys making their way to Russia round the North Cape were vulnerable to attack, since they passed within range of occupied Norway. In the Mediterranean, convoys to Malta ran the gauntlet of sea and air attacks on an increasingly heavy scale. In home waters, losses throughout the war accounted for more than one quarter of the total, due to enemy mines, submarine and light surface craft activity and air attacks.

When the time came to commemorate the men of the Merchant Navy who lost their lives during the Second World War and have no known grave, it was decided to combine the new memorial with the existing one to create a complete whole. Sir Edward Maufe achieved this by designing a semi-circular sunken garden adjoining the original memorial. This created enough wallspace to record almost 24,000 names without building high walls on Tower Hill. The inscription is guarded by sculpted figures representing an officer and seaman of the Merchant Service. Other stone sculptural figures represent the Seven Seas, and there is a central pool of bronze, engraved as a mariners' compass, and set to Magnetic North. The memorial was unveiled by Elizabeth II on 5 November 1955.[27]

After the war, London's great Victorian cemeteries went into terminal decline. Vandalism and neglect completed the destruction started by the Luftwaffe, and family plots were abandoned as the younger generation moved out to the suburbs, reluctant to return to Kensal Green or Highgate and tend the graves. The tightly-knit working-class communities of the East End, which had perpetuated the Victorian funeral tradition, were broken up, as residents of bombed-out squares and terraces were moved to distant estates.[28] The war had irrevocably changed attitudes towards death. As Peter Jupp notes, whilst in 1938, one in ten Londoners wanted a 'proper funeral'[29], by 1945 the war had 'made grief both more public and more private. Grief was increasingly something the family wanted to keep to itself'.[30]

Once again, the dead were banished from the city, but not to 'God's acre beautiful' or the delightful memorial gardens envisaged by Loudon. It was impossible to visualize families promenading through soulless municipal cemeteries, with their strict regulations for monument design, so that gravestones would not impair the performance of industrial mowers. No wildflowers blew in these dispiriting places; no weeping angels stretched out their wings imploringly; no mausolea waited to open their doors to the next generation.

At Highgate, the pinnacles of the magnificent Tudor entrance became so dangerous that they had to be dismantled. The chapels at Nunhead were never rebuilt after bombing; wanton destruction across London left monuments in ruins, trashed by vandals and stripped of valuable bronze and lead. Questions were asked in the House about the future of Highgate Cemetery, and rumours circulated that it might be sold off to a property developer. The imposing gates of Highgate Cemetery's Western Ground were locked for ever in 1973.

Within a generation of death being on everyone's lips, whether at the hands of bomber crews or on the battlefield, it had become the great unmentionable topic. Far from dying contentedly surrounded by a circle of family and friends, the terminally ill were airbrushed out of existence, removed to hospitals, never to be seen again. When

*David Brooks's evocative image of the Egyptian Avenue,
Highgate Cemetery.*

London began to swing, Victorian cemeteries were grim reminders of mortality, fit only for film locations and the attentions of local hooligans.

And then, suddenly, rescue arrived in the form of Sir John Betjeman. A writer, Victorian enthusiast and architectural expert, Betjeman spearheaded the conservation movement in Britain, campaigning for endangered buildings with such books as *Ghastly Good Taste*. Portrayed by the cartoonist Searle as an aesthete version of *The Avengers'* John Steed, Betjeman galvanized the heritage industry.

In 1975, the Friends of Highgate Cemetery was formed. Dedicated to clearing brambles and opening access to graves, the organization subsequently obtained the freehold of the Cemetery and began an impressive programme of restoration. London's other Victorian cemeteries soon developed passionate 'Friends', a trend which was echoed nationally. A growing interest in genealogy and local history sent visitors back to the cemeteries, tracing ancestors or intrigued by the anecdotes of those buried there. Volunteers and preservationists responded in kind, with programmes of tours and lectures. Kensal Green, for instance, hosts an annual 'Day of the Dead' when visitors may view the catacombs and coffin lift, admire parading hearses and even buy jam made from the cemetery's fruit bushes. The event, almost mediaeval in its acceptance of death, also echoes the Victorian sentiment of cemetery tours as a satisfying day out.

As well as attitudes towards death, attitudes towards burial have changed. The Socialist author Paul Foot was buried at Golders Green in a cardboard coffin in 2004. Attitudes towards mourning reflect this change. For example, the announcement of the death of Sheila Gish, the actor, contained this injunction: On Miss Gish's request, no black to be worn, please (unless of course it's your best colour).'[31]

Natural burial grounds, which recall the earliest pagan cemeteries, have been developed where the body is committed to the earth in a simple shell and the memorial consists of a tree. There are now 200 of these woodland meadows in the UK, inspired by concerns about the environmental consequences of conventional burial and cremation. Crematoria have been blamed for at least 16 per cent of the UK's total mercury emissions, as well as carbon monoxide and dioxins. Conventional burial also means that formaldehyde from embalmed bodies will leak into the soil and contaminate nearby water supplies. In 2004, Haringey Council's proposals to dig up parts of Queen's Wood and Highgate Wood for woodland burial plots was a response to the perennial problem of overcrowding in London cemeteries.[32]

From a culture in which it was not permitted to report suicides or mention the word 'cancer' in national newspapers, we now live in a confessional age. Stricken writers record their own decline, meeting the eternal deadline with a dying fall. The terminal illnesses of celebrities are closely monitored; beds of flowers and candles appear at the spots of disasters in apparent spontaneous outpourings of grief. This phenomenon first appeared in Britain after the Hillsborough Stadium football disaster in 1989, but earlier manifestations elsewhere in the world include the shrine which materialized on the spot where John Lennon was shot in 1980 and the reaction to the demise of Eva Peron and Princess Grace of Monaco. Mainland Europe has long had a Roman Catholic tradition of roadside shrines, and now, in Britain, improvised roadside shrines spring up at the site of every murder and fatal accident. Death is even marked in cyberspace: there are now internet memorial sites where we can post a message and sign a guestbook to register our grief.

At some point at the end of the twentieth century, it appears that the stiff upper lip gave way to the bleeding heart. Explanations include a concept of 'Americanism', for which read 'emotional literacy', embracing alternative forms of spirituality and the rise of therapy. At its most extreme, this reaction peaked in the public response to the death of Diana, Princess of Wales.

Diana's death was announced on the last day of summer: 31 August 1997. Within hours of the news of the tragic car crash, crowds had gathered at Kensington Palace and Buckingham Palace in a display of collective grief. Carpets of flowers appeared, accompanied by letters, cards and candles. Within a week, there were fifteen tonnes of tributes. The scene was replicated up and down the land. This appeared to be a public impulse, unlike the national mourning ordained by the Earl Marshall for Prince Albert or Queen Victoria. Strictly speaking, as the ex-wife of a peer, Diana was not in line for a heraldic funeral. However, in her capacity as the 'Princess of Hearts', Diana's funeral represented a political opportunity. There were plans to rename Heathrow Airport after Diana; along with the prediction that Elton John's ballad, 'Goodbye England's Rose' would still top the charts at Christmas (it didn't). Like that of the Duke of Wellington in 1852, Diana's death was the pretext for an elaborate display of national sentiment from a new Government. Within hours, she had earned another soubriquet: the 'People's Princess'. And her funeral was very much the 'People's Funeral', watched on television by thirty-one million people in Britain, and two and a half billion around the world.

While Dodi Al Fayed was buried within twenty-four hours of his death in the accident, according to Islamic law, the body of Diana lay at the Chapel Royal, in St James's Palace, until the evening before the funeral. It was then moved to her apartments at Kensington Palace where it remained overnight. The Bishop of London and the Sub Dean of the Chapels Royal kept a candlelit vigil of prayer over the coffin throughout the night.

On Saturday, 7 September, the coffin left Kensington Palace on a gun carriage of the King's Troop, Royal Horse Artillery, and was escorted on foot by members of the Welsh Guards and mounted police along a route lined by thousands of mourners. An estimated six million people had been expected to attend, but in the event only three million filled the streets, deterred by the prospect of traffic jams.

The coffin, draped with the Royal Standard, bore a card reading MUMMY, from Diana's sons, Prince William and Prince Harry who, along with the Prince of Wales and the Duke of Edinburgh and Diana's brother, Earl Spencer, joined the procession in The Mall and followed her coffin to the Abbey. Meanwhile, the Queen led members of the Royal family in paying their respects outside Buckingham Palace.

The route passed Hyde Park, where many thousands more

watched the procession and service on two giant screens. At Hyde Park Corner the procession passed under Wellington Arch before moving into Constitution Hill. Following the service at Westminster Abbey, Diana's coffin was taken by road to the family estate at Althorp. She was buried, in sanctified ground, on an island in the centre of a lake. The grave faced east, towards the rising sun. Like her aristocratic ancestors, she was buried, not in London, but on her country estate.

There is no doubt that the spontaneous outpouring of grief was fanned by the very newspaper proprietors who had persecuted Diana during life, but another element was also at play. The intense sorrow which greeted Diana's death was the striking of a national chord. The Princess's troubled life story was recognizable from soap operas and our own lives, and her death was curiously familiar: an attractive single mother killed in a car crash on a Saturday night; the bereaved sons, troubled ex-husband and difficult in-laws: the *Dramatis Personae* resonated. Interviewed at vigils, many people explained that the death of Diana and the intense mood that was prevalent allowed them to revisit personal bereavements, in a culture where formal mourning was no longer a regular feature of everyday life. The grief for Diana also seemed to have a particularly feminine quality. Such an emotional response to the death of a (former) female Royal was unprecedented. The subjects of Elizabeth I and Queen Victoria had become critical of their monarchs by the time they died. It is perhaps the feminine aspect of Diana's death and funeral which caused some male commentators to throw up their hands in despair at such overwhelmingly emotional displays.

Diana's was an individual tragedy, inspiring an extraordinary and unique response. The reaction to the London bombings of 2005 presented a far more recognizable picture of Londoners under duress. On 7 July 2005, the day after the capital had been successful in its bid for the 2012 Olympics, four suicide bombers struck in central

London, killing fifty-two people. Three bombs went off at 8.50 a.m. on Underground trains just outside Liverpool Street and Edgware Road Stations, and on another one travelling between King's Cross and Russell Square. The final explosion, about an hour later, was on a bus in Tavistock Square, opposite Euston Station.

The attacks seemed particularly devastating to the London psyche as they took place on public transport. The red bus has always been a symbol of London. To see one bombed felt like a crushing blow to the London spirit. And the very Underground tunnels which had provided shelter from the Blitz became a source of terror.

However, a day after the bombings, Londoners were returning to the Underground with gritted teeth, faced with the prospect of losing their livelihood if they did not show up for work. While the most affluent took to taxis, and corporate buses were laid on in the City, thousands sought other methods of transport – and the sale of bicycles soared.

Amidst the many tales of individual heroism from members of the emergency services and the general public, the bloody-minded stoicism that had seen Londoners through the Black Death, the Plague and the Blitz came into play. One old lady from the East End shook her fist at the heavens and declared that she had survived the Luftwaffe and *she* would decide when it was time for her to go!

The informal memorial garden that sprang up at King's Cross contained a wreath of carnations spelling out the logo of the London Underground – a symbol at once familiar and, in this context, tragic. The funerals of the fifty-two known victims – Humanist, Christian, Muslim, Jewish and other faiths – reflected the fact that London is now multicultural, and that there are many different ways of saying goodbye.

Which is what, ultimately, we must all do. London has seen numberless deaths over the past 2,000 years, and that tumulus on Hampstead Heath has gazed down impassively on many funerals.

But, in the end, we all have to depart. Let me leave you with this beautiful extract from *The Soul of London*, by Ford Madox Ford:

> For all of us it must be again London from a distance, whether it be a distance of six feet underground, or whether we go to rest somewhere on the other side of the hills that ring in this great river basin. For us, at least, London, its problems, its past, its future, will be at rest. At nights the great blaze will shine up at the clouds; on the sky there will still be that brooding and enigmatic glow, as if London with a great ambition strove to grasp at Heaven with arms that are shafts of light. That is London writing its name upon the clouds.
>
> And in the hearts of its children it will still be something like a cloud – a cloud of little experiences, of little personal impressions, of small, futile things that, seen in moments of stress and anguish, have significance so tremendous and meanings so poignant. A cloud – as it were of the dust of men's lives.

# Notes

## 1: A PAGAN PLACE: CELTIC GOLGOTHA AND THE ROMAN CEMETERIES

1  See Taylor, *Burial Practice in Early England*, p. 27.
2  See Baxter, 'Dancing with the dead in a mass grave', *British Archaeology*, 50, December 1999.
3  *ibid.*
4  Translated by Charles W. Kennedy, see Kermode and Hollander, eds, *The Oxford Anthology of English Literature*, vol. 1, pp. 97–8.
5  See De la Bédoyère, Guy http://www.channel4.com/history/microsites/H/history/I-m/london1.html (December 2005).
6  See Ariès, *Western Attitudes Toward Death from the Middle Ages to the Present*, p. 14.
7  See Taylor, *loc. cit.*, p. 89.
8  See Browne, *Hydrotaphia Urne-Buriall, or, A Brief Discourse of the Sepulchrall Urnes Lately Found in Norfolk*, p. 267.
9  *ibid.*, p. 289.
10  http://www.eng-h.gov.uk/ArchRev/rev94_5/eastcem.htm
11  See Thomas, 'Laid to rest on a pillow of bay leaves', *British Archaeology*, 50, December 1999.
12  See Kermode and Hollander, *loc. cit.*, vol. 1, pp. 29–30.

## 2: *DANSE MACABRE*: LONDON AND THE BLACK DEATH

1  'Bones Reveal Chubby Monks Aplenty', *Guardian*, 15 July 2004.
2  See Holmes, *The London Burial Grounds*, pp. 36–7.
3  *ibid.*, pp. 36–7.
4  *ibid.*, p. 33.

5  *ibid.*, p. 34.

6  See Harding, *The Dead and the Living in Paris and London 1500–1670*, p. 46.

7  See Ariès, *Western Attitudes Toward Death from the Middle Ages to the Present*, p. 15.

8  'The Black Death 1348', www.eyewitnesstohistory.com (2001).

9  *ibid.*

10  See Maitland, *History of London*, p. 128.

11  See Hawkins, 'The Black Death and the New London Cemeteries of 1348', *Antiquity*, vol. 64, no, 244, pp. 637–42.

12  See Maitland, *loc. cit.*, p. 128.

13  *ibid.*

14  See Hawkins, *loc. cit.*, pp. 637–42.

15  See Cantor, *In the Wake of the Plague*, p. 207.

16  See White, *loc. cit.*, p. xi.

17  *ibid.*, pp. xiii–xiv.

18  *ibid.*, p. xxiii.

19  *ibid.*, p. xxvii.

20  *ibid.*, p. xxiv.

21  *ibid.*, p. xxiv.

22  *ibid.*, p. 6.

### 3: *MEMENTO MORI*: THE THEATRE OF DEATH

1  See Shakespeare, *Julius Caesar*, II, ii.

2  See Dekker, *The Wonderful Year*, p. 181.

3  See Holmes, *The London Burial Grounds,* p. 98.

4  See Shakespeare, *Hamlet*, V, i.

5  See Holmes quoting Maitland, *loc. cit.,* p. 33.

6  *ibid.*, p. 38.

7  Nashe, Thomas, 'Summer's Last Will and Testament', line 1588.

8  See Holmes, *loc. cit.*, pp. 69–70.

9  See Bell, *Unknown London*, pp. 192–3.

10  *ibid.,* p. 47.

11  See Puckle, *Funeral Customs*, p. 44.

12  See Dekker, *loc. cit.*, p. 168.

13  See Chettle, *Englandes Mourning Garment*.

14  See Woodward, *The Theatre of Death*, pp. 87–117.

15 See Holmes, *loc. cit.*, p. 57.
16 See Dugdale, *History of St Paul's*, p. 129.


4: PESTILENCE: DIARY OF A PLAGUE YEAR

1 See O'Donoghue, *The Story of Bethlehem Hospital*, p. 192.
2 See Dunbar, 'In Honour of the City of London', *The Oxford Book of English Verse*, pp. 26–7.
3 See Defoe, *A Journal of the Plague Year*, p. 3.
4 See Pepys, *Diary*, 30 April 1665.
5 See Defoe, *loc. cit.*, p. 8.
6 See Pepys, *loc. cit.*, 7 June 1665.
7 See Hodges, *Loimologia*.
8 See Pepys, *loc. cit.*, 3 August 1665.
9 See Defoe, *loc. cit.*, p. 38.
10 *ibid.*, p. 175.
11 See Porter, *The Great Plague*, p. 18.
12 See Holmes, *The London Burial Grounds*, p. 124.
13 *ibid.*, p. 124.
14 See Pepys, *loc. cit.*, 15 June 1665.
15 *ibid.*, 17 June 1665.
16 *ibid.*, 23 June 1665.
17 *ibid.*
18 See Defoe, *loc. cit.*, p. 9.
19 See Pepys, *loc. cit.*, 12 August 1665.
20 *ibid.*, 31 August 1665.
21 *ibid.*, 3 September 1665.
22 *ibid.*, 18 July 1665.
23 See Defoe, *loc. cit.*, p. 58.
24 *ibid.*, pp. 58–9.
25 See Pepys, *loc. cit.*, 6 September 1665.
26 See Bell, *The Great Plague in London, 1665*, p. 185.
27 See Pepys, *loc. cit.*, 30 August 1665.
28 See Defoe, *loc. cit.*, p. 59.
29 Thomson, George, *Loimotomia, or The Pest Anatomised*, p. 66.
30 See Hodges, *loc. cit.*
31 See Defoe, *loc. cit.*, p. 218.
32 *ibid.*, p. 219.

33 http://www.zurichmansion.org/parks/.50.html (November 2005).

34 See Bell, *loc. cit.*, p. 284.

35 See Pepys, *loc. cit.*, 30 January 1666.

### 5: *ET IN ARCADIA EGO*: A VISION OF ELYSIAN FIELDS

1 See Aubrey, *Brief Lives*, p. 158.

2 See Puckle, *Funeral Customs*, p. 76.

3 See Holmes, *The London Burial Grounds*, p. 213.

4 *ibid.*, p. 134.

5 See Maitland.

6 See Pepys, *Diary*, 18 March 1664.

7 *ibid.*, 23 February 1668.

8 See Litten, *The English Way of Death*, pp. 41–2.

9 See Donne, 'Devotions', XVII.

10 See Puckle, *Funeral Customs*, p. 55.

11 Evelyn quoted in *ibid.*, p. 62.

12 See Gough, *Sepulchral Monuments*, Introduction.

13 See Litten quoting Walpole, *loc. cit.*, fig. 29.

14 See Curl, *The Victorian Celebration of Death*, pp. 1–3.

15 See Ariès, *Western Attitudes Toward Death from the Middles Ages to the Present*, p. 52.

16 See Young, *Night Thoughts*, lines 160–80.

17 See Blair, *The Grave*, lines 39–42.

18 http://cmpl.ucr.edu/terminals/memento_mori/cemetery.html

19 See Barker, *London As It Might Have Been*, pp. 144–8.

20 See Loudon, Jane, *A Short Account of the Life and Writings of John Claudius Loudon* (reprinted as an appendix in Gloag, *Mr Loudon's England*), pp. 182–219.

21 See Morley quoting Loudon, *Death, Heaven and the Victorians*, p. 46.

22 *ibid.*, p. 48.

### 6: GATHERINGS FROM GRAVEYARDS: THE DEAD ARE KILLING THE LIVING

1 See Porter, *London, A Social History*, p. 257.

2 Chadwick, *Report on the Sanitary Condition of the Labouring*

*Population of Great Britain.*

3  *Punch*, July–December, 1849.

4  'Let the stones speak, the spire and crypt inspire', *A History of St Mary's Church, Islington.*
   http://www.stmaryislington.org/history/036.html (11/02/05).

5  See Simon, *City Medical Reports*, 1849. http://www.victorianlondon.org/

6  See Holmes, *The London Burial Grounds*, pp. 192–3.

7  See Walker, *Gatherings from Graveyards*, p. 1.

8  *ibid.*, p. 150.

9  See Gladstone, quoted
   http://www.somewhatmuchly.co.uk/index.php?cat=Cemeteries
   (03/08/2004).

10  See Walker, *loc. cit.*, p. 7.

11  *The Times*, 25 June 1839.

12  *Weekly Despatch*, 30 September 1838.

13  See Miller, *Picturesque Sketches of London Past and Present*, p. 270.

14  See Dickens, *The Uncommercial Traveller*, p. 234.

15  See Dickens, *Bleak House*, p. 266.

16  See Howarth and Jupp, 'Enon Chapel: No Way for the Dead', *The Changing Face of Death*, pp. 90–104.

17  See Holmes, *loc. cit.*, p.102.

18  Gilbert v. Buzzard (1820).

19  See Miller, *loc. cit.*

20  See Lewis, *Edwin Chadwick and the Public Health Movement 1832–1854*, p. 205.

21  See Porter, *loc. cit.*, p. 265.

22  *ibid.*, p. 266.

23  See Curl, *The Victorian Celebration of Death.*

24  See Jupp, *From Dust to Ashes*, p. 9.

25  See Holmes, *loc. cit.*, p. 214.

26  Walker quoted in *ibid.*

27  *ibid.*, pp. 194–7.

28  *Weekly Dispatch*, 9 September 1838.

29  See Howarth and Jupp, *loc. cit.*, p. 97.

30  See Holmes, *loc. cit.*, p. 215.

31  *ibid.*, pp. 215–6.

32  See Miller, *loc. cit.*

## 7: VICTORIAN VALHALLAS: THE DEVELOPMENT OF THE GREAT VICTORIAN CEMETERIES

1 *Morning Advertiser*, 14 May 1830.
2 See Rugg, 'A new burial form and its meanings: cemetery establishment in the first half of the 19th century' in Cox, ed., *Grave Concerns Death & Burial in England 1700–1850*, p. 44.
3 See Winter, J. in Elliot, ed., *Highgate Cemetery*.
4 See Betjeman, *A Pictorial History of English Architecture*, p. 81.
5 See Clark, *The Gothic Revival*, p. 126.
6 See Meller, *London Cemeteries: An Illustrated Guide and Gazetteer*, p. 182.
7 See Morley, *Death, Heaven and the Victorians*, p. 47.
8 See Pepper, Edward S. *The Mechanical Catafalque at Kensal Green* http://www.virtualnorwood.com/news/005.html
9 See Meller, *loc. cit.*, p. 182.
10 See Brooks, *Mortal Remains*, p. 29.
11 See Blanchard, *Ainsworth's* magazine, p. 178.
12 See Bartlett, *London By Day and Night*, p. 242.
13 See Shelley, *The Complete Poetical Works*, p. 437.
14 *ibid.*, p. 437.
15 See Richardson, *Highgate: Its History Since the Fifteenth Century*, p. 46.
16 See Leon, Robert, 'The Man Who Made King's Cross – The Misfortunes of Stephen Geary', *Camden History Review*, vol. 17, pp. 13–16.
17 See Pateman, *In Highgate Cemetery*.
18 See Barker, *Highgate Cemetery: Victorian Valhalla*, p. 15.
19 See Winter, *loc. cit.*
20 See De Quincey, *Confessions of an English Opium-Eater*, p. 73.
21 See Pateman, *loc. cit*, p. 13.
22 See Richardson, *loc. cit.*, p. 162.
23 See Barker, *loc. cit.*, p. 16.
24 See Woollacott, *Investors in Death*.
25 See Barker, *loc. cit.*, p. 33.
26 See Gaunt, *The Pre-Raphaelite Dream*, pp. 149–50.
27 See Graham Stewart, *Funeral Echoes from Down the Years*, *The Times Online*, 3 December 2005.
28 See Rossetti, Christina, 'Remember', *The Oxford Book of English Verse*.
29 See Barker, *loc. cit.*, p. 41.

30  See Richardson, *loc. cit.*, p. 163.
31  See Barker, *loc. cit.*, p. 32.
32  See Meller, *loc. cit.*, p. 227.


## 8: GREAT GARDENS OF SLEEP

1  See Woollacott, *Investors in Death*.
2  See Bartlett, *London by Day and Night*, p. 244.
3  See Holmes, *The London Burial Grounds*, p. 136.
4  See Brooks, *Mortal Remains*, p. 28.
5  See Meller, *London Cemeteries*, p. 274.
6  See Brooks, *loc. cit.*, p. 29.
7  *Illustrated London News*, 24 March 1849.
8  See Barker, *London As It Might Have Been*, p. 147.
9  See Robinson, *Cremation and Urn Burial or The Cemeteries of the Future*, p. 34.
10  *Illustrated London News*, 25 April 1856.
11  See Clarke, *The Brookwood Necropolis Railway*, p. 13.
12  *ibid.*, p. 3.
13  See Lewis, *Edwin Chadwick and the Public Health Movement 1832–1854*, pp. 252, 324.
14  See Clarke, *loc. cit.*, p. 39.
15  *The Brookwood Necropolis Railway*, pp. 197–8.
16  See Holmes, *loc. cit.*, p. 139.
17  *ibid.*, p. 150.
18  *A Plea for the St Pancras Churchyard: being a remonstrance against its proposed desecration by the Midland Railway Company* http://webp1.mimas.ac.uk/~zzaascs/pan-pamph.html (01/08/2005).
19  See Holmes, *loc. cit.*, p. 186.
20  *ibid.*, p. 175.
21  See Meller, *loc. cit.*, pp. 250–2.
22  See Mayhew, *The Criminal Prisons of London*.
23  www.royal-arsenal.com
24  See Holmes, *loc. cit.*, p. 218.
25  *ibid.*, p. 219.
26  See *A Plea for the St Pancras Churchyard etc*, *loc. cit.*
27  'Reburial to Make Way for Rail Link', *Hampstead and Highgate Express*, 13 December 2004.

28  See Holmes, *loc. cit.*, p. 201.
29  See Dickens, *The Uncommercial Traveller*, p. 233.
30  See Holmes, *loc. cit.*, p. 237.
31  *Illustrated London News*, 23 October 1869.
32  See Holmes, *loc. cit.*, p. 227.
33  *ibid.*, p. 201.
34  *ibid.*, p. 17.
35  *ibid.*, p. 236.
36  *ibid.*, p. 242.
37  *ibid.*, p. 245.
38  *ibid.*, p.276.
39  *ibid.*, p.278.
40  *ibid.*, p. 242.
41  *ibid.*, pp. 256–7.
42  *ibid.*, p. 256.

## 9: THE PEOPLE WHO INVENTED DEATH: THE VICTORIAN FUNERAL

1  See Raitt, *The Life of Villiers de l'Isle-Adam*, p. 319.
2  See Dickens, *The Old Curiosity Shop*, p. 395.
3  *ibid.*, p. 540.
4  See Shelley, *The Complete Poetical Works*, p. 1.
5  See Tennyson, *The Complete Works*, p. 412.
6  See Dickens, *loc. cit.*, p. 542.
7  See Morley, *Death, Heaven and the Victorians*, fig. 20.
8  See Gissing, *Diary*, 1 March 1888.
9  See MacDonald and Murphy, *Sleepless Souls: Suicide in Early Modern England*, pp. 44–6.
10  *ibid.*, pp. 138–9.
11  See Trollope, *The Prime Minister*, p. 194.
12  See Greenwood, *The Wilds of London*, p. 85.
13  See Lewis, *Edwin Chadwick and the Public Health Movement 1832–1854*, p. 73.
14  See *Cassell's Household Guide*, vol. 3, p. 266.
15  See Lewis, *loc. cit.*, p. 72.
16  See Dickens, *Martin Chuzzlewit*, p. 321.
17  See Dickens, *Oliver Twist*, pp. 25–6.

18 See Morley, *loc. cit.*, pp. 30–31.
19 See Puckle, *Funeral Customs*, p. 50.
20 See *Cassell's loc. cit.*, vol. 3, p. 292.
21 *ibid.*
22 See Gordon, *The Horse World of London*, p. 138.
23 See Litten, *The English Way of Death*, pp. 135–6.
24 See Justyne, *Guide to Highgate*.
25 See Greenwood, *loc. cit.*, pp. 127–33.
26 See Davey, *A History of Mourning*.
27 See Holmes, *The London Burial Grounds*, p. 272.
28 See Litten, *loc. cit.*, pp. 47–50.
29 *ibid.*

## 10: THE VALE OF TEARS: THE VICTORIAN CULT OF MOURNING

1 See Davey, *A History of Mourning*.
2 *ibid.*
3 *ibid.*
4 See Dickens, *David Copperfield*, p. 99.
5 See Puckle, *Funeral Customs,* p. 145.
6 *ibid.*, pp. 49–50.
7 See Trollope, *The Prime Minister*, vol. 2, p. 276.
8 *ibid.*, p. 270.
9 *ibid.*, pp. 236–7.
10 *ibid.*, p. 379.
11 See Davey, *loc. cit.*
12 See Lurie, *The Language of Clothes*, p. 258.
13 Henry Mayhew, quoted in Morley, *Death, Heaven and the Victorians*, pp. 74–5.
14 See Bartlett, *London by Day and Night*, pp. 244–5.
15 Henry Kirk White, 'Consumption', *Ainsworth's* magazine, 1842, p. 185.
16 See Hood, Thomas, *The Oxford Book of English Verse*, pp. 758–9.
17 http://homepages.gold.ac.uk/london-journal/march2004/nicoletti.html
18 See Godwin, *Essay on Sepulchres*, p. 78.
19 See Blanchard, *Ainsworth's* magazine, p. 178.
20 *The Builder*, vol. 37, 1878, p. 250.
21 See Richardson, *Highgate*, p. 165.

22  See Blair, quoted in Morley, *Death, Heaven and the Victorians*, p. 53.
23  See Pugin, *An Apology for the Revival of Christian Architecture in England 1843*, p. 6.
24  *ibid.*
25  See Robinson, *God's Acre Beautiful or The Cemeteries of the Future*, p. 82.


## 11: UP IN SMOKE: THE DEVELOPMENT OF CREMATION

1  See Robinson, *God's Acre Beautiful*, p. 1.
2  *ibid.*, p. 2.
3  *Lancet*, 27 September 1879.
4  See Holmes, *The London Burial Grounds*, p. 269.
5  *ibid.*, p. 269.
6  See Browne, *The Major Works*, p. 295.
7  *ibid.*
8  *ibid.*
9  See White, 'Honoretta Pratt – Cremated 1769?' in *Pharos International*, 2001, vol. 67, no. 1, p. 16.
10  See Taylor, *Danger of Premature Interment*, p. 119.
11  See Loudon, *On the Planting and Laying out of Cemeteries*.
12  The Cremation Society of Great Britain, *History* http://www.srgw.demon.co.uk/CremSoc/History/HistSocy.html
13  *ibid.*
14  See Holmes, *loc. cit.*, p. 267.
15  See Taylor, *loc. cit.*, title page.
16  See Curl, *Kensal Green*, p. 121.
17  See Puckle, *Funeral Customs*, p. 10.
18  *ibid.*, p. 11.
19  The Cremation Society of Great Britain, *loc. cit.*
20  *ibid.*
21  *ibid.*
22  See Morley, *Death, Heaven and the Victorians*, pp. 96–7.
23  *ibid.*
24  *ibid.*
25  See Robinson, *loc. cit.*, p. 97.
26  *ibid.*, p. 13.
27  *ibid.*, p. 108.

28 Jupp, Peter, quoted in White, Stephen, 'A burial ahead of its time?' *Mortality*, vol. 7, no. 2, p. 173.

29 See Robinson, *loc. cit*., p. 114.

30 *ibid*., p. 115.

31 See White, Stephen, 'A burial ahead of its time', *Mortality*, vol. 7, no. 2, p. 179.

32 *ibid*.

33 *ibid*.

34 *ibid*.

35 See Puckle, *loc. cit*., p. 118.

36 See Grainger, Hilary J., 'Golders Green Crematorium and the Architectural Expression of Cremation', *Mortality*, vol. 5, no. 1, 2000, p. 5.

37 *ibid*., p. 10.

38 *ibid*., p. 11.

39 *ibid*., p. 6.

40 *ibid*., p. 14.

41 See Robinson, *loc. cit*., p. 28.

42 The Cremation Society of Great Britain, *loc. cit*.

43 See Grainger, *loc. cit*., p. 19.


## 12: OUR DARKEST HOURS: WORLD WAR AND
## THE DECLINE OF MOURNING

1 See Stamp, *Silent Cities*, p. 3.

2 *ibid*., pp. 5–6.

3 http://www.aftermathww1.com/warrior2.asp

4 *Daily Mail*, 12 November 1920.

5 http://www.cwgc.org/cwgcinternet/cemetery_details.aspx? cemetery=90002

6 See Pateman, *In Highgate Cemetery*.

7 http://www.tbcs.org.uk/history.htm

8 See Stamp, *loc. cit*., p. 6.

9 See Gorer, *Death, Grief and Mourning in Contemporary Britain*, pp. 1–2.

10 *ibid*., pp. 2–4.

11 See Taylor, *Mourning Dress: A Costume and Social History*, p. 267.

12 See Gorer, *loc. cit*., p. 6.

13 See Puckle, *Funeral Customs*, p. 66.

14 www.hampsteadscience.ac.uk/HSS
15 See Royall, *The Royall Family and East London History*
   http://www.royall.co.uk/royall/cbrownf1.htm
16 See Ziegler, quoted in *London, the Greatest City, In War and Peace*
   http://www.channel4.com/history
17 *ibid.*
18 Pyle, Ernie, quoted in www.EverywitnesstoHistory.com
19 See Ziegler, *loc. cit.*
20 See Sherry, *The Life of Graham Greene*, vol. 2, p. 63.
21 See Woolf, *Diary*, 10 September 1940.
22 *ibid.*, 20 October 1940.
23 See Ziegler, *loc. cit.*
24 See Woolf, *Diary*, 27 March 1935.
25 The Bethnal Green Tube Disaster, *The People's War*
   http://www.bbc.co.uk/dna/ww2
26 http://www.tbcs.org.uk/history.htm
27 http://www.cwgc.org/cwgcinternet/cemetery
28 See Jupp, *From Dust to Ashes*, p. 24.
29 *ibid.*, p. 24.
30 *ibid.*, p. 17.
31 *Guardian*, 18 March 2005.
32 *Hornsey and Crouch End Journal*, 14 October 2004.

# Bibliography

Ackroyd, Peter, *London: The Biography*, Vintage, London, 2001.

Ariès, Philippe, *The Hour of Our Death*, translated by Helen Weaver, Alfred A. Knopf, New York, 1981.

—— *Western Attitudes Toward Death*, translated by P.M. Ranum, Marion Boyers, London, 1994.

Aubrey, John, *Brief Lives*, ed. Oliver Lawson Dick, Penguin, Harmondsworth, 1972.

Barker, Felix, *Highgate Cemetery: Victorian Valhalla*, John Murray, London, 1984.

—— *London As It Might Have Been*, John Murray, London, 1982.

Bartlett, P.W., *London By Day and Night*, Hurst & Co., New York, 1852.

Baxter, Mary, 'Dancing with the Dead in a Mass Grave', *British Archaeology*, 50, December 1999.

Bédoyère, de la, Guy: http://www.channel4.com/history/microsites/H/history/I-m/london1.html, December 2005.

Bell, Walter, *The Great Plague in London, 1665*, Bodley Head, London, 1924.

—— *Unknown London*, Spring Books, London, 1966.

Betjeman, J., *A Pictorial History of English Architecture*, Penguin, Harmondsworth, 1977.

Blair, Robert, *The Grave, A Poem*, R. Morrison, Perth, 1790.

Blanchard, Samuel Laman, *A Visit to Kensal Green Cemetery*, *Ainsworth's* magazine, London, 1842.

Brooks, Chris, *Mortal Remains: The History and Present State of the Victorian and Edwardian Cemetery*, The Victorian Society, Exeter, 1989.

Browne, Sir Thomas, *The Major Works*, ed. C.A. Patrides, Penguin, London, 1977.

Cantor, Norman F., *In the Wake of the Plague: The Black Death and the World It Made*, Simon & Schuster, London, 2001.

*Cassell's Household Guide*, London, revised 1880s.

Chadwick, Sir Edwin, *Report on the Sanitary Condition of the Labouring Population of Great Britain*, Her Majesty's Stationery Office, London, 1842.

Chettle, Henry, *Englandes Mourning Garment*, London, 1603; *The English Experience Number 579*, De Capo Press Theatrum Orbis Terrarum Ltd, Amsterdam, 1973.

Clark, Kenneth, *The Gothic Revival: An Essay in the History of Taste*, John Murray, London, 1974.

Clarke, John M., *The Brookwood Necropolis Railway*, Oakwood, Oxford 1995.

—— *London's Necropolis: A Guide to Brookwood Cemetery*, Sutton, Stroud, 2004.

Cox, Margaret, ed., *Grave Concerns: Death and Burial in England 1700–1850*, York Council for British Archaeology, York, 1988.

Curl, James Stevens, ed., *Kensal Green Cemetery*, Phillimore & Co Ltd, London, 2001.

—— *The Victorian Celebration of Death*, David & Charles, Newton Abbot, 1972.

—— *The Victorian Celebration of Death* (revised), Sutton, Stroud, 2004.

Davey, Richard, *A History of Mourning*, Jay's, London, 1889.

Defoe, Daniel, *A Journal of the Plague Year*, ed. Cynthia Wall, Penguin, London, 2003.

Dekker, Thomas, *The Wonderful Year* in *Three Elizabethan Pamphlets*, ed. G.R. Hibbard, Harrap & Co, London, 1951.

De Quincey, Thomas, *Confessions of an English Opium Eater and Other Writings*, ed. Grevel Lindrop, World's Classics, Oxford University Press, Oxford, 1985.

Dickens, Charles, *Bleak House*, World's Classics, Oxford University Press, Oxford, 1948.

—— *David Copperfield*, World's Classics, Oxford University Press, Oxford, 1983.

—— *Martin Chuzzlewit*, World's Classics, Oxford University Press, Oxford, 1951.

—— *The Old Curiosity Shop*, World's Classics, Oxford University Press, Oxford, 1951.

—— *Oliver Twist*, Clarendon Press, Oxford, 1966.

—— *The Uncommercial Traveller*, Oxford University Press, 1958.

Donne, John, *Devotions Upon Emergent Occasions* (1624), 'Meditation XVII'.

Dugdale, Sir William, *The History of St Paul's Cathedral in London from its Foundation Until These Times . . .*, London, 1658.

Dunbar, William, 'In Honour of the City of London', *The Oxford Book of English Verse*, Clarendon Press, Oxford, 1912.

Elliott, Brent *et al.*, *Highgate Cemetery*, Friends of Highgate Cemetery, 1978.

Enright, D.J., *The Oxford Book of Death*, Oxford University Press, Oxford, 1983.

Finer, Samuel Edward, *The Life and Times of Sir Edwin Chadwick*, Barnes and Noble, New York, 1970.

Ford Madox Ford, *The Soul of London: A Survey of a Modern City*, ed. Alan G. Hill, Dent, London, 1995.

Gaunt, William, *The Pre-Raphaelite Dream*, The Reprint Society, London, 1943.

Gissing, George, *The Diary of George Gissing*, Plerne Associated University Press, London, 1978.

Gladstone, William, http:somewhatmuchly.co.uk/index.php?cat–Cemeteries

Gloag, John, *Mr Loudon's England: The Life and Work of John Claudius Loudon and his Influence on Architecture and Furniture Design*, Oriel Press, Newcastle upon Tyne, 1970.

Godwin, William, *Essay on Sepulchres; Or, A Proposal for Erecting Some Memorial of the Illustrious Dead in All Ages on the Spot Where Their Remains Have Been Interred*, London, W. Miller, 1809.

Gordon, W.J., *The Horse World of London*, The Religious Tract Society, London, 1893.

Gorer, Geoffrey, *Death, Grief and Mourning in Contemporary Britain*, Crescett Press, London, 1965.

Gough, Richard, *Sepulchral Monuments in Great Britain Applied to Illustrate the History of Families, Manners, Habits and Arts*, London, 1786–96.

Greenwood, J., *The Wilds of London*, Chatto & Windus, London, 1874.

Harding, Vanessa, *The Dead and the Living in Paris and London 1500–1670*, Cambridge University Press, Cambridge, 2002.

—— 'Burial of the Plague Dead in Early Modern London', http://www.history.ac.uk/cmh/epiharding.html

Harrison, Michael, *London Beneath the Pavement*, P. Davies, London, 1971.

Harvey, John, *Men in Black*, Reaktion Books, London, 1995.

Hawkins, Duncan, 'The Black Death and the New London Cemeteries of 1348', *Antiquity*, vol. 64, no, 244, London, 1990.

Hodges, Nathaniel, *Loimologia: Or, An Historical Account of the Plague in London in 1665; With Precautionary Directions Against the Like Contagion*, Bell & Osborn, London, 1720.

Holmes, Isabella (Mrs), *The London Burial Grounds. Notes on Their History from the Earliest Times to the Present Day*, T. Unwin, London, 1896.

Howarth, Glennys and Jupp, Peter C., eds, *The Changing Face of Death: Historical Accounts of Death and Disposal*, Macmillan, Basingstoke, 1997.

Jalland, Pat, *Death in the Victorian Family*, Oxford University Press, Oxford, 1999.

Jones, Barbara, *Design for Death*, Deutsch, London, 1967.

Jupp, Peter C., *From Dust to Ashes: The Replacement of Burial by Cremation in England 1840–1967*, Congregational Memorial Hall Trust, London, 1990.

Justyne, William, *Guide to Highgate Cemetery*, J. Moore, London, 1864.

Lewis, R.A., *Edwin Chadwick and the Public Health Movement 1832–1854*, Longmans, Green, London, 1952.

Litten, Julian, *The English Way of Death: The Common Funeral Since 1450*, Robert Hale, London, 2002.

Lloyd, Alan, *The Great Prize Fight*, Cassell, London, 1977.

Loudon, John Claudius, *On the Laying Out, Planting and Management of Cemeteries*, Longmans, Green, London, 1843.

Lucy, Sam, *The Anglo-Saxon Way of Death: Burial Rites in Early England*, Sutton, Stroud, 2000.

Lurie, Alison, *The Language of Clothes*, Henry Holt, New York, 2000.

MacDonald, Michael, *Sleepless Souls: Suicide in Early Modern England* (with Terence R. Murphy), Clarendon, Oxford, 1990.

Maitland, William, *History of London*, London, 1756.

Matthews, Dr Samantha, *Poetical Remains*, Oxford University Press, Oxford, 2004.

Mayhew, William, *The Criminal Prisons of London*, C. Griffin & Co., London, 1862.

Meller, Hugh, *London Cemeteries: An Illustrated Guide and Gazetteer*, Avebury, Amersham, 1981.

Miller, Thomas, *Picturesque Sketches of London Past and Present*. See also http://www.victorianlondon.org

Moote, Lloyd A. and Dorothy C., *The Great Plague*, Johns Hopkins, Baltimore, 2004.

Morley, John, *Death, Heaven and the Victorians*, Studio Vista, London, 1971.

O'Donoghue, E.G., *The Story of Bethlehem Hospital from its Foundation in 1247*, T. Fisher Unwin, London, 1914.

Pateman, Jean, *In Highgate Cemetery*, Friends of Highgate Cemetery, London, 1992.

Pepys, Samuel, *The Diaries of Samuel Pepys: A New and Complete Transcription*, eds Robert Latham and William Matthews, Bell & Hyman, London, 1970–83.

Pevsner, Nikolaus, *Buildings of England*, vol. 2, Penguin, London, 1974.

Porter, Roy, *London: A Social History*, Penguin, London, 2000.

Porter, Stephen, *The Great Plague*, Sutton, Stroud, 1999.

Puckle, Bertram S., *Funeral Customs: Their Origin and Development*, T. Werner Laurie, London, 1926.

Pugin, A.W.N., *An Apology for the Revival of Christian Architecture in England 1843*, St Barnabus Press, Oxford, 1969.

Raitt, A.W., *The Life of Villiers de l'Isle-Adam*, Clarendon Press, Oxford, 1981.

Richardson, John, *Highgate: Its History Since the Fifteenth Century*, New Barnet Historical Publications, 1983.

Richardson, Ruth, *Death, Dissection and the Destitute: The Politics of the Corpse in Pre-Victorian Britain*, Weidenfeld & Nicolson, London, 2001.

Robinson, William, *God's Acre Beautiful, Or The Cemeteries of the Future*, Cassell, London, 1889.

Shelley, Percy Bysshe, *The Complete Poetical Works*, Oxford University Press, Oxford, 1914. See also http://homepages.gold.ac.uk/london-journal/March2004/nicoletti.html

Sherry, Norman, *The Life of Graham Greene*, vol. 2, 1939–1955, Pimlico, London, 2004.

Simon, Dr John, *City Medical Reports*, 1849 http://www.victorianlondon.org/

Stamp, Gavin, *Silent Cities*, Royal Institute of British Architects, London, 1977.

Steele, Sir Richard, *The Funeral* in *The Plays of Richard Steele*, ed. Shirley Strum Kenny, Clarendon Press, Oxford, 1971.

Stow, John, *The Annals of England, Faithfully Collected Out of the Most Authenticall Authors, Records, and Other Monuments of Antiquities*, London, 1605.

Sweet, Matthew, *Inventing the Victorians*, Faber & Faber, London, 2002.

Taylor, Alison, *Burial Practice in Early England*, Tempus Publishing Ltd, London, 2001.

Taylor, Joseph, *Danger of Premature Interment, Proved from Many Remarkable Instances,* London, 1816.

Taylor, Lou, *Mourning Dress: A Costume and Social History,* Allen & Unwin, London, 1983.

Tennyson, Alfred, *The Complete Works,* Macmillan & Co., London, 1900.

Thomas, Christopher, 'Laid to rest on a pillow of bay leaves', *British Archaeology,* 50, December 1999.

—— *Life and Death in London's East End: 2000 Years at Spitalfields,* Museum of London Archaeology Service, London, 2004.

Thomson, George, *Loimotomia or The Pest Anatomised,* Nathaniel Crouch, London, 1666.

Tinniswood, Adrian, *His Invention So Fertile: A Life of Christopher Wren,* Pimlico, London, 2002.

Tomalin, Claire, *Pepys The Unequalled Self,* Viking, London, 2003.

Trollope, Anthony, *The Prime Minister,* vols 1 and 2, Oxford University Press, London, 1952.

Walker, George, *Gatherings from Graveyards: Particularly Those of London,* Nottingham (printed), London, 1839.

Weever, John, *Ancient Funerall Monuments,* Theatrum Orbis Terrarum, Amsterdam, 1979.

Wheeler, Michael, *Heaven, Hell and the Victorians,* Cambridge University Press, Cambridge, 1994.

White, Beatrice (ed.), *The Dance of Death,* Oxford University Press for the Early English Text Society, London, 1931.

Woodward, Jennifer, *The Theatre of Death: The Ritual Management of Royal Funerals in Renaissance England 1570–1625,* Boydell Press, Woodbridge, 1997.

Woolf, Virginia, *The Diary of Virginia Woolf,* vol. 5, 1936–1941, ed. Anne Olivier Bell, Penguin, London, 1985.

Woollacott, Ron, *Investors in Death,* Friends of Nunhead Cemetery, London, 2005.

Worple, Ken, *Last Landscapes: The Architecture of the Cemetery in the West,* Reaktion Books, London, 2003.

Young, Edward, *Night Thoughts,* ed. Stephen Cornford, Cambridge University Press, Cambridge, 1989.

Ziegler, Philip, *The Black Death,* Collins, London, 1969.

—— *King William IV,* Cassell, London, 1989.

# Web Resources

http://www.aftermathww1.com/warrior2.asp

http://www.bbc.co.uk/dna/ww2

http://www.channel4.com/history/microsites/H/history/I-m/london1.html

http://cmpl.ucr.edu/terminals/memento_mori/cemetery.html

http://cwgc.org/cwgcinternet/cemetery_details.aspx?cemetery=90002

http://cwgc.eng-h.gov.uk/ArchRev/rev945/eastcem.html

http://www.eng-h.gov.uk/ArchRev/rev945/eastcem.html

www.everywitnesstohistory.com

http://homepages.gold.ac.uk/london-journal/march 2004/nicoletti.html

www.hampsteadscience.ac.uk/HSS

http://www.history.ac.uk/cmh/epiharding.html

http://webp1.mimas.ac.uk/-2aacs/pan.pamph.html

www.royal-arsenal.com

http://www.royall.co.uk/royall/cbrownfl.htm

http://somewhatmuchly.co.uk/index.php?cat=Cemeteries

http://www.srgw.demon.co.uk/CremSoc/History/HistSocy.html

http://www.stmaryislington.org/history/036.html

http://www.tbcs.org.uk/history.htm

http://www.victorianlondon.org/

http://www.virtualnorwood.com/news/005.html

http://www.zurichmansion.org/parks/.50.html

# Index

Page numbers in *italics* denote an illustration